D1186614

wittypedia

Published in 2017 by Prion
An imprint of
Carlton Books Limited
20 Mortimer Street
London W1T 3JW

A catalogue record for this book is available from the British Library.

ISBN: 978-1-85375-983-3

Printed and bound by CPI Group (UK) Ltd, Croydon, CR0 4YY

Some of the material in this book was previously published in *Wit*, *Wit Rides Again*, *Wit The Last Laugh* and *Wit The Final Word*

wittypedia

More than
5,000 Quotations!

DES MACHALE

PRION

Contents

Introduction   7

Art   11

Business and Money   23

Drink and other Drugs   45

Education   67

Food   89

Lawyers and other Professions   101

Literature   113

Living – Family and Relations   145

Love, Sex, Marriage, Men and Women   197

Media and Films   249

Medicine and Doctors   291

Music   313

Nationalities and Places   335

Politics   377

Religion   409

Science and Technology   431

Social Behaviour and Manners   443

Sport   465

Theatre and Criticism   497

Miscellaneous   509

Index   541

Introduction

Welcome to Wittypedia, a massive compilation of wit and wisdom on every topic imaginable. Author Des Machale has spent almost thirty years hunting down the brightest verbal and literary gems from books, magazines, newspapers, radio, television, films, word of mouth – you name it! With so many fine quotations to choose from, it seems incredible that we've managed to squeeze the best-of-the-best into just one volume, but we have and now you're reading it!

According to Des (writing in the first of his Wit books) a good, humorous quotation should have the following qualities:

"First of all it should be funny – it should provoke laughter or at least a smile. Too many books of humorous quotations are shamelessly padded with substandard material that is not even remotely funny. I humbly submit that this book is different.

It should be short and pithy, for brevity is the soul of wit: the average quotation in this book has fourteen words, but I have not resisted the temptation to include just a few longer quotes of exceptional merit.

It should be free-standing i.e. it must be independent of the context in which it arises. This rather stringent requirement will undoubtably eliminate some old favourites of yours and mine, but look at it this way – if the explanation of why a quotation is funny because of where it arises is actually longer than the quotation itself, is it really worth the bother?"

The quotes have been arranged into topic categories for handy reference and there is an index of names at the back if you're searching for a pearl of wisdom from a particular personage.

Armed with this book you will always be a fount of mirth at dinner parties and never again be stuck for a caption on a greeting card. Enjoy!

Art

Art

Abstract art is a product of the untalented, sold by the unprincipled, to the utterly bewildered.

Al Capp

I inherited a painting and a violin which turned out to be a Rembrandt and a Stradivarius. Unfortunately Rembrandt made lousy violins and Stradivarius was a terrible painter.

Tommy Cooper

Anyone who sees and paints a sky green and fields blue ought to be sterilised.

Adolf Hitler

Which painting in the National Gallery would I save if there was a fire? The one nearest the door of course.

George Bernard Shaw

The only thoroughly original ideas I have ever heard Mr Whistler express have had reference to his own superiority as a painter over painters greater than himself.

Oscar Wilde

She looks like the Venus de Milo; she is very old, has no teeth, and has white spots on her yellow skin.

Heinrich Heine

She is one of those ladies who pursue culture in bands, as though it were dangerous to meet it alone.

Edith Wharton

There is only one difference between a madman and me. I am not mad.

Salvador Dali

He was as ugly as a gargoyle hewn by a drunken stonemason
for the adornment of a Methodist Chapel in one of the vilest
suburbs of Leeds or Wigan.

Max Beerbohm

You ask me, Sir, for a suitable institution to which you
propose to leave your paintings. May I suggest an asylum for
the blind?

James McNeill Whistler

I don't understand anything about the ballet. All I know is
that during the intervals the ballerinas stink like horses.

Anton Chekhov

Post-Impressionist drawing is on the level of an untaught
child of seven or eight years old, the sense of colour of a tea-
tray painter, the method of a schoolboy who wipes his
fingers on a slate after spitting on them.

Wilfred Blunt

I am lonesome. They are all dying. I have hardly a warm
personal enemy left.

James McNeill Whistler

If it sells, it's art.

Frank Lloyd

Many excellent cooks are spoilt by going into the arts.

Paul Gauguin

All the arts in America are a gigantic racket run by
unscrupulous men for unhealthy women.

Thomas Beecham

Can it be mere coincidence that so many of the best Post-
Impressionists are Poles?

Patrick Murray

Art

It might be an idea if Miss Winterson got out her brushes
and set to painting her masterpiece as soon as possible.
Because the signs are, right now, that she certainly isn't ever
going to write one.

Julie Burchill

It is only an auctioneer who can admire all schools of art
equally.

Oscar Wilde

One reassuring thing about modern art is that things can't be
as bad as they are painted.

Walthall Jackson

Over in the corner the mood was more ruffled, where dense
mobs praised 'The 17th Wedding Anniversary: Our Bedroom
at Mole End', a seven-sided *tour de force* by Anthony Green
RA. It's the kind of picture that induces people to describe it
to their companions beside them as if they were blind.

Alex Hamilton

Excuse me guard, where is the big Mona Lisa?

Dave Barry

I've been doing a lot of abstract painting lately, extremely
abstract. No brush, no paint, no canvas, I just think about it.

Steven Wright

If my husband Picasso ever met a woman in the street who looked like one of his paintings he would faint.

Jacqueline Roque

To the accountants, a true work of art is an investment that hangs on the wall.

Hilary Alexander

Sculpture is what you bump into when you back up to look at a painting.

Ed Reinhart

Art is making something out of nothing and selling it.

Frank Zappa

Varnishing is the only artistic process with which the Royal Academicians are thoroughly familiar.

Oscar Wilde

At the Art Exhibition fruit sold well, and chickens, and items like corks and shoes, though nudes were slow.

Alex Hamilton

The workmanship was fairly neat and resembled in many ways the kind of barely ingenious handicraft pursued in hospitals by the disabled, who are anxious to employ their fingers without taxing their intellect or senses.

Evelyn Waugh

I sculpt by choosing a block of marble and chopping off anything that doesn't look like what I am trying to create.
Auguste Rodin

Art needed Ruskin like a moving train needs one of the passengers to shove it.
Tom Stoppard

When I get to Heaven I mean to spend a considerable portion of my first million years in painting, and so get to the bottom of the subject.
Winston Churchill

The one unforgivable sin in art is to muddle Monet and Manet.
Andrew McEvoy

Sister Wendy is to art what Saint Teresa was to sex education.
A.A. Gill

Of course I can draw Von Hindenberg: I can piss the old boy in the snow.
Max Liebermann

I do not paint a portrait to look like the subject, rather does the person grow to look like his portrait.
Salvador Dali

Renoir's later work was like pastel-coloured sneezes.
David Carritt

Pictures deface more walls than they decorate.

Frank Lloyd Wright

His work was that curious mixture of bad painting and good intentions that always entitles a man to be called a representative British artist.

Oscar Wilde

I simply refuse to countenance paintings that do not have at least a horse, gladioli or a canal in them.

Dylan Moran

I see Jim Morrison's ejaculation as art while he sees it as poetry.

Linda Ashcroft

It is amazing that you can win the Turner Prize with an E in A-level art, twisted imagination and a chainsaw.

Damien Hirst

It's not hard to understand modern art. If it hangs on a wall it's a painting, and if you can walk around it, it's a sculpture.

Simon Updike

When I hear the word culture, I take out my chequebook.

Jean-Luc Goddard

You can't control life: only art you can control. Art and masturbation. Two areas in which I am expert.

Woody Allen

Art

All architecture is great architecture after sunset.

G.K. Chesterton

If you threw every single painting made by a woman into the Atlantic, the only complaint would be that, along with a lot of futile dross, a few pretty boudoir things were gone.

Brian Sewell

If Whistler were not a genius, he would be the most ridiculous man in Paris.

Hilaire Degas

I hate flowers: I paint them because they're cheaper than models and they don't move.

Georgia O'Keeffe

In the afterlife, I wouldn't mind turning into a vermilion goldfish.

Henri Matisse

A Test match is like a painting. A one-day match is like a Rolf Harris painting.

Ian Chappell

Van Gogh became a painter because he had no ear for music.

Nikki Harris

"What are you painting?" I asked him. "Is it the Heavenly Child?" "No," he said, "it is a cow."

Stephen Leacock

This young man is an artist. The other day I saw him in the street in a brown jacket.

Quentin Crisp

A woman is fascinated not by art but by the noise made by those in the field.

Anton Chekhov

The Shakespeare Memorial Theatre, Stratford-upon-Avon, is a courageous and partly successful attempt to disguise a gasworks as a racquets court.

Peter Fleming

Paul Klee's pictures seem to resemble, not pictures, but a sample book of patterns of linoleum.

Cyril Asquith

My friend has chicken pox. He's running a high temperature and his chest looks like a bad Matisse.

Noel Coward

We gotta be out of this joint, the Louvre, in twenny minutes.

Darryl F. Zanuck

For a successful exhibition, you've got to have two out of death, sex and jewels.

Roy Strong

When it comes to ruining paintings, he's an artist.

Samuel Goldwyn

Art

If Michelangelo had been heterosexual, the ceiling of the Sistine Chapel would have been painted basic white and with a roller.

Rita Mae Brown

A highbrow is a person who looks at a sausage and thinks of Picasso.

A.P. Herbert

What does this picture represent? It represents two hundred thousand dollars.

Pablo Picasso

Tintoretto will never be anything but a dauber.

Titian

Artists hate the enlightened amateur unless he buys.

Ernest Dimmet

Sodom-hipped young men, with the inevitable sidewhiskers and cigarettes, the faulty livers and the stained teeth, reading Lawrence as an aphrodisiac, and Marie Corelli in their infrequent baths, spew onto paper and canvas their ignorance and perversions, wetting the bed of their brains with discharges of fungoid verse. This is the art of today.

Dylan Thomas

James Whistler once dyed a rice pudding green so that it wouldn't clash with the walls of his dining room.

Geoff Tibballs

Patriotism is the last refuge of the sculptor.

William Plomer

Art dealers are not happy unless they tell twelve lies before lunchtime.

Damien Hirst

Vincent Van Gogh's mother painted all of his best things. The famous mailed decapitated ear was a figment of the public relations firm engaged by Van Gogh's dealer.

Roy Blount

Rembrandt's first name was Beauregard, which is why he never used it.

Dave Barry

I hate all Boets and Bainters.

King George I

A sculpture is just a drawing you fall over in the dark.

Al Hirschfeld

In the mornings, artists work. They fall in love only in the afternoons.

Frederic Raphael

I will be so brief I have already finished.

Salvador Dali

Business and Money

I've been rich and I've been poor – rich is better.

Sophie Tucker

If you would like to know the value of money, go and try to borrow some.

Benjamin Franklin

I've got all the money I'll ever need if I die by four o'clock this afternoon.

Henny Youngman

October. This is one of the peculiarly dangerous months to speculate in stocks. Other dangerous months are July, January, September, April, November, May, March, June, December, August and February.

Mark Twain

When I was young I used to think that money was the most important thing in life. Now that I am old, I know it is.

Oscar Wilde

I owe much; I have nothing; the rest I leave to the poor.

François Rabelais

A lot of people become pessimists from financing optimists.

C. T. Jones

Money is just the poor man's credit card.

Marshall McLuhan

A man who has a million dollars is as well off as if he were rich.

Cleveland Amory

Dear *Reader's Digest*, we hardly know each other, yet I have been selected from so many millions to enter your free contest in which I may win £25,000. You have made me very happy.

Miles Kington

My luck is so bad that if I bought a cemetery, people would stop dying.

Ed Furgol

Undermine the entire economic structure of society by leaving the pay toilet door ajar so the next person can get in free.

Taylor Meade

I always arrive late at the office, but I make up for it by leaving early.

Charles Lamb

A verbal contract isn't worth the paper it's written on.

Samuel Goldwyn

It is only by not paying one's bills that one can hope to live in the memory of the commercial classes.

Oscar Wilde

Money can't buy you happiness, but it does bring you a more pleasant form of misery.

Spike Milligan

The light at the end of the tunnel is just the light of an oncoming train.

Robert Lowell

When I asked my accountant if anything could get me out of the mess I am in now, he thought for a long time. 'Yes,' he said, 'death would help'.

Robert Morley

Business and Money

They usually have two tellers in my local bank. Except when it's very busy, when they have one.

Rita Rudner

It is morally wrong to allow a sucker to keep his money.

W.C. Fields

Having a little inflation is like being a little bit pregnant.

Leon Henderson

Office Hours: 2 to 2.15 every other Wednesday.

George S. Kaufman

I rob banks because that's where the money is.

Willie Sutton

Statistics indicate that as a result of overwork, modern executives are dropping like flies on the nation's golf courses.

Ira Wallach

We were allowed to accept gifts of flowers, candies, jewels, furs, yachts, castles – but never money.

Quentin Crisp

I always travel first-class on the train. It's the only way to avoid one's creditors.

Seymour Hicks

If only God would give me a clear sign! Like making a large deposit in my name at a Swiss bank.

Woody Allen

I haven't reported my missing credit card to the police because whoever stole it is spending less than my wife.

Ilie Nastase

Business and Money

The holy passion of friendship is of so sweet and steady and loyal and enduring a nature that it will last through a whole lifetime, if not asked to lend money.

Mark Twain

You should always live within your income, even if you have to borrow to do so.

Josh Billings

All students of economics should learn about Marxism, just as all medical students should learn about venereal diseases.

C.K. Grant

Money is better than poverty, if only for financial reasons.

Woody Allen

One of the strangest things about life is that the poor, who need money the most, are the very ones that never have it.

Finley Peter Dunne

I wish that dear Karl could have spent some time acquiring capital instead of merely writing about it.

Jenny Marx

Blessed are the young, for they shall inherit the national debt.

Herbert Hoover

The first rule of business is – do other men for they would do you.

Charles Dickens

Any organisation is like a septic tank. The really big chunks always rise to the top.

John Imhoff

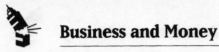

Business and Money

The difference between a man and his valet is that they both smoke the same cigars but only one pays for them.

Robert Frost

To stop telephone salesmen in their tracks I always say 'That's great. I'm very interested but I'm busy right now, so if you could leave your home number I'll call you back tonight at about 11:30pm'.

Bob Jeffay

Banking is the second oldest profession but more profitable than the oldest profession.

Flann O'Brien

An Act of God designation on all insurance policies means roughly that you cannot be insured for the accidents that are most likely to happen to you.

Alan Coren

Noah must have taken into the Ark two taxes, one male and one female and did they multiply beautifully! Next to guinea pigs, taxes must have been the most prolific animals.

Will Rogers

George goes to sleep at a bank every day from ten to four, except Saturdays, when they wake him up and put him outside at two.

Jerome K. Jerome

Business and Money

Things got so bad that I received a letter from The Readers' Digest, saying that I hadn't been included in their prize draw.

John McGrath

Everybody likes a kidder, but nobody will lend him money.

Arthur Miller

An economist is someone who, if you have forgotten your telephone number, will estimate it for you.

Edward Kent

One of the silliest wastes of time is figuring out how much money you'd have if you'd stayed single.

Kin Hubbard

Doubtless there are things money won't buy, but I cannot think of any of them at the moment.

Richard Needham

Time spent in the advertising business seems to create a permanent deformity like the Chinese habit of foot-binding.

Dean Acheson

I'd give a thousand dollars to be a millionaire.

Lewis Timberlake

Business and Money

If you had your life to live over again – you'd need a lot more money.

Robert Orben

I would like to execute everyone who uses the word 'fair' in connection with income tax policies.

William F. Buckley

Nothing in the known universe travels faster than a bad cheque.

Alec Slick

God made gentiles because somebody has to buy retail.

Arthur Naiman

There is a certain Buddhistic calm that comes from having money in the bank.

Tom Robbins

There's no business like show business, but there are several businesses like accounting.

David Letterman

Oil prices have fallen lately. We include this news for the benefit of gas stations, which otherwise wouldn't learn of it for six months.

Bill Tammeus

We will spare no expense to save money on this movie.

Samuel Goldwyn

It is a rather pleasant experience to be alone in a bank at night.

Willie Sutton

I have long admired the unknown genius, larcenous though he must have been, who ran this one-line ad in a Los Angeles newspaper: LAST DAY TO SEND IN YOUR DOLLAR BOX 153. Thousands of idiots sent in their dollars.

Leo Rosten

Breathes there a man with a soul so dead that he doesn't stick two fingers in the coin return box after completing a call?

Richard Needham

I got this letter telling me I may already be a loser.

Rodney Dangerfield

There is a very easy way to return from a casino with a small fortune – go there with a large one.

Jack Yelton

The only difference between a tax collector and a taxidermist is that a taxidermist leaves the hide.

Mortimer Caplan

Business and Money

The trickle-down theory of economics is the less than elegant metaphor that if one feeds the horse enough oats, some will pass through to the road for the sparrows.

J. K. Galbraith

I took out a big life insurance policy because I want to be rich when I die.

Yogi Berra

Bankruptcy is a legal proceeding in which you put your money in your pants pocket and give your coat to the creditors.

Joey Adams

To the Bank of Scotland I bequeath my testicles, because it has no balls.

Lord Erskine

Don't spend two pounds to dry-clean a shirt. Donate it to the Salvation Army instead. They will clean it and put it on a hanger. Then you can buy it back for fifty pence.

Jack Dee

The gambling known as business looks with austere disfavour upon the business known as gambling.

Ambrose Bierce

I was feeling very very irritable. It was that difficult time of the month when the credit card statement arrives.

Julie Walters

Death is the most convenient time to tax rich people.

David Lloyd-George

The son-in-law also rises.

William Goldman

It doesn't matter if you're rich or poor, as long as you've got money.

Joe E. Lewis

A cheque is the only argument I recognise.

Oscar Wilde

You can say it was a real love match. We married for money.

S.J. Perelman

I was on a basic £100,000 a year. You don't make many savings on that.

Ernest Saunders

Ladies and gentlemen, my assistant will pass the plate around, and kindly remember that I am allergic to the sound of silver.

W.C. Fields

When I was young I'd steal from the piggy banks of dear little kiddies. Fortunately, when I got older, there were some habits I didn't change.

W.C. Fields

Jane Fonda didn't get that terrific body from exercise. She got it from lifting all that money.

Joan Rivers

Idealism is fine, but as it approaches reality, the costs become prohibitive.

William F. Buckley

There is only one thing that money can't buy and that's poverty.

Joe E. Lewis

I don't want to be a millionaire. I just want to live like one.

Walter Hagen

My boss carried only one brand of cigar. It sold for three cents. If a customer asked for a ten-cent cigar, he was handed one which sold for three cents. "The customer is always right," my boss would say, "so never allow him to be disappointed."

W.C. Fields

I need to marry someone wealthy. I'd rather not have to turn right on entering an airplane.

Tara Palmer-Tomkinson

I like going into newsagents' shops and saying, "Excuse me, is that Mars bar for sale?" When he says "Yes," I say, "OK, I might be back later, I still have a few other ones to see."

Michael Redmond

So, Debbie McGee, what first attracted you to millionaire
Paul Daniels?

Mrs Merton

H.G. Wells and George Bernard Shaw are opposed to
capitalism but not to capital, when it adopts the form of a
tidy balance in their own name at Barclay's Bank.

Finley Peter Dunne

The quickest way to become a millionaire is to borrow fivers
off everyone you meet.

Richard Branson

The easiest way for your children to learn about money is
not to have any.

Katharine Whitehorn

The business sense of a publisher is in inverse proportion to
the wattage of the bulbs in his firm's toilets.

André Deutsch

A lot of people have asked me how short I am. Since my last
divorce, I think I'm about $100,000 short.

Mickey Rooney

Business and Money

Money is not the most important thing in the world – love is. Fortunately I love money.

Jackie Mason

Don't get mad – get everything.

Ivana Trump

You'd be surprised how much better looking a man gets when you know he's worth a hundred and fifty million dollars.

Joan Rivers

The businessman is a person to whom age brings golf instead of wisdom.

George Bernard Shaw

If you don't believe in the resurrection of the dead, look at any office at closing time.

Robert Townsend

I notice that more and more of our imports seem to be coming from overseas.

George W. Bush

It was said of Andrew Carnegie that he gave money away as silently as a waiter falling down a flight of stairs with a tray of glasses.

Billy Connolly

It's clearly a budget – it's got lots of numbers in it.

George W. Bush

Business and Money

Business clothes are naturally attracted to staining liquids.
This attraction is strongest just before an important meeting.

Scott Adams

Mother always said that honesty was the best policy, and
money wasn't everything. She was wrong about other things
too.

Gerald Barzan

Three years ago I came to Florida without a nickel in my
pocket. And now I've got a nickel in my pocket.

Groucho Marx

They say money talks, but all it ever said to me was
'goodbye'.

Cary Grant

The most expensive thing in the world is a girl who is free
for the evening.

Sheryl Bernstein

The national debt is a trillion dollars. Who do we owe this
money to? Someone named Vinnie?

Robin Williams

Merchandising reached its apogee in the Lux advertisement
which portrayed two articles of lingerie which discussed
their wearer's effluvia, for all the world like rival stamp
collectors.

S. J. Perelman

Business and Money

To become a millionaire, what you have to do is to begin as a billionaire. Then go into the airline business.

Richard Branson

No applications can be received here on Sundays, nor any business done during the remainder of the week.

Richard Brinsley Sheridan

I am so changed that my oldest creditors would hardly know me.

Henry Fox

When creating hand-lettered small-business signs you should put quotation marks as in: TRY "OUR" HOT DOG'S.

Dave Barry

I went to the bank and asked to borrow a cup of money. They asked, 'What for?' I said, 'I'm going to buy some sugar.'

Steven Wright

I taught my child the value of a dollar. This week he wants his allowance in yen.

Milton Berle

Will you marry me? How much money do you have? Answer the second question first.

Groucho Marx

Business and Money

The recipe for my success is, some people strike oil, others don't.

J. Paul Getty

I don't want to retire from business. I'd hate to spend the rest of my life trying to outwit an 18-inch fish.

Harold Geneen

To force myself to earn money, I determined to spend more.

James Agate

To steal from one person is theft. To steal from many is taxation.

John Dixon

Xerox has sued somebody for copying.

Dave Letterman

The most difficult of all tasks that a mortal man can embark on is to sell a book.

Stanley Unwin

A typical conversation between me and my teenage daughter runs as follows – 'You need fifty dollars? Forty dollars, what do you need thirty dollars for?'

Bill Cosby

I'm filthy stinking rich – well, two out of three ain't bad.

Emo Philips

Business and Money

The early bird who catches the worm works for someone who comes in late and owns the worm farm.

John D. MacDonald

I decided long ago never to look at the right-hand side of the menu or the price tag of clothes. Otherwise I would starve, naked.

Helen Hayes

I wasn't always rich. There was a time when I didn't know where my next husband was coming from.

Mae West

All our operators are either drunk or fornicating right now, but if you care to leave a message when you hear the tone...

Hugh Leonard

Who says auditors are human?

Arthur Hailey

If you can afford it, then there is no pleasure in buying it.

Wallis Simpson

A billion dollars is not what it used to be.

J. Paul Getty

I would like to live like a poor person with lots of money.

Pablo Picasso

Business and Money

I was the leading money spender on the PGA Tour.

John Brodie

My husband fell in a river right in front of me and drowned. I rushed to the bank but he had already withdrawn all his money.

Phyllis Diller

Whoever is rich is my brother.

Aristotle Onassis

A manager is a person who looks after visitors so everyone one else can get some work done.

Henry Mintzberg

Money is the root of all evil but man needs roots.

Joe Peers

Bankruptcy is a sacred state, a condition beyond conditions, as theologians might say, and attempts to investigate it are necessarily obscene, like spiritualism.

John Updike

If you can't make your books balance, you take however much they are out by and enter it under the heading ESP, which stands for Error Some Place.

Sam Walton

Money doesn't make you happy. I now have $50 million but I was just as happy when I had $48 million.

Arnold Schwarzenegger

Business and Money

On my income tax form it says 'Check this box if you are blind'. I want to put a check mark about 3 inches away.

Tom Lehrer

Money can't buy everything. That's what credit cards are for.

Ruby Wax

Receiving a million dollars tax-free will make you feel better than being flat broke and having a stomach ache.

Dolph Sharp

Save a little money each month and at the end of the year you'll be surprised at how little you'll have.

Ernest Haskins

Abolish inheritance tax – no taxation without respiration.

Bob Schaffer

If you're given a champagne lunch there's a catch somewhere.

Ben Lyon

Being the boss doesn't make you right, it only makes you the boss.

Milton Metz

You have to be rich to have a swing like Bing Crosby.

Bob Hope

My wife has a complex accounting system. She does an initial scan of the supermarket total and says 'Oh my God.' Then she puts the receipt away carefully in a drawer with all the others which ensures that eventually we will have enough receipts to fill a box.

Frank McNally

Have you ever heard of a kid playing accountant, even if he wanted to be one?

Jackie Mason

Do the people who run the stores at airports have any idea what the prices are everywhere else in the world?

Jerry Seinfeld

Lending money to your children is like lending money to a Third World country – you never get the interest back, let alone the principal.

J. L. Long

I found a wallet the other day containing $150. I was going to return it but I thought that if I lost a wallet with $150 in it, what would I want and I realised I would want to be taught a lesson.

Emo Philips

Don't ever stay in bed unless you can make money in bed.

George Burns

My accountant told me to put my money into land so I buried it all in the back garden.

Ken Dodd

Drink and other Drugs

Drink and other Drugs

I am not a heavy drinker. I can sometimes go for hours without touching a drop.

Noel Coward

I drink therefore I am.

W.C. Fields

If I had my life to live over again, I'd live over a saloon.

W.C. Fields

A woman drove me to drink – and I hadn't even the courtesy to thank her.

W.C. Fields

I feel sorry for people who don't drink. They wake up in the morning and that's the best they are going to feel all day.

Dean Martin

Some American writers who have known each other for years have never met in the daytime or when both are sober.

James Thurber

An alcoholic is anyone you don't like who drinks more than you do.

Dylan Thomas

You're not drunk if you can lie on the floor without holding on.

Dean Martin

The drink in that pub is not fit for washing hearses.

Brendan Behan

Reality is an illusion created by a lack of alcohol.

N.F. Simpson

Drink and other Drugs

A tavern is a place where madness is sold by the bottle.

Jonathan Swift

May I suggest, sir, that if you want an impenetrable disguise for the fancy dress ball, that you go sober?

Samuel Foote

Work is the curse of the drinking classes.

Oscar Wilde

There are more old drunks than old doctors.

François Rabelais

My dad was the town drunk. Most of the time that's not so bad – but New York City?

Henny Youngman

I never drink water because of the disgusting things that fish do in it.

W.C. Fields

A cap of good acid costs five dollars and for that you can hear the Universal Symphony with God singing solo and the Holy Ghost on drums.

Hunter S. Thompson

I always keep a stimulant handy in case I see a snake – which I also keep handy.

W.C. Fields

He once had his toes amputated so he could stand closer to the bar.

Mike Harding

What contemptible scoundrel stole the cork from my lunch?

W.C. Fields

Drink and other Drugs

The trouble with him is that when he is not drunk he is sober.

W.B.Yeats

A debut is the first time a young girl is seen drunk in public.

F. Scott Fitzgerald

Cocaine is God's way of saying you're making too much money.

Robin Williams

I exercise strong self-control. I never drink anything stronger than gin before breakfast.

W.C. Fields

The AAAA is a new organisation for drunks who drive. Give them a call and they'll tow you away from the bar.

Martin Burden

Whiskey is by far the most popular of all the remedies that won't cure a cold.

Jerry Vale

The difference between a drunk and an alcoholic is that a drunk doesn't have to attend all those meetings.

Arthur J. Lewis

The Management of an Irish pub cannot be held responsible for any accidents which occur in the mad rush for the doors at closing time.

Tony Butler

A total abstainer is someone who abstains from everything except abstention.

Ambrose Bierce

Drink and other Drugs

He awoke with a severe hangover. His mouth felt as if it had been used as a latrine by some small animal.

Kingsley Amis

Your superego is that part of you which is soluble in alcohol.

Thomas L. Martin

I'd rather have a full bottle in front of me than a full frontal lobotomy.

Fred Allen

Perfection is such a nuisance that I often regret having cured myself of using tobacco.

Emile Zola

I once shook hands with Pat Boone and my whole right side sobered up.

Dean Martin

I can't die until the government finds a safe place to bury my liver.

Phil Harris

People keep warning me not to smoke too much, but I gotta. It's a matter of principle, like who's running my life – me or the *Reader's Digest*?

Dick Gregory

I got thrown out of Alcoholics Anonymous because when the other clients saw me they thought they were having the DTs.

Dave Dutton

There is nothing wrong with sobriety in moderation.

John Ciardi

Women add zest to the unlicenced hours.

Allen D. Thomas

Drink and other Drugs

In the pub last night I had six beers, two large gins, a couple of Ports, a brandy and a pork pie. On the way home I was as sick as a dog. I don't think that pork pie agreed with me.

Rex Jameson

There was an ancient Greek law which made it a crime not to get drunk during the annual festival of Dionysus.

Bruce Felton

The heavy port drinker must be prepared to make some sacrifice of personal beauty and agility.

Evelyn Waugh

I like the odd drink. Five is odd, seven is odd, nine is odd...

W.C. Fields

The only thing worse than a reformed cigarette smoker is an early Christmas shopper.

Liz Scott

I once ate a cannabis cookie but I didn't swallow.

Sandy Toksvig

I find that red wine improves with age. The older I get the more I like it.

Raymond George

The best temperance lecture I ever heard was delivered by a man under the influence of alcohol.

W.C. Fields

Drink and other Drugs

In 1969 I gave up drinking and sex. It was the worst twenty minutes of my life.

George Best

No, I don't mind if you smoke – not if you don't mind my being sick all over you.

Thomas Beecham

I am so holy that when I touch wine it turns into water.

Aga Khan III

I was with some Vietnamese recently, and some of them were smoking two cigarettes at the same time. That's the kind of customers we need.

Jesse Helms

All roads lead to rum.

W.C. Fields

He was a wine waiter at a great hotel, endowed by nature with a uniquely sensitive nose and a retentive memory. No drop had ever passed his lips, but when it came to the test he was able to name the chateau and year of a dozen clarets merely by putting his nose to the glass. He was like a sanitary inspector smelling drains.

Evelyn Waugh

I myself once woke up in a drawer at the bottom of a wardrobe. That was fairly frightening. Try opening a drawer from the inside. It's quite tricky.

Jeffrey Bernard

Drink and other Drugs

How do you look when I'm sober?

Ring Lardner

When my time comes, I want to die in bed, listening to music and sampling a warming well-rounded twenty-five-year-old. I mean whisky of course.

Tom Brown

When Jack Benny throws a party, you not only bring your own scotch, you bring your own rocks.

George Burns

Whisky-making is the art of making poison pleasant.

Samuel Johnson

The European Parliment has banned smoking by its MPs while it is in session. The reason is that those fellows drink so much that if you lit a match in there the place would explode.

Eamon Morrissey

A soft drink turneth away company.

Oliver Herford

On one occasion some one put a very little wine into a wine-cooler and said that it was sixteen years old. 'It's very small for its age', remarked his guest.

Athenaeus

Drink and other Drugs

Red sky in the morning – red wine the previous evening.
Don Rickles

He'd had so much the night before he was suddenly sick over the bride. The service continued a while and then the groom was sick again, this time over the vicar.
Jeffrey Bernard

A good general rule on wine-tasting is to state that the bouquet is better than the taste, and vice versa.
Stephen Potter

Twenty four hours in a day; twenty four beers in a case – mere coincidence?
Steven Wright

Don't invite drug addicts round for a meal on Boxing Day. They may find your offer of 'cold turkey' embarrassing or offensive.
Steven Howlett

I've been doing the Fonda workout: the Peter Fonda workout. That's where I wake up, take a hit of acid, smoke a joint, and go to my sister's house and ask her for money.
Kevin Meaney

People may say what they like about the decay of Christianity; the religious system that produced green Chartreuse can never really die.
H.H. Munro

Drink and other Drugs

You don't buy beer, you just rent it.

W.C. Fields

What on earth was I drinking last night? My head feels like there's a Frenchman living in it.

Rowan Atkinson

Don't put any ice in my drink. It takes up too much room.

Groucho Marx

The South is dry and will stay dry. That is, everybody that is sober enough to stagger to the polls will.

Will Rogers

Put American beer back in the horse.

H. Allen Smith

My brother Brendan was the sort of man who would get a panic attack if he saw someone wearing a teetotaller's badge.

Brian Behan

There are three things in this world you can do nothing about. Getting AIDS, getting clamped, and running out of Chateau Lafite '45.

Alan Clark

Habitual teetotallers. There should be asylums for such people. But they would probably lapse into teetotalism as soon as they came out.

Samuel Butler

I have no objection to people smoking on my undertaking premises. It's good for business.

Alan Puxley

A total abstainer is the kind of man you wouldn't want to drink with even if he did.

George J. Nathan

I got Mark Helliger so drunk last night it took three bellboys to put me to bed.

W.C. Fields

Don't cry sonny and I'll let you smell my breath.

W.C. Fields

I'd give up smoking but I'm not a quitter.

Jo Brand

Good heavens! How marriage ruins a man! It's as demoralising as cigarettes and far more expensive.

Oscar Wilde

Kids nowadays are no sooner off the pot than they are back on again.

Stu Francis

A friend of mine belongs to Alcoholics Anonymous, but he's not a fanatic about it. He doesn't go to meetings: he just sends in the empties.

Milton Berle

Drink and other Drugs

I feel as though the Russian army has been walking over my
tongue in their stockinged feet.

W.C. Fields

American beer is served cold so you can tell it from urine.

David Moulton

Yes, I do have a drinking problem: there's never enough.

Denis Thatcher

Show me a nation whose national beverage is beer and I'll
show you an advanced toilet technology.

Paul Hawkins

I have had only one glass: maybe it has been refilled a few
times, but it's only one glass.

Raymond George

Cocktails have all the disagreeability of a disinfectant
without the utility.

Shane Leslie

What a strange paradox it is that I would be unemployable if
I were teetotal.

Jeffrey Bernard

You can't be a real country unless you have a beer and an
airline: it helps if you have some kind of football team, or
some nuclear weapons, but at the very least you need a beer.

Frank Zappa

Drink and other Drugs

I have never been drunk, but I have often been overserved.

George Gobel

Yes madam, I am drunk and you are exceedingly ugly; but in the morning I shall be sober.

Winston Churchill

My favourite drink is a cocktail of carrot juice and whisky. I am always drunk but I can see for miles.

Roy Brown

Farrell's Bar in Brooklyn had urinals so large they looked like shower stalls for Toulouse-Lautrec.

Joe Flaherty

He was so full of alcohol, if you put a lighted wick in his mouth, he'd burn for three days.

Groucho Marx

I think this wine has been drunk before.

W.C. Fields

The cognac tasted like semi-viscous airplane fuel from the Amelia Earhart era.

Kinky Friedman

The man was a secular version of the Immaculate Conception. He became an alcoholic without ever buying a drink.

Niall Toibin

Drink and other Drugs

The local drink was rakia which gave off a powerful stench, part sewage, part glue.

Evelyn Waugh

Just my luck to have given up drinking when the pubs are staying open all night.

George Best

Can't we just get rid of wine lists? Do we really have to be reminded every time we go out to a restaurant that we have no idea what we are doing? Why don't they just give us a trigonometry quiz with the menu?

Jerry Seinfeld

There is no hangover on earth like the single malt hangover. It roars in the ears, burns in the stomach and sizzles in the brain like a short circuit. Death is the easy way out.

Ian Bell

The human brain can operate only as fast as the slowest brain cells. Excessive intake of alcohol kills brain cells, but naturally it attacks the slowest and weakest brain cells first. In this way, regular consumption of alcohol eliminates the weaker brain cells, making the brain a faster and more efficient machine.

W. C. Fields

Why are so many of my friends recovering alcoholics? Because they can always be relied upon to drive me home.

Jeremy Clarkson

Drink and other Drugs

Did you know that if you laid every cigarette smoker end-to-end around the world more than 67 per cent of them would drown?

Steve Altman

I was working as a barman and an American asked me for a traditional Scottish drink. So I gave him 18 pints of lager.

Danny Bhoy

I once shared a house with Errol Flynn. It was called Cirrhosis-by-the-Sea.

David Niven

It was a brilliant affair; water flowed like champagne.

William Evarts

I have practically given up drinking – only about seven bottles of wine and three of spirits a week.

Evelyn Waugh

I never drink unless I'm alone or with someone.

W. C. Fields

It is difficult to speak about proper beer, because its friends are its worst enemies. 'Real ale' fans are just like train spotters – only drunk.

Christopher Howse

Drink and other Drugs

Between Scotch and nothing, I suppose I'd take Scotch. It's the nearest thing to good moonshine I can find.

William Faulkner

Beauty is in the eye of the beerholder.

W. C. Fields

Not all chemicals are bad. Without chemicals such as hydrogen and oxygen, for example, there would be no way to make water, a vital ingredient in beer.

Dave Barry

A well-balanced person is someone with a drink in each hand.

Billy Connolly

The first cigar was probably nothing but a bunch of rolled up old tobacco leaves.

Jack Handey

In pubs, spirits are served in mean-spirited measures laughably called singles and doubles. A single is invisible and its presence can be detected only by sniffing the glass. A double whisky can generally be observed through an electron microscope.

Stephen Burgen

Whenever someone asks me if I want water with my Scotch, I say I'm thirsty, not dirty.

Joe E. Lewis

Drink and other Drugs

The greatest invention in the history of mankind is beer. Oh, I grant you the wheel was also a fine invention, but the wheel does not go nearly as well with pizza.

> Dave Barry

When we drink, we get drunk. When we get drunk we fall asleep. When we are asleep, we commit no sin. When we commit no sin, we go to Heaven. So, let's all get drunk and go to Heaven.

> Brian O'Rourke

Never turn down a drink, unless it is of local manufacture.

> George Walden

The wine in Scotland was so weak that there were many people who died of dropsies, which they contracted in trying to get drunk.

> Samuel Johnson

If I had all the money I've spent on drink, I'd go out and spend it all again on drink.

> Vivian Stanshall

You can die from drinking too much of anything – coffee, water, milk, soft drinks and all such stuff as that. And so long as the presence of death lurks with anything one goes through the simple act of swallowing, I will make mine whisky.

> W. C. Fields

Drink and other Drugs

I love drink, so long as it isn't in moderation.

Geoffrey Madan

A guide is a guy who knows where to find whiskey in the jungle.

John Wayne

All my life I have been a very thirsty person.

Keith Floyd

I once saw Michael Scott taking alternate sips of Scotch and Alka Seltzer, thereby acquiring and curing a hangover simultaneously.

Hugh Leonard

My wife clubbed me over the head one night when I came home drunk. It's sweet surprises like that which keep our marriage alive.

Rab C. Nesbitt

Ain't no way I could drink as much as they say I do. Maybe some days I do smoke six packs of cigarettes. Some days maybe I drink twenty to twenty-five beers – but not every day.

Billy Carter

Wine, madame, is God's next best gift to man.

Ambrose Bierce

Drink and other Drugs

I hate white Burgundies – they so closely resemble a blend of cold chalk soup and alum cordial with an additive or two to bring it to the colour of children's pee.

Kingsley Amis

How well I remember my first encounter with the Devil's Brew. I happened to stumble across a case of bourbon – and went on stumbling for several days thereafter.

W. C. Fields

There was a time when I was into acid and finding the most hip joint in town. Now I'm into antacid and hip joints.

Garrison Keillor

What rascal has been putting pineapple juice in my pineapple juice?

W. C. Fields

Booze is the answer. I don't remember the question.

Denis Leary

Cigarettes are a much cheaper and more widely available alternative to nicotine patches.

Bob Davies

It took a lot of bottle for Tony Adams to admit publicly that he had an alcohol problem.

Ian Wright

Drink and other Drugs

On some days, my head is filled with such wild and original thoughts that I can barely utter a word. On other days, the liquor store is closed.

Frank Varano

I am as drunk as a lord, but then, I am one, so what does it matter?

Bertrand Russell

Give a man a fish and he will eat for a day. Teach him how to fish, and he will sit in a boat and drink beer all day.

Paul Hawkins

The church is near, but the road is icy. The bar is far, but we will walk carefully.

Yakov Smirnoff

What's so unpleasant about being drunk? You ask a glass of water.

Douglas Adams

One tequila, two tequila, three tequila, floor.

George Carlin

I don't drink water in case it becomes habit-forming.

W. C. Fields

Drinking makes such fools of people, and people are such fools to begin with, that it's compounding a felony.

Robert Benchley

In the order named, these are the hardest to control: wine, women and song.

Franklin P. Adams

Although man is already ninety per cent water, the Prohibitionists are not yet satisfied.

Josh Billings

I sold my wife to a guy for a bottle of Scotch and now I wish I had her back because I'm thirsty again.

Henny Youngman

The trouble with jogging is that the ice falls out of your glass.

Martin Mull

The five most beautiful words known to man are 'Have one on the house.'

Wilson Mizner

People are really missing why I did this book. This is about alcoholism, my disease. Two years ago I was dead.

Tony Adams

In the first few weeks of pre-season football training, all you do is just sweat out the alcohol.

Pasi Rautianien

Education

Education

'Whom are you?' he said, for he had been to night school.
George Ade

My problems all started with my early education. I went to a
school for mentally disturbed teachers.
Woody Allen

Educational television should be absolutely forbidden. It can
only lead to unreasonable disappointment when your child
discovers that the letters of the alphabet do not leap up out
of books and dance around with royal-blue chickens.
Fran Lebowitz

Anyone who has been to an English public school will
always feel comparatively at home in prison.
Evelyn Waugh

I took a speed reading course and read *War and Peace* in
twenty minutes. It's about Russia.
Woody Allen

I can speak Esperanto like a native.
Spike Milligan

I speak twelve languages – English is the bestest.
Stefan Bergman

My act is very educational. I heard a man leaving the other
night saying 'Well, that's taught me a lesson.'
Ken Dodd

I wish that people who have difficulty in communicating
would just shut up about it.
Tom Lehrer

If a man is a fool, you don't train him out of being a fool by sending him to university. You merely turn him into a trained fool, ten times more dangerous.

Desmond Bagley

'You will all write an essay on "self-indulgence". There will be a prize of half a crown for the longest essay, irrespective of any possible merit.' From then on all was silence until the break.

Evelyn Waugh

Never attribute to malice that which can be adequately explained by straightforward stupidity.

J.C. Collins

The average Ph.D thesis is nothing but the transference of bones from one graveyard to the other.

J.F. Dobie

An intellectual is someone who has found something more interesting than sex.

Edgar Wallace

A lecture is a process by which the notes of the professor become the notes of the students without passing through the minds of either.

R.K. Rathbun

Let me protest against recent attacks on the fagging system at public schools. In all my four years I can recall only eleven deaths from fagging.

J.B. Morton

A man who has never gone to school may steal from a freight car; but if he has a university education, he may steal the whole railroad.

Theodore Roosevelt

Education

Dublin University contains the cream of Ireland – rich and thick.

Samuel Beckett

I expect you'll be becoming a schoolmaster, sir. That's what most of the gentlemen does, sir, that gets sent down for indecent behaviour.

Evelyn Waugh

I don't hold with bilingualism. English was good enough for Jesus Christ.

Ralph Melnyk

Violence is the repartee of the illiterate.

Alan Brien

I cheated in the final of my metaphysics examination. I looked into the soul of the boy sitting next to me.

Woody Allen

I acquired such skill in reading Latin and Greek that I could take a page of either, and distinguish which language it was by merely glancing at it.

Stephen Leacock

A college graduate returned home from his twenty-fifth class reunion and said to his wife – 'My classmates have all gotten so fat and bald they didn't even recognise me.'

Bennett Cerf

Trinity College Cambridge is like a dead body in a high state of putrefaction. The only interest is the worms that come out of it.

Lytton Strachey

Education

Harvard is a storehouse of knowledge because the freshmen bring so much in and the graduates take so little out.

Charles W. Eliot

I used to keep my college roommate from reading my personal mail by hiding it in her textbooks.

Joan Welsh

The ablative absolute is an ancient form of grammatical error much admired by modern scholars.

Ambrose Bierce

We spend the first twelve months of our children's lives teaching them to walk and talk and the next twelve years telling them to sit down and shut up.

Phyllis Diller

Loaded firearms were strictly forbidden at St Trinians to all but Sixth Formers.

Timothy Shy

Ignorance is like a delicate exotic fruit; touch it and the bloom is gone.

Oscar Wilde

He can barely read and write – Eton, of course.

Lawrence Durrell

'Shut up', he explained.

Ring Lardner

When Lord Berners returned, many years later, to visit his old school, he was astonished to observe nothing but smiling faces – only to learn that it was a school no more and that the building was a lunatic asylum.

Arthur Marshall

# Education

In the event of a nuclear attack Scottish children will be
given a day off school.

Vin Shanley

There are only two sorts of job always open under the
English social system – domestic service and education.
However abominable one's record, though one may be fresh
from prison or the lunatic asylum, one can always look after
the silver or teach the young. I had not the right presence for
a footman, so I chose the latter.

Evelyn Waugh

Teaching has ruined more American novelists than drink.

Gore Vidal

And remember, this is the school play. You are not here to
enjoy yourselves.

Alan Bennett

I swear I once saw this notice in a shop window –
            AVAILABLE TOP CLASS TYPISSED.

Patrick Murray

All of my best thoughts were stolen by the ancients.

Ralph Waldo Emerson

Seventy eight percent of our high school students in a recent nationwide multiple choice test, identified Abraham Lincoln as 'a kind of lobster'. That's right: more than three quarters of our nation's youth could not correctly identify the man who invented the telephone.

Dave Barry

H.G. Wells' *History of the World* is very good until the end of the Neolithic.

A.J.P. Taylor

I had an IQ test but the results came back negative.

Steven Wright

The fellow who thinks he knows it all is especially annoying to those of us who do.

Harold Coffin

If a word in the dictionary is misspelled, how would we know?

Steven Wright

I am returning this otherwise good typing paper to you because somebody has printed gibberish all over it and put your name at the top.

Steven Clark

I have never been jealous. Not even when my dad finished fifth grade a year before I did.

Jeff Foxworthy

Education

You live and learn. Well at any rate you live.

Douglas Adams

A gifted teacher is as rare as a gifted doctor and makes far less money.

Tom Lehrer

Don Robustiano had never read Voltaire, but he detested him as much as Gloucester, the Archdeacon, detested him, who hadn't read him either.

Leopoldo Alas

My teacher must have known me, had he seen me as he was wont to see me, for he was in the habit of flogging me constantly. Perhaps he did not recognise me by my face.

Anthony Trollope

When the children at public schools should have been whipped and taught Greek paradigms, they were set arguing about birth control and nationalisation. Their crude little opinions were treated with respect. It is hardly surprising that they were Bolshevik at 18 and bored at 20.

Evelyn Waugh

Force is all that matters. War is sacred. Hanging is excellent. We don't need too much knowledge. Build more prisons and fewer schools.

Victor Hugo

Education

A University President is like the body at an Irish wake. They need you in order to have the party, but no one expects you to say very much.

Anthony Lake

I think the world is run by 'C' students.

Al McGuire

What are we going to do about ignorance and apathy? I don't know and I don't care.

William Safire

Children's alphabet blocks should contain a warning: Letters may be used to construct phrases and sentences that may be deemed offensive.

David Handelsman

If you had to have a diploma to collect unemployment benefit, you'd see a lot more kids staying in school.

Wayne Knight

The private schools of England are to the educated classes what the Union Workhouses are to the very poor. Relief is granted to all who come but it is provided in as unpalatable a form as possible.

Evelyn Waugh

The need to use the lavatory is not related to biological urges but an urge to get out of class.

William Marsano

Graduates are entitled to bleat B.A. after their names.
D. S. MacColl

My school report on mathematics read "Four per cent: effortlessly achieved."
Godfrey Smith

This college is neglecting football for education.
Groucho Marx

I wrote my name at the top of the page. I wrote down the number of the question, "1". After much reflection, I put a bracket round it thus: "(1)". But thereafter I could not think of anything connected with it that was either relevant or true. It was from these slender indications of scholarship that Mr. Weldon drew the conclusion that I was worthy to pass into Harrow. It was very much to his credit.
Winston Churchill

My school colours were "clear".
Steven Wright

Fifty per cent of this country's schoolchildren have I.Q.s below average. Under our education policy, we can turn that around.
John Clarke

The most formidable headmaster I ever met was a
headmistress. She had X-ray pince-nez and that undivided
bust popularised by Queen Mary. I think she was God in
drag.

Nancy Banks-Smith

Given a choice of weapons with you, sir, I would choose
grammar.

Halliwell Hobbes

One legend that keeps recurring throughout history, in every
culture, is the story of Popeye.

Jack Handey

All the convent taught me was that if you spit on a pencil
eraser, it will erase ink.

Dorothy Parker

I hated school: arson was an option.

Alan Davies

Mamma, whose views on education are remarkably strict,
has brought me up to be extremely short-sighted; it is part of
her system.

Oscar Wilde

In elementary school, in case of fire, you have to line up
quietly in a single file line from smallest to tallest. What is
the logic? Do tall people burn slower?

Jack Handey

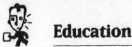 **Education**

Fourteen years in the professor dodge have taught me that one can argue ingeniously on behalf of any theory, applied to any piece of literature. This is rarely harmful, because normally no one reads such essays.

Robert Parker

Our history master was also known to possess a pair of suede shoes, a sure sign in the Melbourne of the period of sexual ambivalence.

Barry Humphries

In this address at the beginning of the new academic year I intended to give you some advice, but now I remember how much is left over from last year unused.

George Harris

The intelligent are to the intelligentsia what a gentleman is to a gent.

Stanley Baldwin

There is much to be said in favour of modern journalism. By giving us the opinions of the uneducated, it keeps us in touch with the ignorance of the community.

Oscar Wilde

School is just a jail with educational opportunities.

Robertson Davies

I have lectured on campuses for a quarter of a century, and it is my impression that after taking a course in The Novel, it is an unusual student who would ever want to read a novel again.

Gore Vidal

When bad ideas have nowhere else to go, they emigrate to America and become university courses.

Frederic Raphael

History is just a distillation of rumour.

Thomas Carlyle

As long as there are tests, there will be prayer in public schools.

David Letterman

Colleges hate geniuses just as convents hate saints.

Ralph Waldo Emerson

I told my father I was punished in school because I didn't know where the Azores were. He told me to remember where I put things in future.

Henny Youngman

A professor at a British university can be fired for only two reasons; first, gross immorality on the office furniture (I think the floor is all right) and second and worse, pinching the tea-things.

Isaac Asimov

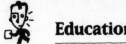

After finding no qualified candidates for the position of principal, the school board is extremely pleased to announce the appointment of David Steele to the post.

Philip Streifer

After he has served his jail sentence for perjury, Jonathan Aitken will be accepted at Oxford University to read theology. A statement from the University said: "We are satisfied that he has met the full requirements for his intended course of academic study."

Andrew Pierce

I have three A-levels: one in pure mathematics and one in applied mathematics.

Spike Milligan

I knew this girl who was a terrible speller: she worked for two years in a warehouse.

Larry Wilde

A class reunion is a meeting where three hundred people hold in their stomachs for four hours while writing down the names and addresses of friends they'll never contact.

Brenda Davidson

Instead of giving money to found colleges to promote learning, why don't they pass a constitutional amendment prohibiting anybody from learning anything? If it works as good as the Prohibition one did, in five years we would have the smartest race of people on earth.

Will Rogers

Education

Our principal writers have nearly all been fortunate in escaping regular education.

Hugh Macdiarmuid

A mother recently moaned to me that she had her Fiona tested, but sadly she wasn't dyslexic: "Oh, so she's just normal then. I am sorry."

A.A. Gill

I acquired my first motorbike, left behind by one of the masters who had to go because he had V.D.

Jennifer Patterson

There is no limit to stupidity. Space itself is said to be bounded by its own curvature, but stupidity continues beyond infinity.

Gene Wolfe

The chapter on the Fall of the Rupee you may omit. It is somewhat too sensational.

Oscar Wilde

A fool's brain digests philosophy into folly, science into superstition, and art into pedantry. Hence university education.

George Bernard Shaw

A school bus driver is someone who thought he liked children.

John Rooney

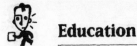
A woman who has a head full of Greek or carries on fundamental controversies about mechanics might as well have a beard.

Immanuel Kant

You didn't understand this at first, but my CONVINCING USE OF CAPITAL LETTERS HAS MADE IT ALL CLEAR TO YOU.

J. Nairn

The worst problem in the world has got to be missing children but they got the wrong people looking for those kids: the F.B.I.: and they can't find them. You got to get the Student Loan Association looking for them. I graduated from the University of Iowa nine years ago, I've moved fifty times, never left any forwarding address anywhere, I'm walking through the casino in Atlantic City and a payphone rings. It was the S.L.A.

Tom Arnold

Homework is something teenagers do during commercials.

Brenda Davidson

Eton was an early introduction to human cruelty, treachery and extreme physical hardship.

Alan Clark

The more tolerant among us regard foreign languages as a kind of speech impediment that could be overcome by willpower.

Barbara Ehrenreich

Learning has gained most by those books which the printers have lost.

Thomas Fuller

It distresses me, this failure to keep pace with the leaders of thought as they pass into oblivion.

Max Beerbohm

Why is "abbreviation" such a long word?

Steven Wright

School is where you go between when your parents can't take you and industry can't take you.

John Updike

I actually do think I'm quite intelligent. But my intelligence seems to be a different type from everyone else's.

Tara Palmer-Tomkinson

I am not an intellectual but I have this look.

Woody Allen

It is too early to form a judgement about the French Revolution.

Zhou Enlai

I have tried to know absolutely nothing about a great many things, and I have succeeded fairly well.

Robert Benchley

Education

Butler's Education Act provided for the free distribution of university degrees to the deserving poor.

Evelyn Waugh

I speak about six or seven languages – Spanish, Argentinian, Cuban, Mexican...

Seve Ballesteros

The head cannot take in more than the seat can endure.

Winston Churchill

The historian Henry Adams was the only man in America who could sit on a fence and see himself go by.

E. W. Howe

At Princeton University, we guarantee you satisfaction or you get your son back.

Woodrow Wilson

I managed to fail my 11-plus by refusing point-blank to do a maths paper. I put my hand up, gave it back and said 'I'm sorry, I don't do this'.

Nigella Lawson

The easiest way to change history is to become a historian.

Paul Dickson

Whatever people may say against Cambridge, it is certainly the best preparatory school of Oxford that I know.

Oscar Wilde

I read Shakespeare and the Bible and I can shoot dice. That's what I call a liberal education.

Tallulah Bankhead

Learning is the kind of ignorance distinguishing the studious.

Ambrose Bierce

Oxford is the best of our provincial universities.

Lord Annan

Now let me correct you on a couple of things, OK? Aristotle was not Belgian. The central message of Buddhism is not every man for himself; and the London Underground is not a political movement.

Jamie Lee Curtis

For your information, let me ask you a question.

Marshall McLuhan

University printing presses exist, and are subsidised by the Government for the purpose of producing books which no one can read; and they are true to their high calling.

Francis Cornford

The thing that best defines a child is the total inability to receive information from anything not plugged in.

Bill Cosby

Cultural Studies is the vacuous pondering of the absent.

David Womersley

A seminar is a gathering of purportedly intelligent people who sit around pooling their ignorance until group findings emerge.

Bryan Wilson

The main aim of education should be to send children out into the world with a reasonably sized anthology in their heads so that while seated on the lavatory, waiting in doctors' surgeries, on stationary trains or watching interviews with politicians, they may have something interesting to think about.

John Mortimer

Although this work is History, I believe it to be true.

Mark Twain

Why send your kids to college when for the same money you can take them to Disneyland?

Bruce Lansky

What you don't know would make a great book.

Sydney Smith

If Thomas Edison went to business school, we would all be reading by bigger candles.

Mark McCormack

The world can never be considered educated until we spend as much on books as we do on chewing gum.

Elbert Hubbard

In high school, my sister went out with the captain of the chess team. My parents loved him because they figured that any guy that took hours to make a move was OK with them.

Brian Kiley

Prison holds no terror for me because I lived in Eton in the 1950s.

Jonathan Aitken

Losing money is what university publishing is all about.

Thomas McFarland

Shirley Williams' abolition of grammar schools did more damage to the country than Hitler.

Auberon Waugh

The little I know, I owe to my ignorance.

George Bernard Shaw

Food

Food

We lived for days on nothing but food and water.

W.C. Fields

Cucumber should be well sliced, dressed with pepper and vinegar, and then thrown out.

Samuel Johnson

If a lump of soot falls into the soup, and you cannot conveniently get it out, stir it well in, and it will give the soup a French taste.

Jonathan Swift

The cook was a good cook, as cooks go; and as cooks go, she went.

H.H. Munro

Cursed is he that uses peanuts when the recipe calls for almonds.

Christopher Driver

The secret of staying young is to live honestly, eat slowly and lie about your age.

Lucille Ball

Two sharks met and one said to the other 'My dear, I've discovered the most wonderful Italian restaurant. It's called the Andrea Doria.'

John Hollander

Eat at this restaurant and you'll never eat anywhere else again!

Bob Phillips

House-warming at Zola's – a very tasty dinner, including some grouse whose scented flesh Daudet compared to an old courtesan's flesh marinated in a bidet.

Edmond de Goncourt

I personally stay away from natural foods. At my age I need all the preservatives I can get.

George Burns

Americans will eat garbage provided you sprinkle it liberally with ketchup.

Henry Miller

Not alone is it quite acceptable to breast-feed in a restaurant, but it comes in quite handy when the waiter is late with the cream.

Blanche Knott

No one goes to that restaurant anymore – it's too crowded.

Yogi Berra

Whenever cannibals are on the brink of starvation, Heaven, in its infinite mercy, sends them a fat missionary.

Oscar Wilde

I'm at the age when food has taken the place of sex in my life. In fact, I've just had a mirror put over my kitchen table.

Rodney Dangerfield

I refuse to spend my life worrying about what I eat. There is no pleasure worth foregoing just for an extra three years in the geriatric ward.

John Mortimer

The most remarkable thing about my mother is that for thirty years she served the family nothing but leftovers. The original meal has never been found.

Calvin Trillin

I'm on a grapefruit diet. I eat everything except grapefruit.

Chi Chi Rodriguez

Food

No request is too much in this restaurant – I shall of course be delighted to change your colostomy bag Ma'am.

Jonathan Meades

Soup is food – not musical instrument.

Charlie Chan

Diamond Jim Brady was the best twenty-five customers I ever had in my restaurant.

Charles Rector

My uncle Charlie showed me where milk comes from, but I still like it.

Hank Ketcham

I'm trying to lose some weight so I've gone on a garlic diet. You eat garlic with everything. It doesn't make you lose any weight but people stand further back and you look thinner at a distance.

Noel Britton

Bread that must be sliced with an axe is bread that is too nourishing.

Fran Lebowitz

The two biggest sellers in any bookshop are the cookbooks and the diet books. The cookbooks tell you how to prepare the food and the diet books tell you how not to eat any of it.

Andy Rooney

Food

At my lemonade stand I used to give the first glass away free and charge five dollars for the second glass. The refill contained the antidote.

Emo Philips

The proof that God has a very weird sense of humour is that, having invented the sublime mystery of haute cuisine, he went and give it to the French.

A.A. Gill

One of the main arguments in favour of fox hunting is that foxes kill chickens. But so does Bernard Matthews and nobody advocates chasing him across the country with a pack of dogs and tearing him to pieces.

Alexei Sayle

Shake and shake the ketchup bottle. First none'll come and then a lott'ill.

Richard Armour

There is a machine that dispenses liquids that are allegedly 'coffee', 'tea', 'hot chocolate' and even 'soup', which all come from the same orifice and all taste exactly the same.

Dave Barry

Another machine dispenses bags containing a grand total of maybe three potato chips each and packages of crackers smeared with a bizarre substance called 'cheez', which is the same bright-orange colour as marine rescue equipment.

Dave Barry

Food

Dried fish is a staple food in Iceland: it varies in toughness. The tougher kind tastes like toenails, and the softer kind like the skin off the soles of one's feet.

W. H. Auden

I went into McDonald's the other day and asked for some fries. The girl at the counter said, "Would you like some fries with that?"

Jay Leno

Her cooking suggested that she had attained the Cordon Noir.

Leo Rosten

One thing my mother could never say to me is that my eyes were bigger than my belly.

Roy Brown

No Roman was ever able to say, "I dined last night with the Borgias."

Max Beerbohm

I will never understand why they cook on TV. I can't smell it. Can't eat it. Can't taste it. At the end of the show they hold it up to the camera. "Well here it is. You can't have any. Thanks for watching. Goodbye."

Jerry Seinfeld

I'd like to live on Mars.

Jo Brand

Airline food is gastronomic murder, preceded by culinary torture.

Egon Ronay

A diet is a system of starving yourself to death so you can live a little longer.

Totie Fields

The older you get, the better you get: unless you're a banana.

Rose Nylund

If you are in the process of preparing something, food licked off knives and spoons has no calories, e.g. peanut butter on a knife or spoon.

Lewis Grizzard

You seem quite out of sorts. You haven't quarrelled with your cook, I hope? What a tragedy that would be for you; you would lose all your friends.

Oscar Wilde

Whenever you get sick at a party there will always be carrots. You may never have eaten a carrot in your life, you may have led a totally carrot-free existence, but there they are, bloody carrots.

Mike Harding

Never trust a thin cook.

Charlotte Wright

Food

When drinking a diet soda while eating a candy bar, the calories in the candy bar are cancelled by the diet soda. And cookie pieces contain no calories. The process of breaking the cookie causes calorie leakage.

Lewis Grizzard

My mother is the only person in the world who cooks lumpy boiled water.

David Brenner

I live in a place called Green Lanes, but that's a misnomer. The only green you see is on a Saturday night when people are throwing up the salad off their kebabs.

Alan Davies

It is time to go on a diet when the Prudential offers you group insurance.

Totie Fields

I just love animals, especially in good gravy.

Freddie Starr

There is only one secret to bachelor cooking: not caring how it tastes.

P. J. O'Rourke

Good mashed potato is one of the great luxuries of life and I don't blame Elvis for eating it every night for the last year of his life.

Lindsey Bareham

"Turbot, sir," said the waiter, placing before me two wishbones, two eyeballs and a bit of black mackintosh.

Thomas E. Welby

It has been said that fish is good brain food. That's a fallacy. But brains are good fish food.

Mel Brooks

As a child my family's menu consisted of two choices: take it or leave it.

Buddy Hackett

Coffee in England is just toasted milk.

Christopher Foy

Now all your doughnuts can be like Fanny's.

Johnny Craddock

A delicatessen is a shop selling the worst parts of animals more expensively than the nice parts.

Mike Barfield

Large, naked, raw carrots are acceptable food only to those who live in hutches eagerly awaiting Easter.

Fran Lebowitz

Why do people who work in health food shops always look so unhealthy?

Victoria Wood

Food

Asquith's two lifelong aversions were to eating rabbit and the Roman Catholic Church.

Selina Hastings

I haven't clawed my way to the top of the food chain just to eat vegetables.

Charles Jarvis

I don't even butter my bread; I consider that cooking.

Merla Zellerbach

NAAFI – where you can eat dirt cheap.

Frank Muir

In bush cooking, you always want to garnish when it's off.

Bill Harney

To cook meat, I put a little roast and a big roast in the oven at the same time. When the little one burns, the big roast is done.

Gracie Allen

This restaurant is full at 8.55 p.m. There are obviously a lot of people in Paris who know nothing about food.

Michael Winner

I make a lot of jokes about vegetarians in my act but most of them don't have enough strength to protest.

Ardal O'Hanlon

Food

When I invite a woman to dinner I expect her to look at my face. That's the price she has to pay.

Groucho Marx

If the Chinese are so clever, why can't they do puddings?

Jonathan Ross

I can recommend this restaurant to Hindus out for a good night's fasting.

Denis Leary

Home-made dishes are ones that drive one from home.

Thomas Hood

You'll eat anything when you're a kid – snots, ear wax, toenail clippings, scabs. But not sprouts.

Tony Burgess

This restaurant is very consistent – steak, coffee and ice cream – all the same temperature.

Michael Winner

Never eat any product on which the listed ingredients cover more than one-third of the package.

Herb Caen

I went on a diet – but I had to go on another one at the same time because the first diet wasn't giving me enough food.

Barry Marter

Lawyers and other Professions

Lawyers and other Professions

An actuary is someone who cannot stand the excitement of chartered accountancy.

Glan Thomas

Justice must not only be done, it must be seen to be believed.

J.B. Morton

I have nothing against undertakers personally. It's just that I wouldn't want one to bury my sister.

Jessica Mitford

Only lawyers and mental defectives are automatically exempt from jury duty.

George Bernard Shaw

When I came back to Dublin I was court-martialed in my absence and sentenced to death in my absence, so I said they could shoot me in my absence.

Brendan Behan

It's not the people who are in prison that worry me. It's the people who aren't.

Arthur Gore

A person guilty of rape should be castrated. That would stop him pretty quick.

Billy Graham

No brilliance is required in the law, just common sense and relatively clean fingernails.

John Mortimer

Lawyers and other Professions

The thrill of hearing a jury return a guilty verdict is the ultimate sexual experience.

Judge Gregory Wallance

I am on record as saying that Simon Cameron would not steal a red-hot stove. I now wish to withdraw that statement.

Thaddeus Stevens

A lawyer is a learned gentleman who rescues your estate from your enemies and keeps it to himself.

Henry Brougham

Probably the only place where a man can feel really secure is in a maximum security prison, except for the imminent threat of release.

Germaine Greer

The court was not previously aware of the prisoner's many accomplishments. In view of these, we see fit to impose the death penalty.

Quentin Crisp

I went to see him hanged, drawn, and quartered, which was done, he looking as cheerful as any man could do in that condition.

Samuel Pepys

The only difference between doctors and lawyers is that lawyers merely rob you, whereas doctors rob you and kill you, too.

Anton Chekhov

Curiosity killed the cat, but for a while I was a suspect.

Steven Wright

Lawyers and other Professions

This book is dedicated to Gollancz's libel lawyer, John Rubinstein, without whom it would have been considerably longer.

Victor Lewis-Smith

Your honour, as I was overtaking the other car quite legally, the policeman was hiding in the bushes with a bucket of whitewash, and when he saw me approach he rushed out and painted double lines on the road.

Spike Milligan

I was going to be a shrink but I thought if their stories got dull, I'd have to kill them.

Ruby Wax

We had a guy who was absent from work so much that he celebrated his 25th anniversary with the company after 35 years.

Gene Perret

Of this I am certain, when the Antichrist comes, he will have a law degree.

John F. Curran

Pool hustling is life – work is for cowards.

U.J. Puckett

The witness will please state her age, after which the clerk will swear her in.

Norton Plasset

We have a criminal jury system which is superior to any in the world; and its efficiency is marred only by the difficulty of finding twelve men every day who don't know anything and can't read.

Mark Twain

If I was being executed by injection, I'd clean up my cell real neat. Then, when they came to get me I'd say, 'Injection?' I thought you said 'inspection'. They'd probably feel real bad, and maybe I could get out of it.

Jack Handey

The comparative of lawyer is "liar" and the superlative is "expert".

Pierre Bernthsen

When Lem Moon was acquitted for the murder of his wife and the judge asked him if he had anything to say he replied, 'If I had known I'd have to go through so much red tape, I never would have shot her'.

Kin Hubbard

Anyone who supports capital punishment should be shot.

Colin Crompton

The First Amendment states that members of religious groups, no matter how small or unpopular, shall have the right to hassle you in airports.

Dave Barry

Lawyers are the opposite of sex. Even when they're good they're lousy.

Dave Barry

Wretches hang that jurymen may dine.

Alexander Pope

The ugliest of trades have their moments of pleasure. Now if I were a grave-digger, or even a hangman, there are some people I could work for with a great deal of enjoyment.

Douglas Jerrold

Lawyers and other Professions

A journalist is someone who stays sober right up to lunch time.

Godfrey Smith

The judge asked me where I was in the interim. I told him I had never been near the place.

Jimmy Durante

I don't mind hecklers, because I know how to ignore people: I was an airline stewardess.

Jo-Ann Deering

You may leave the court with no other stain on your character other than the fact that you have been acquitted by an Irish jury.

Maurice Healy

A lawyer with his briefcase can steal more than a thousand men with guns.

Mario Puzo

The crime rate in Mexico City is so high because the police wear uniforms and the criminals always spot us.

Francisco Luna

Frankly, I don't believe people think of their office as a workplace anyway. I think they think of it as a stationery store with Danish. You want to get your pastry, your envelopes, your supplies, your toilet paper, six cups of coffee and you go home.

Jerry Seinfeld

Lawyers and other Professions

I read the other day of a man who was cleared of causing cruelty to animals in Maryland. The prosecution said he had had sex with a raccoon but in his defence he said the animal was dead at the time and therefore could not have suffered.

Jeremy Clarkson

I should urge your client to observe, and to ensure that his dog observes, the standards of behaviour proper to their respective levels of creation.

Geoffrey Madan

I have all the Christian virtues except that of resignation.

Lord Denning

The defendant aroused the landlord's suspicion as he was the only one in the pub wearing prison uniform.

Mick Potter

In Washington, D.C, there are more lawyers than people.

Sandra O'Connor

The firm of Batten, Barton, Durstine & Osborne sounds like a trunk falling downstairs.

Fred Allen

Epitaph on a dead waiter: By and by, God caught his eye.

David McCord

Four-fifths of the perjury in the world is expended on tombstones, women and competitors.

Lord Dewar

Lawyers and other Professions

I was a witness in a road accident case. All I could testify is that the cars hit each other at about the same time.

Steven Wright

The policeman who arrested me said I was doing between 106 and 108 miles an hour. "107 then," I said.

Alan Davies

Hijackers should be given a rapid trial with due process of law, then hanged.

Edward Davis

The main difference between O.J. Simpson and Christopher Reeves is that O.J. walked while Christopher Reeves got the electric chair.

Tim Dedopulos

The long and distressing controversy over capital punishment is very unfair to anyone contemplating murder.

Geoffrey Fisher

Nothing is more annoying than to be obscurely hanged.

Voltaire

There are many different jobs for cops these days. It seems to me that the Chalk Outline Guy is one of the better jobs you can get. It's not too dangerous, the criminals are long gone: that seems like a good one. I don't know who those guys are. I guess they're people who wanted to be sketch artists but they couldn't draw too well.

Jerry Seinfeld

It is probably no mere chance that in legal textbooks the problems relating to married women are usually considered immediately after the pages devote to idiots and lunatics.

A.P. Herbert

Dorothy Parker and I once shared the tiniest office space imaginable. One cubic foot less of space and it would have constituted adultery.

Robert Benchley

They were as scarce as lawyers in heaven.

Mark Twain

With Congress, every time they make a joke it's a law and every time they make a law it's a joke.

Will Rogers

The only difference between a pigeon and a farmer today is that a pigeon can still make a deposit on a tractor.

M.E. Kerr

In America they lock up juries and let the defendants out on bail.

Herbert Prochnow

Death is one of the worst things that can happen to a Mafia member, and many prefer to pay a fine.

Woody Allen

An executive is just an ulcer with authority.

Fred Allen

Economics is the only profession where you can gain great eminence without ever being right.

George Meany

Lawyers are like rhinoceroses: thick-skinned, short-sighted and always ready to charge.

David Mellor

He might have brought an action against his countenance for libel, and won heavy damages.

Charles Dickens

I didn't steal it. It was 'differently acquired'.

Sara Cytron

I have forgotten more law than you ever knew, but allow me to say, I have not forgotten much.

John Maynard

My father, a teacher at an inner-city comprehensive, once taught a family where all five boys were named Eugene so as to confuse the police.

Joanna Coles

My lawyer is so good they've named a loophole after him.

Steven Wright

A solicitor is a man who calls in a person he does not know, to sign a contract he hasn't seen to buy a property he does not want with money he hasn't got.

Dingwall Bateson

Lawyers and Other Professions

A historian is merely an unsuccessful novelist but then so are most novelists.

H. L. Mencken

Capital punishment would be more effective as a preventive measure if it were administered prior to the crime.

Woody Allen

Remember at the Preston A. Mantis Consumers Retail Law Outlet, our motto is: 'It is very difficult to disprove certain kinds of pain.'

Dave Barry

A cavity is a tiny hole in your child's tooth that takes many, many dollars to fill.

Bill Dodds

You have the right to remain silent, so please shut up.

Denis Leary

He had faced death in many forms but he had never faced a dentist. The thought of dentists gave him just the same sick horror as the thought of Socialism.

Evelyn Waugh

Good news – they've found Hitler. He's alive, living in Buenos Aires and they're bringing him to trial. The bad news – they're holding the trial in L.A.

Alice Kahn

Literature

Literature

I never read a book before reviewing it. I find that it just prejudices me.

Sydney Smith

Read over your compositions, and wherever you meet with a passage which you think is particularly fine, strike it out.

Samuel Johnson

The dawn is a term for the early morning used by poets and other people who don't have to get up.

Oliver Herford

He has produced a couplet. When our friend is delivered of a couplet, with infinite labour and pain, he takes to his bed, has straw laid down, the knocker tied up, and expects his friends to call and make enquiries.

Sydney Smith

Two people getting together to write a book is like three people getting together to have a baby. One of them is superfluous.

George Bernard Shaw

I never travel without my diary. One should always have something sensational to read in the train.

Oscar Wilde

My only claim to literary fame is that I used to deliver meat to a woman who became T. S. Eliot's mother-in-law.

Alan Bennett

If you want to get rich from writing, write the sort of thing that's read by persons who move their lips when they're reading to themselves.

Don Marquis

Literature

You may certainly not kiss the hand that wrote *Ulysses*. It's done lots of other things as well.

James Joyce

An editor should have a pimp for a brother so he can have someone to look up to.

Gene Fowler

Your manuscript is both good and original; but the part that is good is not original, and the part that is original is not good.

Samuel Johnson

Immature poets imitate; mature poets steal.

T.S. Eliot

This is not a book to be tossed aside lightly. It should be thrown with great force.

Dorothy Parker

I am sitting in the smallest room in the house. I have your review before me. It will soon be behind me.

Max Reger

I have been told by hospital authorities that more copies of my works are left behind by departing patients than those of any other author.

Robert Benchley

George Bernard Shaw writes like a Pakistani who has learned English when he was twelve years old to become a chartered accountant.

John Osborne

The Poems of Seth will be remembered long after those of Homer and Virgil are forgotten – but not until then.

Richard Porson

Literature

Reading Proust is like bathing in someone else's dirty water.

Alexander Woollcott

Finishing a book is just like you took a child out in the yard and shot it.

Truman Capote

For those who like this sort of thing, this is the sort of thing they will like.

Max Beerbohm

Donne's verses are like the peace and mercy of God. Like His peace, they pass all understanding, and like His mercy they seem to endure forever.

King James I

I was working on the proofs of one of my poems all day. In the morning I put a comma in and in the afternoon I took it back out again.

Oscar Wilde

Originality is undetected plagiarism.

W.R. Ince

Free verse is like playing tennis with the net down.

Robert Frost

I have read only one book in my life, and that is *White Fang*. It's so frightfully good I've never bothered to read another.

Nancy Mitford

There are two ways of disliking poetry. One way is to dislike it, and the other is to read Pope.

Oscar Wilde

Many thanks for your book – I shall lose no time in reading it.

Benjamin Disraeli

Warren Harding, the only man, woman, or child who ever wrote a simple declarative sentence with seven grammatical errors, is dead.

e.e. cummings

To me Poe's prose is unreadable – like Jane Austen's. No, there is a difference. I could read Poe's prose on a salary, but not Jane Austen's.

Mark Twain

Mr Irvin Cobb took me into his library and showed me his books, of which he has a complete set.

Ring Lardner

Mr Waugh is a parochial English writer (tautologies gush from my pen!)

Gore Vidal

Writers of thrillers tend to gravitate to the Secret Service as the mentally unstable become psychiatrists and the impotent become pornographers.

Malcolm Muggeridge

On the day when a young writer corrects his first proof sheets, he is as proud as a schoolboy who has just got his first dose of pox.

Charles Baudelaire

His books are going like wildfire – everybody is burning them.

George de Witt

I am addicted to literature. I never go anywhere without a Trollope.

Alec Guinness

Literature

Your function as a critic is to show that it is really you yourself who should have written the book, if you had had the time, and since you hadn't you are glad that someone else had, although obviously it might have been done better.

Stephen Potter

Shakespeare said pretty well everything and what he left out, James Joyce, with a nudge from meself, put in.

Brendan Behan

When I want to read a book, I write one.

Benjamin Disraeli

Paradise Lost is a book that, once put down, is very hard to pick up again.

Samuel Johnson

Oscar Wilde paraphrased and inverted the witticisms and epigrams of others. His method of literary piracy was on the lines of the robber Cacus, who dragged stolen cows backwards by the tails to his cavern so that their hoofprints might not lead to detection.

George Moore

This book of Italian literature shows a want of knowledge that must be the result of years of study.

Oscar Wilde

If you steal from one author, it's plagiarism; if you steal from many, it's research.

Wilson Mizner

I've given up reading books. I find it takes my mind off myself.

Oscar Wilde

Jeffrey Archer is proof of the proposition that in each of us there lurks a bad novel.

Julian Critchley

He was an author whose works were so little known as to be almost confidential.

Stanley Walker

There are just three rules for writing – but nobody knows what they are.

Somerset Maugham

G.K. Chesterton and Hilaire Belloc were the two buttocks of one bum.

T. Sturge Moore

This book is dedicated to the one woman fate created just for me. So far I've managed to avoid her.

Jon Winokur

Thomas Gray walks as if he had fouled his small-clothes, and looks as if he smelt it.

Christopher Smart

Perhaps the saddest lot that can befall mortal man is to be the husband of a lady poet.

George Jean Nathan

George Sand was a great cow-full of ink.

Gustave Flaubert

My brother-in-law wrote an unusual murder story. The victim got killed by a man from another book.

Robert Sylvester

Literature

You've got to be one of two ages to appreciate Walter Scott.
When you're eighteen you can read *Ivanhoe*, and you want to
wait until you are ninety to read some of the rest. It takes a
pretty well-regulated abstemious critic to live ninety years.

Mark Twain

I cannot choose one hundred best books because I have
written only five.

Oscar Wilde

I wouldn't drop God if I were Graham Greene. It would be
like P.G. Wodehouse dropping Jeeves halfway through the
Wooster series.

Evelyn Waugh

I trust that the Brownings' marriage will be a happy one and
that they will speak more intelligibly to each other than they
have yet done to the public.

William Wordsworth

I was once gratified to receive a cheque from a magazine for
a joke I had stolen from its own pages.

Bernard Braden

And now kind friends, what I have wrote
I hope you will pass over,
and not criticise as some have done
Hitherto herebefore.

Julia A. Moore

I have met people who have borrowed my books from the library; I have met others more enterprising, who have stolen them from the library; but I have never met anyone who has *bought* any of my books.

Russell Braddon

A prose style may often be improved by striking out every other word from each sentence when written.

Sydney Smith

I hear the little children say
(For the tale will never die)
How the old pump flowed both night and day
When the brooks and the wells ran dry.
This verse has all the ring of Macaulay in it, and is a form of poetry which cannot possibly harm anybody, even if translated into French.

Oscar Wilde

On looking over at Sir Walter Scott, I was painfully struck by the utter vacancy of his look. How dreadful if he should live to survive that mighty mind of his.

Thomas Moore

Literature

This book was written in those long hours I spent waiting for my wife to get dressed to go out. And if she had never gotten dressed at all, this book would never have been written.

Groucho Marx

My talent I put into my writing; my genius I have saved for living.

Oscar Wilde

Writers have two main problems. One is writer's block, when words won't come at all, and the other is logorrhoea, when the words come so fast that they can hardly get to the wastebasket in time.

Cecilia Bartholomew

The football memoir is a literary form that ranks at least two grades below the trashiest airport novel.

Alan English

Women write novels because there is this tremendous desire to expose themselves; with men the motive is often some kind of obscure revenge.

Auberon Waugh

I once came across a book I had signed 'With compliments' to a friend in a second hand bookshop. So I bought it and sent it to him 'With renewed compliments'.

George Bernard Shaw

In truth, Wycherley's indecency is protected against the critics as a skunk is protected against the hunters. It is safe because it is too filthy to handle, and too noisome to approach.

Thomas B. Macaulay

Always be nicer to writers younger than you, because they are the ones who will be writing about you.

Cyril Connolly

William Faulkner was a great friend of mine. Well as much as you could be a friend of his unless you were a fourteen-year-old nymphet.

Truman Capote

The few bad poems which occasionally are created during abstinence are of no great interest.

Wilhelm Reich

Henry Miller was writing a huge book on Hamlet but could not bring himself to read Shakespeare's version; so he asked Lawrence Durrell to give him the low-down on it.

D.J. Enright

Where do I find all the time for not reading so many books?

Karl Kraus

There must be five hundred signed copies for particular friends; six for the general public; and one for America.

Oscar Wilde

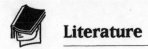

Literature

I do not want Miss Mannin's feelings to be hurt by the fact that I have never heard of her. At the moment I am debarred from the pleasures of putting her in her place by the fact that she has not got one.

Edith Sitwell

Pope's verses, when they were written, resembled nothing so much as spoonfuls of boiling oil, ladled out by a fiendish monkey at an upstairs window upon such of the passers-by whom the wretch had a grudge against.

Lytton Strachey

The Chronicle of Mites is a mock-heroic poem about the inhabitants of a decaying cheese who speculate about the origin of their species and hold learned discussions upon the meaning of evolution and the Gospel according to Darwin. This cheese-epic is a rather unsavoury production and the style is at times so monstrous and so realistic that the author should be called the Gorgon-Zola of literature.

Oscar Wilde

Except for a sense of humour, Hemingway had everything.

Quentin Crisp

From my close observation of writers, they fall into two groups – those who bleed copiously and visibly at any bad review and those who bleed copiously and secretly at any bad review.

Isaac Asimov

My dog ate *Of Mice and Men* but was unable to finish *Moby Dick*.

George Steinbeck

Literature

The original of Beckford's *Vathek* is not faithful to Henley's translation.

Jorge Luis Borges

Conrad is pretty certain to come back into favour. One of the surest signs of his genius is that women dislike his books.

George Orwell

George Orwell was Don Quixote on a bicycle.

Paul Potts

It seems a great pity they allowed Jane Austen to die a natural death.

Mark Twain

Ten years of rejection slips is nature's way of telling you to stop writing.

Ralph Geiss

We were put to Dickens as children but it never quite took. That unremitting humanity soon had me cheesed off.

Alan Bennett

Somerset Maugham – that old lady is a crashing bore.

Dorothy Parker

I don't think anyone should write their autobiography until after they are dead.

Samuel Goldwyn

Literature

In the pages of Pater, the English language lies in state.

George Moore

Until twelve years ago, I didn't realise that books were translated. I thought Proust wrote in English.

Beryl Bainbridge

Last night I dined out in Chelsea and mauled the dead and rotten carcasses of several works written by my friends.

Virginia Woolf

I know I have won the Nobel Prize for literature. Stop babbling man: how much?

W. B. Yeats

Whitman was not only eager to talk about himself but reluctant to have the conversation stray from the subject for too long.

Henry D. Thoreau

There are passages of Joyce's *Ulysses* which should be read only in the toilet: if one wants to extract the full flavour of their content.

Henry Miller

It is a sad feature of modern life that only women for the most part have the time to write novels, and they seldom have much to write about.

Auberon Waugh

John Millicent Synge.

James Joyce

Metaphors be with you.

Harvey Mindess

The success of many books is due to the affinity between the mediocrity of the author's ideas and those of the public.

Sébastien Roch Nicolas Chamfort

For those sated readers of my work who ardently wish I would stop, the future looks very dark indeed.

Noel Coward

Your life would not make a good book. Don't even try.

Fran Lebowitz

I am sick and tired of obscure English towns that exist seemingly for the sole accommodation of these limerick writers: and even sicker of their residents, all of whom suffer from physical deformities and spend their time dismembering relatives at fancy dress balls.

Flann O'Brien

At certain points reading Tom Wolfe's *A Man in Full* can be said to resemble the act of making love to a 300lb woman. Once she gets on top it's all over. Fall in love, or be asphyxiated.

Norman Mailer

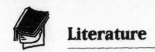

Literature

A magazine editor asked me if I would consider turning one of my plays into a short story for five hundred dollars. I reflected gleefully that for five hundred dollars I would gladly consider turning *War and Peace* into a music-hall sketch.

Noel Coward

Do we need another dictionary of quotations? Hell, yes! Like underpants in the Urals, you can never have enough of them.

Reginald Hill

I refused the Nobel Prize for literature on the grounds that I wish to be read by people who feel like reading my books and not by celebrity collectors.

Jean-Paul Sartre

My wife pleased me by laughing uproariously when reading my manuscript, only to inform me that it was my spelling that amused her.

Gerald Durrell

Reviewers seemed to fall into two classes: those that had little to say and those that had nothing.

Max Beerbohm

I have always been an avid reader; ever since I grew hair I could sit on, I could always be found with a torch under the sheets, until a doctor advised me to give it up and take up reading. Since then I've never looked back or up again.

Edna Everage

Life and Laughter Amidst the Cannibals relates the hilarious story of a sailor visiting the Solomon Islands who avoided being eaten by cannibals but whose false teeth fell overboard; in attempting to retrieve them, he was eaten alive by a shark.

Russell Ash

I read a book twice as fast as anybody else. First I read the beginning, then I read the ending and then I start in the middle and work towards whichever end I like best.

Gracie Allen

Everything I've said will be credited to Dorothy Parker.

George Kaufman

Here lies that peerless peer Lord Peter
Who broke the laws of God and man and metre.

John Lockhart

Balzac was so conceited that he raised his hat every time he spoke of himself.

Robert Broughton

The affair between Margot Asquith and Margot Asquith will live as one of the prettiest love stories in all literature.

Dorothy Parker

I was a genius and therefore unemployable.

Patrick Kavanagh

Literature

To hear W. B. Yeats read his own verses was as excruciating a torture as anyone could be exposed to.

Somerset Maugham

Critics are just cut-throat bandits in the paths of fame.

Robert Burns

I don't split infinitives. When I get to work on them, I break them into little pieces.

Jimmy Durante

Literary confessors are contemptible, like beggars who exhibit their sores for money, but not so contemptible as the public that buys their books.

W. H. Auden

All books over five hundred pages that weren't written by Dickens or a dead Russian are better left on the shelf.

William Blundell

I'm really into bondage. When I'm in the mood I'll tie my wife up and gag her and go into the living room and watch a football game.

Tom Arnold

There is obviously a right and a wrong time for any book and attempting as a seventeen-year-old to tackle Virginia Woolf's subtle essay in modernism, *To the Lighthouse*, on a topless beach in Biarritz was almost certainly a mistake.

Richard Beswick

I do not think I had ever seen a nastier-looking man than Percy Wyndham Lewis. Under a black hat, when I had first seen them, the eyes had been those of an unsuccessful rapist.

Ernest Hemingway

When I am asked what kind of writing is the most lucrative, I have to say, ransom notes.

H.N. Swanton

If Malcolm Hardee is as good between the covers of this book as he is between the sheets, put the book back on the shelf.

Jo Brand

Similes are like defective ammunition: the lowest thing I can think of at this time.

Ernest Hemingway

Authors should be paid by the quantity of works not written.

Jack Kirwan

Mr. Hall Caine writes at the top of his voice.

Oscar Wilde

Last thing at night I go over what I'm working on: it's the best sleeping pill.

Jilly Cooper

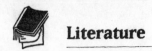

My father adored Shakespeare. Every time he caught sight of me he would say: "Is execution done on Cawdor?" When you are four, that's a pretty tough question.

John Mortimer

A man told me that he had been reading my works all his life. I observed that he must be very tired.

Samuel Beckett

All women poets, dead or alive, who smoke cigars, are major. All poets named Edna St. Vincent Millay are major.

E. B. White

Booksellers drink of their wine in the manner of the heroes in the hall of Odin: out of authors' skulls.

Peter Pindar

The llama is a woolly sort of fleecy hairy goat, with an indolent expression and an undulating throat like an unsuccessful literary man.

Hilaire Belloc

Oxymoron is a literary device whereby two contradictory concepts are juxtaposed: as for example in "the witty Jane Austen".

Patrick Murray

No animal was harmed in the making of this book.

Simon Rose

Publishing pays: if you don't charge for your time.

Jonathan Cape

I know everything. One has to, to write decently.

Henry James

I have given my memoirs far more thought than any of my marriages. You can't divorce a book.

Gloria Swanson

No one reads modern poetry, other than professional poets, professional poets' families, and the poetry reviewer of the *Sunday Times*.

Marcus Berkman

I always told James that he should give up writing and take up singing.

Nora Joyce

I found it impossible to work with security staring me in the face.

Sherwood Anderson

I gave my young nephew a book for Christmas. He's spent six months looking for where to put the batteries.

Milton Berle

Literature

I've just been reading the dictionary. It turns out the zebra did it.

Steven Wright

The great American novel has not only already been written, it has already been rejected.

Frank Dane

Lyric Inditer and Reciter. Poetry Promptly Executed.

W. M. McGonagall

If someone complains that punning is the lowest form of humour, you can tell them that poetry is verse.

Bob Davis

Rod McKuen's poetry is not even trash.

Karl Shapiro

When I see someone asleep over one of my books I am pleased that I have induced healthful slumber.

William M. Thackeray

Baldrick, I'd rather French kiss a skunk than listen to your poetry.

Rowan Atkinson

Poetry is so undervalued in our society that no one should be discouraged from writing it, even Jewel.

Kim Carlin

My cousin Jimmy Burke was the only one of us who could write. I mean, his name.

Brendan Behan

There comes the dreaded moment in any anthology when yours truly decides to include: himself. This fact alone is enough to condemn the book out of hand; if the anthologist cannot see the huge gap between his own pathetic offering and the others, he is obviously not fit to do the job in the first place.

Des MacHale

My name is an anagram of toilets.

T. S. Eliot

Fat people are brilliant in bed. If I'm sitting on top of you, who's going to argue?

Jo Brand

In the course of the book *250 Times I Saw a Play*, the author fails to mention what the play was, who wrote it, where it was performed and who acted in it.

Brian Lake

An author's first duty is to let down his country.

Brendan Behan

Now Barabbas was a publisher.

Thomas Campbell

Literature

I was sent an author's questionnaire to help Norwegian sales. Under "Hobbies?" I listed "Tattooing snakes on sailors' bottoms".

Evelyn Waugh

The ideal reader of my novels is a lapsed Catholic and a failed musician, short-sighted, colour-blind, auditorily biased, who has read the same books that I have read.

Anthony Burgess

It's no fun having dinner with other writers. They have crap social skills, poor personal hygiene and toxic jealousy.

Celia Brayfield

I have known her pass the whole evening without mentioning a single book, in fact anything unpleasant at all.

Henry Reed

Publishers' offices are now crammed with homosexuals who have a horror of any writing with balls in it.

Marshall McLuhan

William Wordsworth keeps one eye on a daffodil and the other on a canal share.

Walter Savage Landor

With sixty staring me in the face, I have developed inflammation of the sentence structure and a definite hardening of the paragraphs.

James Thurber

If only I had taken up golf earlier and devoted my whole time to it instead of writing stories and things, I might have my handicap down to under eighteen.

P.G. Wodehouse

Your Majesty, do not hang George Wither lest it be said that I am the worst poet in the kingdom.

John Denham

The more I read Socrates, the less I wonder they poisoned him.

Thomas B. Macaulay

Watership Down: frankly I would prefer to read a novel about civil servants written by a rabbit.

Craig Brown

In the case of poets, the most important thing for them to do is to write as little as possible.

T.S. Eliot

Carlyle finally compressed his *Gospel of Silence* into thirty handsome octavo volumes.

Lord Morley

Always read stuff that will make you look good if you die in the middle of it.

P.J. O'Rourke

# Literature

One should never read the latest books. Instead, wait for a few years and watch most of them disappear into well-deserved oblivion. This eliminates much unnecessary reading.

Somerset Maugham

Seamus Heaney couldn't write out a shopping list without winning some kind of award.

Cosmo Landesman

I am writing a history of the QE2. I have a good track record with larger-than-life Iron Ladies.

Carol Thatcher

The material of *A Tourist in Africa* was so thin that I suggested to Chapman and Hall that I insert adverbs before all the adjectives in an attempt to lengthen the text.

Evelyn Waugh

Max Beerbohm has the most remarkable and deductive genius – and I should say about the smallest in the world.

Lytton Strachey

I found nothing wrong with Gertrude Stein's autobiography except her poor choice of subject.

Clifton Fadiman

David Halberstam's book on the 1950s, called *The Fifties*, is as inspired and clever as its title.

John Podhoretz

I'm a lousy writer but a helluva lot of people have lousy taste.

Grace Metalous

Fine writing, next to doing nothing, is the best thing in the world.

John Keats

The literary biography is the Meals-on-Wheels service of the book world.

Sheridan Morley

I called my first book 'Collected Works Vol 1'.

Max Beerbohm

Henry Miller is not really a writer but a non-stop talker to whom someone has given a typewriter.

Gerald Brenan

They say my writings have made me immortal. But what is the use of immortality to a man when he's dead?

George Moore

The most violent action W. H. Auden ever saw was when he was playing table tennis at Tossa del Mar on behalf of the Spanish Republicans – apart from the violent exercise he got with his knife and fork.

Roy Campbell

He did nothing; he was a poet.

Sheila Mooney

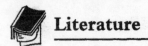 **Literature**

Anyone could write a novel given six weeks, pen, paper, and no telephone or wife.

Evelyn Waugh

Did you know that Jane Austen had an unpublished manuscript in her drawers called Farts and Flatulence?

Patrick Murray

I have crossed out the parts of your script that I did not like. What I haven't crossed out I'm not happy with.

Cecil B. De Mille

Literature is written material that, a hundred years after the death of the author, is forced upon high school students.

Tom Clancy

That's Kingsley Amis, and there's no known cure.

Robert Graves

Circumlocution is a literary trick whereby the writer who has nothing to say breaks it gently to the reader.

Ambrose Bierce

If it were thought that anything I wrote were influenced by Robert Frost, I would take that particular piece of mine, shred it, and flush it down the toilet, hoping not to clog the pipes.

James Dickey

Literature

I became a writer in the same way that a woman becomes a prostitute. First I did it to please myself, then I did it to please my friends and finally I did it for money.

Ferenc Molnar

Substitute 'damn' every time you're inclined to write 'very'; your editor will delete it and the writing will be just as it should be.

Mark Twain

There is only one way to make money at writing and that is to marry a publisher's daughter.

George Orwell

The world's thinnest book is *My Plan To Find The Real Killers* by O. J. Simpson.

Mike McQueen

Edward Gibbon is an ugly, affected, disgusting fellow, and poisons our literary club for me. I class him among infidel wasps and venomous insects.

James Boswell

I would rather endure the pain of a kidney stone the size of a golf ball than to be forced to read this book again.

Ronald Berk

The best place for a female author to discuss terms with an editor is in bed after a couple of double martinis.

Donald MacCampbell

Literature

Times are bad. Children no longer obey their parents and everyone is writing a book.

Cicero

To save my mother from the electric chair I couldn't read three pages of James Cavell's The Silver Stallion.

Dorothy Parker

The foundation of T. S. Eliot's work was self-contempt, well-grounded.

F. R. Leavis

You can't fake bad writing. It's a gift.

Richard Le Gallienne

Writing about travels is nearly always tedious, travelling being, like war and fornication, exciting but not interesting.

Malcolm Muggeridge

Censors read a book only with great difficulty, moving their lips as they puzzle out each syllable, when someone tells them that the book is unfit to be read.

Robertson Davies

Sinclair Lewis was a writer who drank, not, as so many have believed, a drunk who wrote.

James Lundquist

Audiences don't know anybody writes a picture. They think the actors just make it up as they go along.

William Holden

Comedy writing is a very difficult competitive job and I say to aspiring writers, 'Don't do it. Don't do it.'

Mel Brooks

I see Sylvia Plath as a kind of Hammer films poet.

Philip Larkin

Truman Capote's book, *In Cold Blood*, when it came out in 1965, was considered an instant classic, largely because Capote told everyone it was.

Bill Bryson

Literature is an occupation in which you have to keep proving your talent to people who have none.

Jules Renard

Authors have the power to bore people long after we are dead.

Sinclair Lewis

It's red hot, mate. I hate to think of this sort of book getting into the wrong hands. As soon as I've finished it, I shall recommend they ban it.

Tony Hancock

Autobiography is the most respectable form of lying.

Humphrey Carpenter

The book of mine enemy has been remaindered. And I am pleased.

Brian James

Living — Family and
Relations

If you don't clean your house for two months it doesn't get any dirtier.

Quentin Crisp

Never go to bed mad – stay up and fight.

Phyllis Diller

The General was essentially a man of peace – except of course in his domestic affairs.

Oscar Wilde

Insanity is hereditary; you can get it from your children.

Sam Levenson

I love children. Especially when they cry – for then someone takes them away.

Nancy Mitford

It's better to be black than gay because when you're black you don't have to tell your mother.

Charles Pierce

Every time a child says 'I don't believe in fairies', there's a little fairy somewhere that falls down dead.

J.M. Barrie

Why should we do anything for posterity? What has posterity ever done for us?

Joseph Addison

Children really brighten up a household – they never turn the lights off.

Ralph Bus

I have never understood this liking for war. It panders to instincts already well catered for within the scope of any respectable domestic establishment.

Alan Bennett

Any astronomer can predict with absolute accuracy just where every star in the universe will be at 11.30 tonight. He can make no such prediction about his teenage daughter.

James T. Adams

Watching your daughter being collected by her date feels like handing over a million dollar Stradivarius to a gorilla.

Jim Bishop

My husband and I have decided to start a family while my parents are still young enough to look after them.

Rita Rudner

You cannot be happy with a woman who pronounces the first 'd' in Wednesday.

Peter de Vries

When I go to the beauty parlour, I always use the emergency entrance. Sometimes I just go for an estimate.

Phyllis Diller

Most women are not as young as they are painted.

Max Beerbohm

My aunt once sent me a postal order for five pounds for coming top of a list.

F. W. Abernathy

Have you ever had one of those days when you have had to murder a loved one because he is the devil?

Emo Philips

Living — Family and Relations

Another good thing about being poor is that when you are seventy your children will not have you declared legally insane in order to gain control of your estate.

Woody Allen

Your mother, sir, under the pretence of keeping a bawdy house, was in reality a receiver of stolen property.

Samuel Johnson

Some mornings it just doesn't seem worth it to gnaw through the leather straps.

Emo Philips

There are three stages of man: he believes in Santa Claus; he does not believe in Santa Claus; he is Santa Claus.

Bob Phillips

To watch a child drowning within a few yards of me has a dispiriting effect upon my appetite.

Harry Graham

The child was a keen bed-wetter.

Noel Coward

She invariably was first over the fence in the mad pursuit of culture.

George Ade

I never met a kid I liked.

W.C. Fields

Few misfortunes can befall a boy which bring worse consequences than to have a really affectionate mother.

Somerset Maugham

Anyone who hates children and animals can't be all bad.

W.C. Fields

I have good looking kids; thank goodness my wife cheats on me.

Rodney Dangerfield

The flashier kind of widow may insist on sleeping with only black men during the first year after the death.

P.J. O'Rourke

My folks first met on the subway trying to pick each other's pockets.

Freddie Prinze

I cannot tell you if genius is hereditary, because heaven has granted me no offspring.

James McNeill Whistler

He is like a mule, with neither pride of ancestry nor hope of posterity.

Robert G. Ingersoll

Whatever women do they must do twice as well as men to be thought half as good. Luckily, this is not difficult.

Charlotte Whitton

Even if your father had spent more of your mother's immoral earnings on your education you would still not be a gentleman.

Frank Otter

Last week I stated that this woman was the ugliest woman I had ever seen. I have since been visited by her sister and now wish to withdraw that statement.

Mark Twain

Living — Family and Relations

The best way to find something you have lost is to buy a replacement.

Ann Landers

I hate housework! You make the beds, you do the dishes — and six months later you have to start all over again.

Joan Rivers

There are three ages of man — youth, age, and 'you're looking wonderful'.

Francis Spellman

In general my children refuse to eat anything that hasn't danced on television.

Erma Bombeck

An extravagance is anything you buy that is of no earthly use to your wife.

Franklin P. Adams

Children nowadays are tyrants. They contradict their parents, gobble their food, and tyrannise their teachers.

Socrates (425 B.C.)

A genius is a man who can rewrap a new shirt and not have any pins left over.

Dino Levi

It was very good of God to let Thomas and Mrs Carlyle marry one another and so make only two people miserable instead of four.

Samuel Butler

Wealth is any income that is at least one hundred dollars a year more than the income of one's wife's sister's husband.

H.L. Mencken

All a child can expect is that its father be present at the conception.

Joe Orton

Having a family is like having a bowling alley installed in your head.

Martin Mull

I like children – fried.

W.C. Fields

There are only two things that a child will share willingly – communicable diseases and its mother's age.

Benjamin Spock

Man is not born free, he is attached to his mother by a cord and is not capable of looking after himself for at least seven years (seventy in some cases).

Katharine Whitehorn

I was much distressed by the next door people who had twin babies and played the violin; but one of the twins has died, and the other has eaten the fiddle – so all is peace.

Edward Lear

The baby is fine. The only problem is that he looks like Edward G. Robinson.

Woody Allen

My wife has a slight impediment in her speech – every now and then she stops to breathe.

Jimmy Durante

I have never got over the embarrassing fact that I was born in bed with a woman.

Wilson Mizner

She was one of those women who go through life demanding to see the manager.

G. Patrick

When you see a married couple coming down the street, the one who is two or three steps ahead is the one that's mad.

Helen Rowland

A lot of people would rather tour sewers than visit their cousins.

Jane Howard

I love mankind – it's people I can't stand.

Charles Schultz

Childhood is that wonderful time of life when all you need to do to lose weight is to take a bath.

Richard S. Zera

Alimony is like buying oats for a dead horse.

Louis A. Safian

To lose one parent may be regarded as a misfortune; to lose both looks like carelessness.

Oscar Wilde

The ultimate penalty for bigamy is two mothers-in-law.

George Russell

Retirement at sixty-five is ridiculous. When I was sixty-five I still had pimples.

George Burns

Leon Brittain looked like a bloke in the sixth form who never had a date.

Simon Hoggart

I don't feel old – I don't feel anything until noon. Then it's time for my nap.

Bob Hope

When I was a boy, the Dead Sea was only sick.

George Burns

Why a four year old child could understand this report. Run out and find me a four year old child. I can't make head nor tail out of it.

Groucho Marx

Every day, in every way, I get worse and worse.

Patrick Murray

He was watching the moon come up lazily out of the old cemetery in which nine of his daughters were lying, and only two of whom were dead.

James Thurber

Santa Claus has the right idea – visit people only once a year.

Victor Borge

Isn't it funny how everyone in favour of abortion has already been born?

Patrick Murray

No man who has wrestled with a self-adjusting card table can ever be quite the man he once was.

James Thurber

The main difference between an Essex girl and a supermarket trolley is that a supermarket trolley has a mind of its own.

Ray Leigh

I know I was cruel to other children because I remember stuffing their nostrils with putty, and beating a little boy with stinging nettles.

Vita Sackville-West

The real menace in dealing with a five year old is that in no time at all you begin to sound like a five year old.

Jean Kerr

When Lady Louise Moncrieff's sixteenth child was born, her sister was present and called out 'It's all right Louise, and you have got another little boy'. And the reply of the poor tired lady was 'My dear, I really don't care if it is a parrot'.

Lord Ormathwaite

I love to go to the playground and watch the children jumping up and down. They don't know I'm firing blanks.

Emo Philips

The male is a domestic animal which, if treated with firmness and kindness, can be trained to do most things.

Jilly Cooper

I'd love to slit my mother-in-law's corsets and watch her spread to death.

Phyllis Diller

You know you're getting old when you stoop to tie your shoes and wonder what else you can do while you're down there.

George Burns

I was the kid next door's imaginary friend.

Emo Philips

I am the only woman in the world who has her dresses rejected by the Salvation Army.

Phyllis Diller

Living — Family and Relations

The highlight of my childhood was making my brother laugh so hard the food came out of his nose.

Garrison Keillor

The worst sensation I know of is getting up at night and stepping on a toy train.

Kin Hubbard

My grandfather started walking five miles a day when he was sixty. Now he's eighty-five and we don't know where the hell he is.

Ellen de Generis

Two can live as cheaply as one, but it costs them twice as much.

Frank Sullivan

My parents warned me never to open the cellar door or I would see things I shouldn't see. So one day when they were out I did open the cellar door and I did see things I shouldn't see – grass, flowers, the sun ...

Emo Philips

Tell your nice mummies and daddies to buy this book for you and hit them until they do.

Spike Milligan

Distant relatives are the best kind and the further away the better.

Kin Hubbard

When you see what some girls marry, you realise how they must hate to work for a living.

Helen Rowland

He was an honest man who deserved to live longer; he was intelligent and agreeable, resolute and courageous, to be depended upon, generous and faithful – provided he is really dead.

La Bruyère

If you want to get rid of stinking odours in the kitchen, stop cooking.

Erma Bombeck

I don't know how you feel about old age, but in my case, I didn't even see it coming. It hit me from the rear.

Phyllis Diller

Many are called but few get up.

Oliver Herford

In this world nothing is certain except death and taxes.

Benjamin Franklin

She's the sort of woman who lives for others and you can tell the others by their hunted expression.

C.S. Lewis

An optimist is the kind of person who believes that a housefly is looking for a way out.

George Nathan

The wife was up. I could hear her scraping the toast.

Les Dawson

Cleaning your house while your kids are still growing, is like shovelling the walk before it stops snowing.

Phyllis Diller

In spite of the cost of living, it's still very popular.

Laurence J. Peter

There is only one rule of living – live alone.

Quentin Crisp

The best revenge you can have on intellectuals is to be madly happy.

Albert Camus

The five most terrible words in the English language are 'We've got the builders in'.

Godfrey Smith

Oh, are there two nine o'clocks in the day?

Tallulah Bankhead

I have called my house The Blind Architect.

Spike Milligan

If it weren't for the fact that the TV set and the refrigerator are so far apart, some of us wouldn't get any exercise at all.

Joey Adams

It is better to be rich and healthy than to be poor and sick.

Mark Twain

Living — Family and Relations

Am I the only person in Britain who was not sexually abused as a child? Every day, I hear adults blaming their dysfunctional personalities on unwanted advances during childhood, yet the bitter truth is that I was a plain boy, and nobody really fancied me. Scout masters, vicars, little old ladies in tea-shops – not one of them offered me so much as a sweetie or muttered, 'It's our little secret', and I've been traumatised ever since by the rejection. And worse, because of their callousness, I'm unable to appear on television, dimly lit and in silhouette, smoking nervously and dumping all my inadequacies on to a long-forgotten grope.

Victor Lewis-Smith

Kids, you tried your best and you failed miserably. The lesson is, never try.

Homer Simpson

I'm not saying I'm old but at my last birthday the candles cost more than the cake.

Bob Hope

It's too bad that whole families have been torn apart by something as simple as wild dogs.

Jack Handey

Don't you hate when your hand falls asleep and you know it will be up all night.

Steven Wright

I don't buy temporary insanity as a murder defence.
Temporary insanity is breaking into someone's home and
ironing all their clothes.

Sue Kolinsky

A child develops individuality long before he develops taste.
I have seen my kids straggle into the kitchen in the morning
with outfits that need only one accessory: an empty gin
bottle.

Erma Bombeck

There is no accounting for tastes, as the woman said when
somebody told her that her son was wanted by the police.

Franklin P. Adams

Parents like the idea of kids, they just don't like their kids.

Morley Saefer

The trick of not working yourself to death is to take a break
as soon as you see a bright light and hear dead relatives
beckon.

Scott Adams

You see more of your children once they leave home.

Lucille Ball

Don't worry about temptation – as you grow older, it starts
avoiding you.

Elbert Hubbard

My roommate got a pet elephant. Then it got lost. It's in the apartment somewhere.

Steven Wright

I'm a simple man. All I want is enough sleep for two normal men, enough whiskey for three and enough women for four.

Joel Rosenberg

If the shoe fits – I buy it in every available colour.

Imelda Marcos

I come from a rough neighbourhood. If anyone ever paid their rent, the police immediately came round to see where they got the money from.

Alexei Sayle

Middle age is when you have the choice of two temptations and you choose the one that will get you home earlier.

Edgar Howe

A signature always reveals a man's character – and sometimes even his name.

Evan Esar

I dislike monkeys: they always remind me of my poor relations.

Henry Luttrel

Living — Family and Relations

Genius may have its limits, but stupidity is not thus handicapped.

Elbert Hubbard

Sex is something that children never discuss in the presence of their elders.

Arthur Roche

A child of one can be taught not to do certain things such as touch a hot stove, turn on the gas, pull lamps off their tables by their cords, or wake mommy before noon.

Joan Rivers

You know when you're young, you think your dad is Superman. Then you grow up and you realise he's just a regular guy who wears a cape.

Dave Atell

He'd make a lovely corpse.

Charles Dickens

Some men are alive simply because it is against the law to kill them.

Edgar Howe

The moment you're born you're done for.

Arnold Bennett

Life is something that everyone should try at least once.

Henry J. Tillman

Living — Family and Relations

Learning to dislike children at an early age saves a lot of expense and aggravation later in life.

Robert Byrne

I am not lost. I am merely locationally challenged.

John M. Ford

I come from a small town where the population never changes. Every time a baby is born some guy immediately leaves town.

Michael Prichard

Barnum was wrong – it's more like every thirty seconds.

Eric Moore

My mother used to say there are no strangers, only friends you haven't met yet. She's now in a maximum security twilight home in Australia.

Edna Everage

I like life – it gives you something to do.

Ronnie Shakes

It is hard to disguise your feelings when you put a lot of relatives on the train for home.

Edgar Howe

A perfume is any smell that is used to drown a worse one.

Elbert Hubbard

Anyone who uses the phrase 'easy as taking candy from a baby' has never tried taking candy from a baby.

Fran Lebowitz

I have noticed your hostility towards him. I ought to have guessed you were friends.

Malcolm Bradbury

A sobering thought: what if, at this very moment I am living up to my full potential?

Jane Wagner

When you are down and out, something always turns up, usually the noses of your friends.

Orson Welles

Have you ever noticed that on those rare occasions when you do need turpentine, the can, which you bought in 1978, and have been moving from household to household ever since, is always empty?

Dave Barry

Laziness is nothing more than resting before you get tired.

Jules Renard

You have to get up early if you want to get out of bed.

Groucho Marx

Ambition is a poor excuse for not having sense enough to be lazy.

Charlie McCarthy

There was a time when father amounted to something in the United States. He was held with some esteem in the community; he had some authority in his own household; his views were sometimes taken seriously by his children; and even his wife paid heed to him from time to time.

Adlai Stevenson

When the Black Camel comes for me, I am not going to go kicking and screaming. I am, however, going to try to talk my way out of it. 'No, no, you want the other Walter Slovotsky.'

Walter Slovotsky

An eternity with Beelzebub and all his hellish instruments of death shall be a picnic compared to five minutes with me and this pencil.

Rowan Atkinson

If you're a really good kid, I'll give you a ride on a buzz-saw.

W.C. Fields

Children are natural mimics who act like their parents, despite every effort to teach them good manners.

P.J. O'Rourke

Living — Family and Relations

When your mother asks, 'Do you want a piece of advice?' it's a mere formality. It doesn't matter if you answer yes or no. You're going to get it anyway.

Erma Bombeck

Douglas Fairbanks has always faced a situation in the only way he knew how, by running away from it.

Mary Pickford

If paternity leave was granted it would result in a direct incitement to a population explosion.

Ian Gow

You can calculate Zsa Zsa Gabor's age by the rings on her fingers.

Bob Hope

Bring the little ones to me and I will get a good price for them.

Eugene Fegg

How little it takes to make life unbearable: a pebble in the shoe, a cockroach in the spaghetti, a woman's laugh.

H.L. Mencken

Times were tough when I was a child but they were tough for everyone. If you wanted a new pair of shoes, you went to the baths on a Saturday night.

Tommy Docherty

Living — Family and Relations

If you want the world to beat a path to your door, just try to take a nap on a Saturday afternoon.

Sam Ewing

The years between fifty and seventy are the hardest. You are always asked to do things and yet you are not decrepit enough to turn them down.

T.S. Eliot

I've been forty and I've been fifty and I can tell you forty is better.

Cher

In high school my acne was so bad, blind people tried to read my face.

Joan Rivers

We stayed at the Royal Marin Hotel where we collapsed into bed only to be eaten alive by mosquitoes which could break a child's leg with a kick.

W.C. Fields

Any resemblance between Chico and Harpo and living persons is purely coincidental.

Groucho Marx

Never play peekaboo with a child on a long plane trip. There's no end to the game. Finally you have to grab him by the bib, and shout, "Look it's always going to be me!"

Rita Rudner

Where are you dying tonight?

Evelyn Waugh

I have so many skeletons in the cupboard I can hardly shut the door.

Alan Clark

The proof that we don't understand death is that we give dead people a pillow.

Jerry Seinfeld

I take my children everywhere, but they always find their way back home again.

Robert Orben

My father was quite eccentric: he once told staff not to accept faxes from India because there was a plague outbreak there.

Antonia Owen

I never go to bed because so many people die there.

Mark Twain

The only two things that middle-aged men do with greater frequency are urinate and attend funerals.

Fred Shoenberg

Living — Family and Relations

The baby is wonderful: it has a bridge to its nose which the nurse says is a proof of genius! It also has a superb voice, which it freely exercises: its style is essentially Wagnerian.

Oscar Wilde

You can take it as understood, that your luck changes only if it's good.

Ogden Nash

It never amazes me that a baby can be born unable to see hear, speak, walk or even solve *The Sun*'s coffee-time crossword, but is capable of generating a sound so loud it can dislodge masonry at forty paces.

Jeremy Clarkson

This time of year fills me with sadness. It was ten years ago today that I lost my wife. I'll never forget that poker game.

Henny Youngman

If Einstein and Shaw couldn't beat death, what chance have I got?

Mel Brooks

Having one child makes you a parent; having two makes you a referee.

David Frost

If you have money, spend it. First on necessities such as drink, and then if there is anything left over, on food, shelter and clothing.

Stephen Behan

Nowadays, two can live as cheaply as one large family used to.

Joey Adams

You kids are disgusting, skulking around here all day, reeking of popcorn and lollipops.

W.C. Fields

When my wife is away and I am left to keep house for myself, I know it is time to do the washing-up when I put something on the kitchen table and something falls off the other end.

John D. Sheridan

I knew I was an unwanted baby when I saw my bath toys were a toaster and a radio.

Joan Rivers

A good place to meet a man is at the dry cleaners. These men usually have jobs and bathe.

Rita Rudner

The natural term of the affection of the human animal for its offspring is six years.

George Bernard Shaw

Living — Family and Relations

Not everybody hates me: only the people who've met me.

Emo Philips

I think women deserve to have more than twelve years between the ages of twenty-eight and forty.

James Thurber

Bachelorhood, like being alive, is more depressing than anything but the known alternative.

P. J. O'Rourke

If a man's character is to be abused, say what you will, there's nothing like a relation to do the business.

William Makepeace Thackeray

I pick the loser every time. If ever you see me in a queue at the railway booking office, join the other one; because there'll be a chap at the front of mine who is trying to send a rhinoceros to Tokyo.

Basil Boothroyd

It sometimes happens, even in the best families, that a baby is born. This is not necessarily a cause for alarm. The important thing is to keep your wits about you and borrow some money.

Elinor Smith

I am often asked which of us Gabor girls is the eldest. Actually, it's Mama, but she would never admit it.

Zsa Zsa Gabor

When I was born, I was so surprised I couldn't talk for a year and a half.

Gracie Allen

I'm in pretty good shape for the shape I'm in.

Mickey Rooney

The greatest advantage of not having children must be that you can go on believing that you are a nice person. Once you have children, you realise how wars start.

Fay Weldon

Husbands are a small band of men, armed only with wallets, besieged by a horde of wives and children.

P. J. O'Rourke

Hawaii: it's got everything. Sand for the children, sun for the wife and sharks for the mother-in-law.

Ken Dodd

All I desire for my own burial is not to be buried alive.

Lord Chesterfield

John Adams was a man of great, if intermittent, magnanimity.

Denis Brogan

My son has taken up meditation. At least it's better than sitting and doing nothing.

Max Kauffman

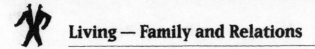

I cannot see why there is all this fuss about the human race being perhaps wiped out in the near future. It certainly deserves to be.

Philip Larkin

My husband and I have discovered a foolproof method of birth control. An hour with the kids before bedtime.

Roseanne Barr

I grew up with six brothers. That's how I learned to dance: waiting for the bathroom.

Bob Hope

The only time a bachelor's bed is made is when it is in the factory.

P. J. O'Rourke

I read one psychologist's theory that said "Never strike a child in anger". When should I strike him? When he is kissing me on my birthday?

Erma Bombeck

Nobody ever knew exactly how much Cordie Mae weighed but her daddy used to say, "If I could get $1.25 a pound for that child, I could pay off my truck."

Lewis Grizzard

They told me that as I got older, I would get wiser. At that rate I should be a genius by now.

George Burns

Living — Family and Relations

It is true that I was born in 1962. And the room next to it was 1963.

Joan Rivers

You know you are getting old when everything hurts. And what doesn't hurt, doesn't work.

Hy Gardner

A woman knows all about her children. She knows about dental appointments and football games and romances and best friends and favourite foods and secret fears and hopes and dreams. A man is vaguely aware of some short people living in the house.

Dave Barry

Babies are too vulgar for me. I cannot bring myself to touch them.

H.L. Mencken

Inside every seventy-year-old is a thirty-five-year-old asking, "What happened?"

Ann Landers

The parents complained that the youngsters never wrote but Grandma said she'd sent a letter and got a reply within days. She received a pleasant page of happy chatter, ending with, "And Grandma, you did mention that you were enclosing a cheque, but there was none in the letter."

Gene Perrett

"You will not find your father greatly changed," remarked Lady Moping, as the car turned into the gates of the County Asylum.

Evelyn Waugh

A woman just had her fourteenth child and ran out of names: to call her husband.

Milton Berle

Birth was the death of him.

Samuel Beckett

Practically anything you say will seem amusing if you're on all fours.

P. J. O'Rourke

The trouble about being retired is that you never get a break from it.

Tom Farmer

Meal time is the only time in the day when children resolutely refuse to eat.

Fran Lebowitz

My uncle was a great man, he told me so himself. "I am a great man," he said, and you cannot argue with facts like that.

Spike Milligan

Living — Family and Relations

The great secret in life is not to open your letters for a fortnight. At the expiration of that period you will find that nearly all of them have answered themselves.

Arthur Binstead

Early one June morning in 1872 I murdered my father: an act which made a deep impression on me at the time.

Ambrose Bierce

Key to the door: eighteen, twenty-one or five if both parents are working.

Mike Barfield

Personally I have nothing against work, particularly when performed quietly and unobtrusively by someone else.

Barbara Ehrenreich

As far as I know, a single man has never vacuumed behind a couch.

Rita Rudner

My wife and I traipsed along to natural childbirth classes, breathing and timing. We were a terrific team and had a swell time. The actual delivery was slightly more difficult. I don't want to name names, but I held my end up.

Dave Barry

Big-money national lottery winners have been found statistically to be no happier than those paralysed following a major car accident, six months after each event.

Raj Persaud

Think about it. You're lying paralysed, have been for six months, but you think, ah well, it could be worse, I could have won the lottery.

Hunter Davies

I don't know if he is dead or not, but they took the liberty of burying him.

James Joyce

The best thing to do is to behave in a manner befitting one's age. If you are sixteen or under, try not to go bald.

Woody Allen

Having dinner with my mother-in-law was quite an experience: watching her pick the cabbage out of her teeth with her Iron Cross.

Les Dawson

It's really posh in the area I've moved to. Dog muck's in real neat piles and no rent-men's eyelashes hanging out of the letterboxes.

Bobby Thompson

Of all forty-two alternatives, running away is best.

Will Rogers

All happiness depends on a leisurely breakfast.

John Gunther

I am the oldest living man, especially at seven in the morning.

Robert Benchley

I hate the word housewife; I don't like the word home-maker either. I want to be called "domestic goddess".

Roseanne Barr

When a man has a birthday he takes a day off. When a woman has a birthday, she may take as much as five years off.

E.C. McKenzie

If you have never seen a total eclipse just watch the groom at a wedding.

Herbert V. Prochnow

If God had to give a woman wrinkles, he might at least have put them on the soles of the feet.

Ninon de Lenclos

Ask not for whom the bell tolls: let the answering machine get it.

Jean Kerr

I have my eighty-seventh birthday coming up soon and people ask me what I'd most appreciate getting. I'll tell you: a paternity suit.

George Burns

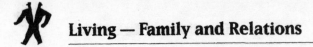

Living — Family and Relations

True maturity is reached only when a man realises he has become a father figure to his girlfriends' boyfriends: and he accepts it.

Larry McMurty

A solved problem creates two new problems and the best prescription for happy living is not to solve any more problems than you have to.

Russell Baker

I admire a housewife who can stand there and watch her husband pack his own lunch in the morning.

Brenda Davidson

Having a baby is like suddenly getting the world's worst roommate, like having Janis Joplin with a bad hangover and P.M.S. come to stay with you.

Anne Lamott

I have found little good about human beings. In my experience most of them, on the whole, are trash.

Sigmund Freud

When in doubt, use brute force.

Ken Thompson

Although prepared for martyrdom, I was willing to have it postponed.

Winston Churchill

Living — Family and Relations

It is an unwritten law that teenagers must dress alike to assert their independence.

Joyce Armor

Am I happy? What do you take me for, an idiot?

Charles De Gaulle

I told my mother-in-law that my house was her house and she said, "Get the hell off my property."

Joan Rivers

When your furnace explodes you call in a so-called professional to fix it. The "professional" arrives in a truck with lettering on the sides and deposits a large quantity of tools and two assistants who spend the better part of the week in your basement whacking objects at random with heavy wrenches, after which the "professional" returns and gives you a bill for slightly more money than it would cost you to run a successful campaign for the U.S. Senate.

Dave Barry

What do I dislike about death? Perhaps it's the hours.

Woody Allen

Nothing you can't spell will ever work.

Will Rogers

May your troubles in the coming New Year be as short-lived as your resolutions.

E.C. McKenzie

When you get married, the man becomes the head of the house. And the woman becomes the neck, and she turns the head any way she wants to.

Yakov Smirnoff

A man who goes into a supermarket for a few items would rather walk around the market balancing them than put them in one of those little baskets.

Rita Rudner

If Mr. Vincent Price were to be co-starred with Miss Bette Davis in a story by Mr. Edgar Allen Poe directed by Mr. Roger Corman, it could not fully express the pent-up violence and depravity of a single day in the life of the average family.

Quentin Crisp

A sweater is a garment worn by a child when its mother is feeling chilly.

Ambrose Bierce

Everyone who has ever walked barefoot into his child's room late at night hates Lego.

Tony Kornheiser

My father left when I was quite young. Well actually, he was asked to leave.

George Carlin

Living — Family and Relations

Notoriously insensitive to subtle shifts in mood, children will persist in discussing the colour of a recently sighted cement mixer long after one's own interest in the topic has waned.

Fran Lebowitz

My father won his great gamble with the future. He died.

Quentin Crisp

If you stay in a house and you go to the bathroom and there is no toilet paper, you can always slide down the banisters. Don't tell me you haven't done it.

Paul Merton

The truly enchanting thing about small children is that they don't insist on showing you photographs of their grandparents.

Niall Toibin

One cat in a house is a sign of loneliness, two of barrenness and three of sodomy.

Edward Dahlberg

I believe John Gotti wears $2,000 suits. I didn't know it was possible to buy one so cheaply.

Alan Clark

Peter O'Toole looks as if he's walking around just to save on funeral expenses.

John Huston

The wolf will never come to my door. He knows I'd drag him in and eat him.

Brendan Behan

When I am trying to manage the kids at Christmas I can understand why some animals eat their young.

Brendan O'Carroll

Excuse me, I didn't recognise you. I've changed so much.

Oscar Wilde

Father's Day is like Mother's Day, except the gift is cheaper.

Gerald F. Lieberman

The sins of the father are often visited upon the sons-in-law.

Joan Kiser

There is no such thing as a tough child. If you boil them first for seven hours, they all come out tender.

W.C. Fields

When a kid asks an experienced father how much a certain building weighs, he doesn't hesitate for a second. "Three thousand, four hundred and fifty-seven tons," he says.

Dave Barry

"You should see what a fine-looking man he was before he had all those children," the Arapesh tribesman told me.

Margaret Mead

My mother hated me. She once took me to an orphanage and told me to mingle.

Phyllis Diller

The sexual briefing that I got from my father was memorable for the way that it avoided textbook jargon and came directly to the point. He told me I was never to use a men's room in the Broadway subway. This dissertation left a certain gap in the story of procreation.

Ralph Schoenstein

Laundry increases exponentially with the number of children.

Miriam Robbins

Next to striking of fire and the discovery of the wheel, the greatest triumph of what we call civilisation was the domestication of the human male.

Max Lerner

Most men are secretly still mad at their mothers for throwing away their comic books which would be very valuable now.

Rita Rudner

At age fifty-eight I am in the prime of senility.

Joel C. Harris

McAvity accused him of canine ancestry on his mother's side.

Bob Hope

You think you'll do some little job, perfectly simple, but Fate
isn't going to have it. I once sat down to put some new
cotton wool in a cigarette lighter and before I'd finished I'd
got all the floorboards up in the spare bedroom.

Basil Boothroyd

I haven't heard of anybody who wants to stop living on
account of the cost.

Kin Hubbard

I ask people why they have deer heads on their walls and
they say, "Because it's such a beautiful animal." Well I think
my mother is attractive, but I have photographs of her.

Ellen DeGeneres

He was hairy. This man was not born, she thought. He was
knitted by his grandmother on a cold day.

Isla Dewar

"Listen, love," I said to the wife, "you just stop at home and
do the cooking and the cleaning and the washing and the
ironing and the gardening and the shopping and the painting
and the decorating, because I don't want my wife to work."

Johnny Carson

I hear the newspapers say I am dying. The charge is not true.
I would not do such a thing at my time of life.

Mark Twain

If you think women are the weaker sex, try pulling the blankets back to your side.

Stuart Turner

Longevity is one of the more dubious rewards of virtue.

Ngaio Marsh

A kid knocked over my beer with a frisbee at the beach once. I threatened him with a lawsuit and then put this curse on him: "May your voice never change and your zits win prizes at county fairs."

Lewis Grizzard

The only advantage of old age is that you can sing while you brush your teeth.

George Burns

There is only one thing wrong with the younger generation: a lot of us don't belong to it any more.

Bernard Baruch

Native Americans give each other names which reflect their behaviour and personality. That's why I call my bloke, "Sits in Front of the Telly Farting".

Jo Brand

A parent is a person who gives a lecture on nutritional values to a youngster who has reached six foot by eating potato crisps.

Dan Looby

With my luck, if I went into the pumpkin business, they'd probably outlaw Hallowe'en.

Larry Ziegler

Dudley Moore is my son – my smallest son.

Roger Moore

George Burns is old enough to be his father.

Red Buttons

My parents were so strict we weren't allowed to read *Goldilocks and the Three Bears*. It wasn't so much Goldilocks going into all those beds as the implied marital tension in the bear family.

Ardal O'Hanlon

To me, funerals are like bad movies. They last too long, everybody is overacting and the ending is completely predictable.

George Burns

Ashes to ashes and clay to clay; if the enemy don't get you, your own folk may.

James Thurber

Even if you haven't got a baby, when you're going out, hire a babysitter. As you're leaving say, 'check out the baby in about half an hour'. Better still, mark one of the rooms 'Baby's room', and leave the window open with a little rope ladder hanging out.

Harry Hill

If you let that sort of thing go on, your bread and butter will be cut from right under your feet.

Ernest Bevin

I'd like to marry a nice, domesticated homosexual with a fetish for wiping down formica and different vacuum-cleaner attachments.

Jenny Eclair

Families is where our nation finds hope, where wings take dream.

George W. Bush

My mother from time to time puts on her wedding dress. Not because she's sentimental. She just gets really far behind in her laundry.

Brian Kiley

If the child is a boy, he is to be named James; if a girl, it would be kinder to drown her.

Evelyn Waugh

No man was ever so low as to have respect for his brother-in-law.

Finley Peter Dunne

Where have you been, who've you been with, what have you been doing and why?

Arthur Lucan

My favourite way to wake up is to have a certain French movie star whisper to me softly at two-thirty in the afternoon that if I want to get to Sweden in time to pick up my Nobel Prize for literature, I had better ring for breakfast.

Fran Lebowitz

My new son has a face like that of an ageing railway porter who is beginning to realise that his untidiness has meant that he'll never get that ticket-collector's job he's been after for twenty years.

Kingsley Amis

It was our son that kept our marriage together – neither of us wanted custody of him.

Chubby Brown

I was an unwanted child. When my parents gave me a rattle it was still attached to the snake.

Joan Rivers

You know your children are growing up when they stop asking you where they come from and refuse to tell you where they are going.

P. J. O'Rourke

There are only three occasions in Ireland when you'll find the whole family together – a wedding, a funeral, or if I've brought home a bag of chips.

Ardal O'Hanlon

Living — Family and Relations

An advantage of having only one child is that you always know who did it.

Erma Bombeck

You feel completely comfortable entrusting your baby to your parents for long periods, which is why most grandparents flee to Florida at the earliest opportunity.

Dave Barry

Whatever is on the floor will wind up in the baby's mouth. Whatever is in the baby's mouth will wind up on the floor.

Bruce Lansky

If Abraham's son had been a teenager, it wouldn't have been a sacrifice.

Scott Spendlove

Do not, on a rainy day, ask your child what he feels like doing because I assure you that what he feels like doing, you won't feel like watching.

Fran Lebowitz

You know your family is really stressed when conversations often begin with 'Put the gun down and then we can talk.'

Mike McQueen

Say what you like about Genghis Khan but when he was around, old ladies could walk the streets of Mongolia safely at night.

Jo Brand

Living — Family and Relations

Where did you go? Out. What did you do? Nothing.

Richard Armour

If you cannot open a childproof bottle, use pliers or ask a child.

Bruce Lansky

Freud is all nonsense; the secret of all neurosis is to be found in the family battle of wills to see who can refuse longest to help with the dishes.

Julian Mitchell

A friend of mine was caring for his mother as her Alzheimer's disease progressed. When the time came to discuss her burial wishes, he asked whether she wanted to be cremated or buried. His mother replied, 'Surprise me.'

Allen Klein

My friend Winnie is a procrastinator. He didn't get his birthmark until he was eight years old.

Steven Wright

When your first baby drops its pacifier, you sterilize it. When your second baby drops its pacifier, you tell the dog 'Fetch'.

Bruce Lansky

In spite of the seven thousand books of expert advice, the right way to discipline a child is still a mystery to most fathers and mothers. Only grandmother and Genghis Khan know how to do it.

Bill Cosby

Living — Family and Relations

If you wonder where your child left his roller skates, try walking around the house in the dark.

Leopold Fechtner

You know children are growing up when they start asking questions that have answers.

John Plomp

We've been having some trouble with the school bus. It keeps bringing the kids back.

Bruce Lansky

When I have a kid, I'm going to get one of those strollers for twins. Then put the kid in and run around, looking frantic. When he gets older, I'll tell him he used to have a brother, but he didn't obey.

Steven Wright

It's amazing. One day you look at your phone bill and realise your children are teenagers.

Milton Berle

My socks DO match. They're the same thickness.

Steven Wright

I was doing the family grocery shopping accompanied by two children, an event I hope to see included in the Olympics in the near future.

Anna Quindlen

My mother phones daily to ask, 'Did you try to reach me?'
When I reply, 'No,' she adds, 'So, if you're not too busy, call
me while I'm still alive,' and hangs up.

> Erma Bombeck

I lost my parents on the beach when I was a kid. I asked a
lifeguard to help me find them. He said, 'I don't know, kid,
there are so many places they could hide.'

> Rodney Dangerfield

You're a disgrace to our family name of Wagstaff, if such a
thing is possible.

> Groucho Marx

A wonderful woman my grandmother – eighty-six years old
and not a single grey hair on her head. She's completely bald.

> Dick Bentley

A man has six items in his bathroom: a toothbrush, shaving
cream, razor, a bar of soap and a towel from the Holiday Inn.
The average number of items in the typical woman's
bathroom is 337. A man would not be able to identify most
of these items.

> Dave Barry

I love all my children, but some of them I don't like.

> Lillian Carter

Not a single member of the under-age set has yet to propose
the word chairchild.

> Fran Lebowitz

The greatest single cause of unhappiness in Britain today is the modern British woman's hatred of housework.

Auberon Waugh

If you see a well-dressed man you know at once his wife is good at picking out clothes.

Joan Rivers

Children aren't happy with nothing to ignore, and that's what parents were created for.

Ogden Nash

A woman who does a man's work is just a lazy cow.

Jo Brand

A self-made man is one who believes in luck and sends his son to Oxford.

Christina Stead

For most of history, baby-having was in the hands of women. Many fine people were born under this system.

Dave Barry

Adolescence is a time of rapid change. Between the ages of twelve and seventeen, for example, a parent can age as much as twenty years.

Dale Baughman

Life is like a dog-sled team. If you ain't the lead dog, the scenery never changes.

Lewis Grizzard

Mixed-faith marriages were frowned upon in Killcock. Both parents had to sign a declaration that any babies that resulted from the union had to be brought up as children.

James McKeon

Never give your boy all the allowance you can afford. Keep some in reserve to bail him out.

Josh Billings

Everyone knows how to raise children except the people who have them.

P. J. O'Rourke

Children have become so expensive that only the poor can afford them.

Mark Twain

You can always get someone to love you – even if you have to do it yourself.

Tom Masson

If I had to choose between my wife and my putter – I'd miss her.

Gary Player

In the algebra of psychology, X stands for a woman's mind.

Ambrose Bierce

I long for my baby boy to be a homosexual because homosexuals are so good to their mothers.

Ruth Sansom

Chloe has just expressed herself all over the floor.

Hannah Betts

I have a horror of leaving this world and not having anyone in the family know how to replace a toilet-roll holder.

Erma Bombeck

What women want is men, careers, money, children, friends, independence, freedom, respect, love, and a three-dollar pantyhose that won't run.

Phyllis Diller

My mother joined the peace corps when she was seventy; my sister Gloria is a motorcycle racer; my other sister Ruth is a holy roller preacher and my brother Jimmy thinks he's going to be President of the United States. Shucks, I'm really the only normal one in the family.

Billy Carter

I told my child there were two words I wanted her never to use – one was 'swell' and the other was 'lousy'. 'OK mum,' she said, 'What are the words?'

Phyllis Diller

Bluebeard was a husband with the neatest solution to the alimony problem.

Leonard Levison

Whoever said you can't take it with you has never seen the family car packed for a vacation trip.

Lester Klimek

Love, Sex, Marriage, Men and Women

Love, Sex, Marriage...

He said it was artificial respiration, but now I find that I am to have his child.

Anthony Burgess

Sara could commit adultery at one end and weep for her sins at the other, and enjoy both operations at once.

Joyce Cary

Sex without love is an empty experience, but as empty experiences go, it's a pretty good empty experience.

Woody Allen

All this fuss about sleeping together. For physical pleasure I'd sooner go to my dentist any day.

Evelyn Waugh

It's so long since I've had sex I've forgotten who ties up whom.

Joan Rivers

The world is full of people who are ready to think the worst when they see a man sneaking out of the wrong bedroom in the middle of the night.

Will Cuppy

The majority of husbands remind me of an orangutang trying to play the violin.

Honoré de Balzac

It is well to write love letters. There are certain things it is not easy to ask your mistress for face to face – like money for instance.

Henri de Regnier

In the circles in which I move, sleeping with a woman does not constitute an introduction.

Virginia McLeod

I thought men like that shot themselves.

King George V

The quickest way to a man's heart is through his chest.

Roseanne Barr

If it wasn't for pickpockets and frisking at airports I wouldn't have any sex life at all.

Rodney Dangerfield

A lady is a woman who never shows her underwear unintentionally.

Lillian Day

I'm such a good lover because I practise a lot on my own.

Woody Allen

A eunuch is a man who has had his works cut out for him.

Robert Byrne

His designs were strictly honourable; that is to rob a lady of her fortune by way of marriage.

Henry Fielding

Sex between a man and a woman can be wonderful – provided you get between the right man and the right woman.

Woody Allen

What a blonde – she was enough to make a bishop kick a hole in a stained glass window.

Raymond Chandler

I blame my mother for my poor sex life. All she told me was 'the man goes on top and the woman underneath'. For three years my husband and I slept in bunk beds.

Joan Rivers

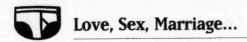

The Love Bird is one hundred per cent faithful to his mate – as long as they are locked together in the same cage.

Will Cuppy

There is nothing in the world like the devotion of a married woman. It's a thing no married man knows anything about.

Oscar Wilde

I'd marry again if I found a man who had fifteen million dollars, would sign over half of it to me before the marriage, and guarantee he'd be dead within a year.

Bette Davis

Women are like elephants – everyone likes to look at them but no one likes to have to keep one.

W.C. Fields

My best birth control now is to leave the lights on.

Joan Rivers

Happiness is watching TV at your girlfriend's house during a power failure.

Bob Hope

Oh Lord, give me chastity, but do not give it yet.

St Augustine

She was so ugly she could make a mule back away from an oat bin.

Will Rogers

Divorce is the sacrament of adultery.

Jean Guichard

What would men be without women? Scarce, sir, mighty scarce.

Mark Twain

Niagara Falls is the bride's second great disappointment.
Oscar Wilde

My love life is terrible. The last time I was inside a woman was when I visited the Statue of Liberty.
Woody Allen

How I wish that Adam had died with all his ribs in his body.
Dion Boucicault

I was actually the first birth from an inflatable woman.
Tony de Meur

I would rather go to bed with Lillian Russell stark naked than with Ulysses S. Grant in full military regalia.
Mark Twain

I think people should be free to engage in any sexual practices they choose – they should draw the line at goats though.
Elton John

A woman's mind is cleaner than a man's – that's because she changes it more often.
Oliver Herford

A man ought not to marry without having studied anatomy, and dissected at least one woman.
Honoré de Balzac

A man who marries his mistress creates a vacancy in the position.
James Goldsmith

Sex is an act which on sober reflection one recalls with repugnance and in a more elevated mood even with disgust.
A. Schopenhauer

Love, Sex, Marriage...

The trees along the banks of the Royal Canal are more sinned against than sinning.

Patrick Kavanagh

My wife is the sort of woman who gives necrophilia a bad name.

Patrick Murray

It is bad manners to begin courting a widow before she gets home from the funeral.

Seumas MacManus

Drying a widow's tears is one of the most dangerous occupations known to man.

Dorothy Dix

Boy was my wife romantic! When I first met her she used to go round with a mattress strapped to her back.

Roy Brown

Marriage is like putting your hand into a bag of snakes in the hope of pulling out an eel.

Leonardo da Vinci

Sexual intercourse is a grossly overrated pastime; the position is undignified, the pleasure momentary and the consequences utterly damnable.

Lord Chesterfield

Every woman is entitled to a middle husband she can forget.

Adela Rogers St. Johns

I had bad luck with both my wives. The first one left me and the second one didn't.

Patrick Murray

I go from stool to stool in singles bars hoping to get lucky, but there's never any gum under any of them.

Emo Philips

Men and women, women and men. It will never work.

Erica Jong

When a man steals your wife, there is no better revenge than to let him keep her.

Sacha Guitry

So little time, so many beautiful women to make love to.

Arturo Toscanini

I am the only man in the world with a marriage licence made out 'to whom it may concern'.

Mickey Rooney

Women's intuition is the result of millions of years of not thinking.

Rupert Hughes

My wife and I pondered for a while whether to take a vacation or get a divorce. We decided that a trip to Bermuda is over in two weeks, but a divorce is something you always have.

Woody Allen

Splendid couple – slept with both of them.

Maurice Bowra

Men are superior to women. For one thing, men can urinate from a speeding car.

Will Durst

I'm dating a woman now who, evidently, is unaware of the fact.

Garry Shandling

Love, Sex, Marriage...

She was stark naked except for a PVC raincoat, dress, net stockings, undergarments, shoes, rain hat and gloves.

Keith Waterhouse

What is wrong with a little incest? It's both handy and cheap.

James Agate

I'm a wonderful housekeeper. Every time I get a divorce, I keep the house.

Zsa Zsa Gabor

She had once heard a semi-drunken peer say on TV that marriage without infidelity was like a salad without dressing.

Keith Waterhouse

Love is temporary insanity curable by marriage.

Ambrose Bierce

Love is the delusion that one woman differs from another.

H.L. Mencken

Bisexuality doubles your chances of a date on a Saturday night.

Woody Allen

Never make a task of pleasure, as the man said when he dug his wife's grave only three feet deep.

Seumas MacManus

It doesn't matter what you do in the bedroom as long as you don't do it in the streets and frighten the horses.

Mrs Patrick Campbell

She dresses to the left.

Patrick Murray

Love, Sex, Marriage...

Love is the answer – but while you're waiting for the answer, sex raises some pretty good questions.

Woody Allen

My boyfriend and I broke up. He wanted to get married and I didn't want him to.

Rita Rudner

Ten men waiting for me at the door? Send one of them home, I'm tired.

Mae West

My wife is a sex object – every time I ask for sex, she objects.

Les Dawson

When a woman behaves like a man, why doesn't she behave like a nice man?

Edith Evans

A successful man is one who makes more money than his wife can spend. A successful woman is one who can find such a man.

Lana Turner

The people I'm furious with are the women's liberationists. They keep getting up on soapboxes and proclaiming women are brighter than men. That's true, but it should be kept quiet or it ruins the whole racket.

Anita Loos

There are only about twenty murders a year in London and not all are serious – some are just husbands killing their wives.

G.H. Hatherill

Sending your girl's love letters to your rival after he has married her is one form of revenge.

Ambrose Bierce

Love, Sex, Marriage...

I sold the memoirs of my sex life to a publisher – they are going to make a board game out of it.

Woody Allen

He kissed me as though he was trying to clear the drains.

Alida Baxter

My wife Mary and I have been married for forty-seven years and not once have we had an argument serious enough to consider divorce; murder, yes, but divorce, never.

Jack Benny

Some women's idea of being faithful is not having more than one man in bed at the same time.

Frederic Raphael

The main difference between men and women is that men are lunatics and women are idiots.

Rebecca West

Basically my wife was immature. I'd be at home in my bath and she'd come in and sink my boats.

Woody Allen

I've been married six months. She looks like a million dollars, but she only knows a hundred and twenty words and she's only got two ideas in her head. The other one is hats.

Eric Linklater

Love is just a dirty trick played on us to achieve the continuation of the species.

Somerset Maugham

A terrible thing happened to me last night again – nothing.

Phyllis Diller

Love, Sex, Marriage...

I married beneath me. All women do.

Nancy Astor

I chased a woman for almost two years only to discover her tastes were exactly like mine – we were both crazy about girls.

Groucho Marx

Here's to woman! Would that we could fall into her arms without falling into her hands.

Ambrose Bierce

She said he proposed something on their wedding night that even her own brother wouldn't have suggested.

James Thurber

I like George and Harriet Grote. I like him; he's so lady-like. And I like her; she's such a perfect gentleman.

Sydney Smith

The chain of wedlock is so heavy that it takes two to carry it, sometimes three.

Alexandre Dumas

The ideal marriage consists of a deaf husband and a blind wife.

Padraig Colum

Every man should have the opportunity of sleeping with Elizabeth Taylor – and at the rate she's going, every man will.

Nicky Hilton

A nymphomaniac is a woman as obsessed with sex as the average man.

Mignon McLaughlin

My wife is as cold as the hairs on a polar bear's bum.

Les Dawson

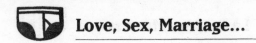

I like younger women. Their stories are shorter.

Tom McGuane

The only thing my husband and I have in common is that we were married on the same day.

Phyllis Diller

I don't know what the Left is doing, said the Right Hand, but it looks fascinating.

James Broughton

I bequeath to my wife the sum of one shilling for a tram fare so she can go somewhere and drown herself.

Francis Lord

Where did I first kiss my present partner? On her insistence.

Daire O'Brien

I used to be Snow White, but I drifted.

Mae West

I haven't spoken to my wife for over a month. We haven't had a row – it's just that I'm afraid to interrupt her.

Les Dawson

I dislike the idea of wives about a house: they accumulate dust. Besides, so few of the really nice women in my set could afford to marry me.

H.H. Munro

One hard and fast rule of my sex life is only one willy in the bed at a time.

A.A. Gill

All that this humourless document, the Kinsey Report, proves is:
(a) that all men lie when they are asked about their adventures in amour, and
(b) that pedagogues are singly naïve and credulous creatures.

H.L. Mencken

Every time Magda Goebbels saw Hitler, her ovaries rattled.

Peter Watson

Never try to impress a woman: because if you do she'll expect you to keep up the standard for the rest of your life. And the pace, my friends, is devastating.

W.C. Fields

If a woman has had more than three husbands, she poisons them; avoid her.

William Maguire

The only time a woman really succeeds in changing a man is when he is a baby.

Natalie Wood

Love, Sex, Marriage...

If a tree falls in the woods and there is nobody there to hear it fall, does it still make a sound? And if a man speaks and there is no woman there to correct him, is he still wrong?

Camille Paglia

I'm too shy to express my sexual needs except over the phone to people I don't know.

Gary Shandling

Women should never wear anything that panics the cat.

P.J. O'Rourke

Lord Ormsby 85 has just married Lady Astorite 18. The groom's gift to the bride was an antique pendant.

Peter Shaw

Did I sleep with her? Not a wink, father, not a wink.

Brendan Behan

When men are angry and upset, they rebel by hurting others; when women are angry and upset, they rebel by hurting themselves: bulimia, anorexia, self-mutilation, suicide, getting married to members of the Windsor family.

Julie Burchill

A bridegroom is a man who has spent a lot of money on a suit that no one notices.

Josh Billings

A girl should marry for love, and keep on marrying until she finds it.

Zsa Zsa Gabor

A man can sleep around, no questions asked, but if a woman makes nineteen or twenty mistakes, she's a tramp.

Joan Rivers

I couldn't tell if the streaker was a man or a woman because it was wearing no clothes.

Yogi Berra

I remember the first time I had sex – I still have the receipt.

Groucho Marx

The only females that pursue me are mosquitos.

Emo Philips

The way to tell if a man is sexually excited is if he's breathing.

Jo Brand

Everybody considers her very beautiful, especially from the neck down.

Damon Runyon

Just two more laser treatments and the "Rosanne" tattoo is gone from my chest.

Tom Arnold

Love, Sex, Marriage...

The problem which confronts homosexuals is that they set out to win the love of a 'real' man. If they succeed, they fail. A man who goes with other men is not what they would call a real man.

Quentin Crisp

If love means never having to say you're sorry, then marriage means always having to say everything twice.

Estelle Getty

Before I met my husband, I'd never fallen in love. I stepped in it a few times.

Rita Rudner

A man can have two, maybe three, love affairs while he's married. But three is the absolute maximum. After that you're cheating.

Yves Montand

A woman will sometimes forgive the man who tries to seduce her, but never the man who misses the opportunity when offered.

Charles de Talleyrand

I can provide temporary relief for nymphomaniacs.

Larry Lee

I am told he has fallen in love. Against whom?

Alfred Adler

A wife lasts only for the length of the marriage, but an ex-wife is there for the rest of your life.

Jim Samuels

I have difficulty in avoiding the persistent attentions of ladies of the street. It's a case of the tail dogging the wag.

S.J. Perelman

Have the florist send some roses to Mrs Upjohn and write, 'Emily, I love you', on the back of the bill'.

Groucho Marx

When widows exclaim loudly against second marriages, I would always lay a wager, that the man, if not the wedding-day is absolutely fixed upon.

Henry Fielding

I can honestly say that I always look on Pauline as one of the nicest girls I was ever engaged to.

P.G. Wodehouse

Only one man in a thousand is a leader of men – the other nine hundred and ninety-nine follow women.

Groucho Marx

The purpose of sexual intercourse is to get it over with as long as possible.

Steven Max Singer

A woman who takes her husband about with her
everywhere is like a cat that goes on playing with a mouse
long after she's killed it.

H.H. Munro

It is only rarely that one can see in a little boy the promise of
a man, but one can almost always see in a little girl the threat
of a woman.

Alexandre Dumas

The proliferation of massage establishments in London in
the last few years appears to indicate a dramatic increase in
muscular disorders amongst the male population.

Evelyn Waugh

I have such poor vision I can date anybody.

Gary Shandling

I would go out with women my age, but there are no
women my age.

George Burns

In biblical times, a man could have as many wives as he could
afford. Just like today.

Abigail Van Buren

I don't know how much it costs to get married – I'm still
paying for it.

Les Dawson

God gave men a penis and a brain, but not enough blood to use both at the same time.

Robin Williams

A married couple playing cards together is just a fight that hasn't started yet.

George Burns

The feller that puts off marrying until he can support a wife ain't much in love.

Kin Hubbard

Guns don't kill people; husbands that come home early kill people.

Don Rose

I once placed an ad in the personal columns of *Private Eye* saying that I wanted to meet a rich well-insured widow with a view to murdering her. I got 48 replies.

Spike Milligan

I am not against hasty marriages, where a mutual flame is fanned by an adequate income.

Wilkie Collins

They say that the daughter-in-law of the Spanish Ambassador is not ugly, and has as good a set of teeth as one can have, when one has but two and those black.

Horace Walpole

Love, Sex, Marriage...

I bank at this women's bank. Everybody is in the red three or four days a month.

Judith Carter

I haven't had any open marriages, though quite a few have been ajar.

Zsa Zsa Gabor

The most romantic thing any woman ever said to me in bed was 'Are you sure you're not a cop?'

Larry Brown

As Major Denis Bloodnok exclaimed when told there were only two sexes: 'It's not enough, I say'.

Albert Hall

Fat generally tends to make a man a better husband. His wife is happy in the knowledge she is not married to a woman chaser. Few fat men chase girls, because they get winded so easily.

Hal Boyle

It wasn't exactly a divorce – I was traded.

Tim Conway

By love, of course, I refer to romantic love – the love between man and woman, rather than between mother and child, or a boy and his dog, or two headwaiters.

Woody Allen

I have little experience of marriage, having been married only once.

Oscar Wilde

There is a way of transferring funds that is even faster than electronic banking. It's called marriage.

James McGavran

If you have to ask if somebody is male or female, don't.

Patrick Murray

Transsexuals always seem to feel that they have been Shirley Bassey trapped inside a man's body rather than an assistant from an Oxfam Shop trapped inside a man's body.

Paul Hoggart

I require only three things of a man. He must be handsome, ruthless and stupid.

Dorothy Parker

I told him that I would give him a call but what I really meant was that I would rather have my nipples torn off by wild dogs than see him again.

Rita Rudner

Men are people, just like women.

Fenella Fielding

What attracted me to Lytton in the first place was his knees.

Carrington Strachey

If a woman hasn't met the right man by the time she's twenty-four, she may be lucky.

Deborah Kerr

Women like silent men. They think they are listening.

Marcel Achard

My girlfriend has the most beautiful breasts in the world: five.

Emo Philips

When you get married you forget about kissing other women.

Pat Boone

I can see you now, bending over a hot stove: but I can't see the stove.

Groucho Marx

I never knew any woman who could compare with Dolly Lestrange in the art of drawing out and waking into rampant life any spice of the devil which might be lurking latent in a man's soul.

Rhoda Broughton

No wonder that girl was licking David Mellor's toes. She was probably trying to get as far away from his face as possible.

Tommy Docherty

I was in San Francisco when the great earthquake struck, but we were kinda busy in the bedroom and we didn't notice what was going on outside.

John Barrymore

When a man talks dirty to a woman, it's sexual harassment.
When a woman talks dirty to a man, it's $3.95 a minute.

Steven Wright

Women will sometimes admit making a mistake. The last man
who admitted that he was wrong was General George Custer.

Rita Rudner

One of the principal differences between a woman and a
volcano is that a volcano doesn't fake eruptions.

Tim Dedopulos

Dear wife, I acknowledge receipt of your complaint number
387,501.

W. C. Fields

The morning the wife and I broke up you could hear a pin
drop in our house. I didn't see the hand grenade in her
other hand.

Roy Brown

A man who won't lie to a woman has very little
consideration for her feelings.

Olin Miller

It is only man, whose intellect is clouded by his sexual
impulses, that could give the name of "the fairer sex" to that
undersized, narrow-shouldered, broad-hipped and short-
legged race.

Arthur Schopenhauer

Bridge is not a sex substitute. Sex is a bridge substitute. The partnership is as intimate as marriage.

Helen Knott

She said she would scream for help. I told her I didn't need any help.

Bob Hope

The first man that can think up a good explanation of how he can be in love with his wife and another woman is going to win that prize they're always giving out in Sweden.

Mary Cecil

I wasn't being free with my hands: I was trying to guess her weight.

W. C. Fields

Love is being able to squeeze your lover's spots.

Zoe Ball

There is nothing wrong with pregnancy. Half of the people in the world wouldn't be here today if it wasn't for women being pregnant.

Sarah Kennedy

Whatever you say against women, they are better creatures than men, for men were made of clay, but women were made of man.

Jonathan Swift

A man who says his wife can't take a joke forgets she took him.

John Simpson

During sex my girlfriend always wants to talk to me. Just the other night she called me from a motel.

Rodney Dangerfield

Before getting married, find out if you're really in love. Ask yourself, "Would I mind getting financially destroyed by this person?"

Johnny Carson

Two is company. Three is fifty bucks.

Joan Rivers

Be careful of men who are bald and rich; the arrogance of "rich" usually cancels out the niceness of "bald".

Rita Rudner

All men make mistakes, but married men find out about them sooner.

Red Skelton

I refuse to take a D.N.A. test to establish if I am the father of an eighteen-year-old beauty queen. I admit I have fathered at least eleven children by five different women, but this case could open the floodgates to dozens of other claims. I might run out of blood.

Joseph Estrada

Anyone who thinks that marriage is a fifty-fifty proposition doesn't understand women or fractions.

Jackie Mason

After seven years of marriage, I'm sure of just two things: first, never wallpaper together, and second, you'll need two bathrooms, both for her.

Dennis Miller

Then I said to her, "So you're a feminist: how cute."

Robin Williams

Women do laundry every couple of days. A man will wear every article of clothing he owns, including his surgical pants that were hip about eight years ago, before he will do his laundry. When he is finally out of clothes, he will wear a dirty sweatshirt inside out, rent a U-haul and take his mountain of clothes to the Laundromat, and expect to meet a beautiful woman there.

Dave Barry

Three wise men? You must be joking.

Rita Rudner

I never saw two fatter lovers, for she is as big as Murray. Seriously speaking it is a very good marriage, and acting under the direction of medical men, with perseverance and the use of a stimulating diet, there may be an heir to the house of Henderland.

Sydney Smith

One night I made love from one o'clock to five past two. It was the time they put the clocks forward.

Gary Shandling

Never marry a widow unless her first husband was hanged.

James Kelly

I am the most desirable man in the world. Indeed, if I put my mind to it, I am sure I could pass the supreme test and lure Miss Taylor away from Mr. Burton.

Noel Coward

My name is Grace but everyone calls me Gracie for short.

Gracie Allen

Marry me Emily and I'll never look at another horse.

Groucho Marx

Dior's New Look: these are clothes worn by a man who doesn't know women, never had one and dreams of being one.

Coco Chanel

Marriage is natural: like poaching, or drinking or wind in the stummick.

H. G. Wells

When a man's best friend is his dog, that dog has a problem.

Edward Abbey

She was built like a brick chickenhouse.

W. C. Fields

For their twenty-fifth wedding anniversary, they gave each other inscribed tombstones. Hers read "Here lies my wife, cold as usual" while his read "Here lies my husband, stiff at last".

Jack South

Lewis Carroll was as fond of me as he could be of anyone over the age of ten.

Ellen Terry

Personally I don't see why a man can't have a dog and a girl. But if you can afford only one of them, get a dog.

Groucho Marx

I was married by a judge but I should have asked for a jury.

Groucho Marx

Some people think my wife is pretty and others think she's ugly. Me: I think she's pretty ugly.

Les Dawson

We had a lot in common. I loved him and he loved him.

Shelley Winters

Husbands are like fires. They go out when unattended.

Zsa Zsa Gabor

The only woman I have ever loved has left me and finally married: my mother.

Emo Philips

You may marry the man of your dreams, ladies, but fourteen years later you're married to a couch that burps.

Roseanne Barr

I knew right away that Rock Hudson was gay when he did not fall in love with me.

Gina Lollobrigida

To have a happy marriage, tell your spouse everything, except the essentials.

Cynthia Nelms

Both marriage and death ought to be welcome. The one promises happiness, doubtless the other assures it.

Mark Twain

There is, of course, no reason for the existence of the male sex except that sometimes one needs help with moving the piano.

Rebecca West

Nothing in our culture, not even home computers, is more overrated than the epidermal felicity of two featherless bipeds in desperate congress.

Quentin Crisp

Love, Sex, Marriage...

Marriage is an outmoded silly convention started by the cavemen and encouraged by the florists and the jewellers.

Olivia de Havilland

A girl phoned me the other day and said, "Come on over, there's nobody home." I went over. Nobody was home.

Rodney Dangerfield

Sex is something the children never discuss in the presence of their elders.

Rodney Dangerfield

Ms. is a syllable which sounds like a bumblebee breaking wind.

Hortense Calisher

It was out of the closet and into the streets for the nation's homosexuals in the 1970s. This didn't do much for the streets but, on the other hand, your average closet has improved immeasurably.

John Weidman

It takes only four men to wallpaper a house, but you have to slice them thinly.

Jo Brand

I didn't get too many women running after me. It was their husbands who'd be after me.

Charlie George

When I was young it was considered immodest for the bride to do anything on the honeymoon except to weep gently and ask for glasses of water.

Noel Coward

Madam, if you wish to have a baby by me, surely you don't mean by unartificial insemination.

James Thurber

I have known couples stay up till three in the morning, each hoping that the other would finally give in and make the bed.

Katharine Hepburn

How many husbands have I had? You mean apart from my own?

Zsa Zsa Gabor

If you want to find out some things about yourself – and in vivid detail too – just try calling your wife fat.

P. J. O'Rourke

Stan Waltz has decided to take unto himself a wife but he hasn't decided whose yet.

Peter de Vries

Men don't shop even for their own underpants.

Germaine Greer

I don't worry about terrorism. I was married for two years.

Sam Kinison

Two cures for love: 1. Don't see him. Don't phone or write a letter. 2. The easy way: get to know him better.

Wendy Cope

Marilyn Monroe and Joe Demaggio have divorced. It just goes to show that no man can be expert at our two national pastimes.

Joe E. Brown

Men are always better at offering women things that men like: a man will give his wife a pair of fishing boots in his size.

Katharine Whitehorn

Don't you realise that as long as you have to sit down to pee, you'll never be a dominant force in the world? You'll never be a convincing technocrat or middle manager. Because people will know. She's in there sitting down.

Don DeLillo

One thing men can do better than women is read a road map. Men read maps better because only a male mind could conceive of an inch equalling a hundred miles.

Roseanne Barr

The trouble with men is that there are not enough of them.

Hermione Gingold

She was the original good time that was had by all.

Bette Davis

A sure sign a man is going to be unfaithful is if he has a penis.

Jo Brand

Sex at ninety-three is like playing snooker with a rope.

George Burns

I'm always attracted to the wrong kind of guy: like the Pope.

Carol Leifer

I read recently that love is entirely a matter of chemistry. That must be why my wife treats me like toxic waste.

David Bissonette

Whatever you may look like, marry a man of your own age: as your beauty fades, so will his eyesight.

Phyllis Diller

"Duck behind the sofa," she told me. "There's no duck behind the sofa," I told her.

Groucho Marx

We were fast and furious: I was fast and she was furious.

Max Kauffman

Is that a gun in your pocket, or are you just pleased to see me?

Mae West

Commitment is what every woman wants; men can't even spell it.

Laura Zigman

The high-heeled shoe is a marvellously contradictory item; it brings a woman to a man's height but makes sure she cannot keep up with him.

Germaine Greer

Marriage is very difficult. Very few of us are fortunate enough to marry multimillionaire girls with thirty-nine-inch busts who have undergone frontal lobotomies.

Tony Curtis

If I never see that woman again, it's too soon.

Groucho Marx

At every party there are two kinds of people: those who want to go home and those who don't. The trouble is they are usually married to each other.

Ann Landers

No two women are alike, in fact no one woman is alike.

Alfred Austin

Love, Sex, Marriage...

My wife and I were married in a toilet: it was a marriage of convenience.

Tommy Cooper

My wife and I have enjoyed over forty years of wedded blitz.

Hugh Leonard

Men get such brilliant ideas during sex because they are plugged into a genius.

Mary Lynch

How do you know if it's time to wash the dishes and clean your house? Look inside your pants. If you find a penis in there, it's not time.

Jo Brand

Fighting is essentially a masculine idea; a woman's weapon is her tongue.

Hermione Gingold

Never trust a woman who wears mauve, whatever her age may be, or a woman over thirty-five who is fond of pink ribbons. It always means they have a history.

Oscar Wilde

Marriage is a triumph of habit over hate.

Oscar Levant

I walked into that wedding with both eyes shut. Her brother shut one and her father shut the other.

Billy Bennett

I have learned that only two things are necessary to keep one's wife happy. First, let her think she's having her own way. And second, let her have it.

Lyndon Johnson

I am sorry to say that the generality of women who have excelled in wit have failed in chastity.

Elizabeth Montagu

I live by a man's code, designed to fit a man's world, yet at the same time I never forgot that a woman's first job is to choose the right shade of lipstick.

Carole Lombard

It is when your boyfriend asks you to accompany him on a river trip, at night, in the boat he has built at evening classes that a crisis comes. There is no tactful way to tell a man he has a leaky vessel.

Grace Bradbury

The word androgyny is misbegotten: conveying something like John Travolta and Farrah Fawcett-Majors Scotch-taped together.

Mary Daly

If you have been married more than ten years, being good in bed means you don't steal the covers.

Brenda Davidson

I saw on television the other day some men who like to dress up as women and when they do they can no longer parallel park.

Roseanne Barr

Do you realise that Eve was the only woman who ever took a man's side?

Milton Berle

Women do not find it difficult nowadays to behave like men, but they often find it extremely difficult to behave like gentlemen.

Compton Mackenzie

A wife can often surprise her husband on their wedding anniversary by merely mentioning it.

E. C. McKenzie

My sister gives me the creeps: all her old boyfriends.

Terri Kelly

I think the only good thing to be said about leotards is that they're a very effective deterrent against any sort of unwanted sexual attention. If you're wearing stretch knickers, and stretch tights, and a stretch Lycra leotard, you might as well try and sexually harass a trampoline.

Victoria Wood

I am tired of being a free finishing school for men.

Suzanne Wolstenholme

One special form of contact which consists of mutual approximation of the mucous membranes of the lips in a kiss has received a sexual value among the civilised nations, though the parts of the body do not belong to the sexual apparatus and merely form the entrance to the digestive tract.

Sigmund Freud

My husband and I didn't sign a pre-nuptial agreement. We signed a mutual suicide pact.

Roseanne Barr

Do we have impotent men in here tonight? Oh, I see, you can't get your arms up either.

Roseanne Barr

Woman is fickle. Give her a tickle.

Ken Dodd

Rule One: The sun will rise in the East. Rule Two: As long as there are rich men trying not to feel old, there will be young girls trying not to feel poor.

Julie Burchill

If I did not wear torn pants, orthopaedic shoes, frantic dishevelled hair, that is to say, if I did not tone down my beauty, people would go mad. Married men would run amuck.

Brenda Ueland

Kathy Sue Loudermilk was a lovely child and a legend before her sixteenth birthday. She was twenty-one, however, before she knew an automobile had a front seat.

Lewis Grizzard

Women are most fascinating between the ages of thirty-five and forty, after they have won a few races and know how to pace themselves. Since few women ever pass forty, maximum fascination can continue indefinitely.

Christian Dior

Most married couples, even though they love each other very much in theory, tend to view each other in practice as large teeming flaw colonies, the result being that they get on each other's nerves and regularly erupt into vicious emotional shouting matches over such issues as toaster settings.

Dave Barry

Women have simple tastes. They can get pleasure out of the conversation of children in arms and men in love.

H.L. Mencken

I hate the sound of an ambulance. My first wife ran away with an ambulance driver and every time I hear a siren, I get the shakes thinking he might be bringing her back.

Jackie Martling

When women go wrong, men go right after them.

Mae West

Alan Clark is not sixty-five going on sixteen. He is sixty-five going on twelve.

Jane Clark

She was about six feet tall and had a bosom as shapeless as a plate of scrambled eggs.

Richard Gordon

Dolly Parton has a yacht in Seattle and it's windy there. One day she hung her bra to dry and woke up in Brazil.

Phyllis Diller

I bought my wife a sex manual but half the pages were missing. We went straight from foreplay to post-natal depression.

Bob Monkhouse

My girlfriend was so big she could breastfeed Watford.

Brian Conley

Most husbands remember where and when they got married. What stumps them is why.

E.C. McKenzie

Before we got married, my wife was my secretary, now she's my treasurer.

Bob Goddard

In olden times, sacrifices were made at the altar, a custom which is still continued.

Helen Rowland

If you want to stay single, look for the perfect woman.

Ken Alstad

She was a pretty nice guy: for a girl.

Robert Mitchum

Women don't gamble as much as men because their total instinct for gambling is satisfied by marriage.

Gloria Steinem

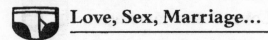

Love, Sex, Marriage...

A journalist once asked me if I had ever slept with a woman.
I replied that I had been accused of being many things in my
life but never of being a lesbian.

> Micheal MacLiammoir

If there is anybody out there who has just bought the book
The Joy of Sex, there is a misprint on page 206.

> Phyllis Diller

I don't mind my wife having the last word. In fact I'm
delighted when she reaches it.

> Walter Matthau

It was not a bosom to repose upon, but it was a capital
bosom to hang jewels on.

> Charles Dickens

I like you so much that sometimes it's an effort to remember
that you're a woman at all.

> Terence Rattigan

Ernest Hemingway's effect upon women is such that they
want to go right out and get him and bring him home
stuffed.

> Dorothy Parker

I've had so many men, the FBI come to me for fingerprints.

> Mae West

My wife gives very good headache.

> Rodney Dangerfield

Love, Sex, Marriage...

My advice to girls is first, don't smoke – to excess; second, don't drink – to excess; third, don't marry – to excess.

Mark Twain

Only time can heal a broken heart, just as only time can heal his broken arms and legs.

Miss Piggy

The closest I ever came to a menage à trois was once when I dated a schizophrenic.

Rita Rudner

The women's movement would probably be more successful if men were running it.

Jimmy Williams

Whenever you apologise to your wife the answer is always the same – 'It's too late now and it's the wrong kind of apology.'

Dave Barry

I dated this girl for two years and then the nagging started – 'Tell me your name, tell me your name.'

Mike Binder

The sock is a highly sensitive conjugal object.

Jean-Claude Kaufman

If Jack Lemmon was a homosexual, I'd marry him.

Walter Matthau

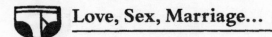# Love, Sex, Marriage...

A man is simply a woman's way of making another woman.

Samuel Butler

When I said I had sex for seven hours, that included dinner and a movie.

Phil Collins

I'm not offended by all the dumb-blonde jokes because I know I'm not dumb. I also know I'm not blonde.

Dolly Parton

A man without a woman is like a neck without a pain.

W. C. Fields

Catherine Deneuve is the man I would have liked to be.

Gerard Depardieu

Men don't understand washing machine controls because they are written in woman.

Jeremy Clarkson

I don't think my wife likes me very much. When I had a heart attack she wrote for an ambulance.

Frank Carson

I love being married. I was single for a long time and I just got sick of finishing my own sentences.

Brian Kiley

All I have to say about men and bathrooms is that they're happy if they hit something.

Rita Rudner

I reckon it is easier to shoot your wife than to have to shoot a different man every week.

Dick Hills

I have a mirrored ceiling over my bed because I like to know what I am doing.

Mae West

O, she is the antidote to desire.

William Congreve

My husband said he needs more space. So I locked him outside.

Roseanne Barr

Greta Garbo was every man's harmless fantasy mistress. She gave you the impression that, if your imagination had to sin, it could at least congratulate itself on its impeccable taste.

Alistair Cooke

You can tell it's love, the real thing, when you dream of slitting his throat.

Wendy Cope

Every night when the moon is full a werewolf turns into a wolf – him and thirty million other guys.

Lou Costello

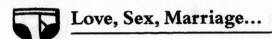

Love, Sex, Marriage...

Most men in this town think monogamy is some kind of wood.

Mike Werb

I have chosen a very plain girlfriend – buggers can't be choosers.

Maurice Bowra

He asked me if I wanted to go back to his place. I told him I didn't know if two people could fit under a rock.

Rita Rudner

How do I feel about women's rights? Just the same way as I feel about women's lefts.

Groucho Marx

I know that blokes have feelings too – but who cares?

Jo Brand

New lovers should have a minimum isolation period of say, six months, so as not to nauseate everyone they meet.

Kathy Lette

A psychiatrist told me and my wife that we should have sex every night – now we never see each other.

Rodney Dangerfield

You get to go through 36 hours of contractions; he gets to hold your hand and say 'focus, breathe, push'.

Joan Rivers

Love, Sex, Marriage...

What's wrong with you men? Would hair stop growing on your chests if you asked directions somewhere?

Erma Bombeck

If your girlfriend wants to leave you, she should give you two weeks' notice, there should be severance pay, and before they leave, they should have to find you a temp.

Bob Ettinger

Men who have fought in the world's bloodiest wars are apt to faint at the sight of a truly foul diaper.

Gary Christenson

To intimidate your daughter's date when he picks up, let him see you sprinkling some dust on her before she leaves. Say, 'It makes fingerprinting easier.'

Mike McQueen

I think, therefore I am single.

Liz Winstead

In lovemaking, what my ex-husband lacked in size, he made up for in speed.

Roseanne Barr

The two times they pronounce you anything in life is when you are man and wife or when they pronounce you dead on arrival.

Dennis Miller

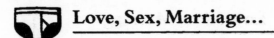

Marriage is the only legal form of pickpocketing.

Alice Kahn

Here's a bit of advice for office managers – keep the sexual harassment complaint forms in the bottom drawer so you'll get a great view of the secretary's butt as she gets one out.

Denis Leary

The difference between a man and a municipal bond is that municipal bonds eventually mature.

Agnes Langer

Heidi Abromowitz has had more hands up her dress than the Muppets.

Joan Rivers

I don't think it's a big deal that swans mate for life. If you're a swan, you're probably not going to find a swan that looks much better than the one you've got, so why not mate for life?

Jack Handey

There ain't nothin' an ol' man can do but bring me a message from a young one.

Moms Mabley

I'm getting old. When I squeeze into a tight parking space, I'm sexually satisfied for the day.

Rodney Dangerfield

If he asks 'Your place or mine?' say, 'Both. You go to your place and I'll go to mine.'

Bette Midler

I have known and respected your husband for many years and what is good enough for him is good enough for me.

Groucho Marx

In the last stage of labour I threatened to take my husband to court for concealing a lethal weapon in his boxer shorts.

Linda Fiterman

If you love someone, set them free. If they come back, they're probably broke.

Rhonda Dickson

Women should not be enlightened or educated in any way. They should, in fact, be segregated as they are the cause of hideous and involuntary erections in holy men.

St Augustine

A control freak is any man who behaves like a woman and a nymphomaniac is any woman who behaves like a man.

Patrick Murray

I'm looking for a perfume to overpower men – I'm sick of karate.

Phyllis Diller

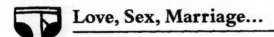

My Uncle Harry was an early feminist. At a race-meeting in Ayr, he threw himself under a suffragette.

Arnold Brown

It is not good enough to spend time and ink in describing the penultimate sensations and physical movements of people getting into a state of rut, we all know them too well.

John Galsworthy

Lo, an intelligent opinion in the mouth of a woman horrifieth a man even as the scissors in the mouth of a babe.

Helen Rowland

Men wake up as good-looking as they went to bed. Women somehow deteriorate during the night.

Jerry Seinfeld

The only really firm rule of taste about cross-dressing is that neither sex should ever wear anything they haven't figured out how to go to the bathroom in.

P. J. O'Rourke

In a world without men, there would be no war – just intense negotiations every 28 days.

Robin Williams

It is my observation that women who complain of sexual harassment are, more often than not, revoltingly ugly.

Auberon Waugh

Love, Sex, Marriage...

Women who insist upon having the same options as men would do well to consider the option of being the strong silent type.

Fran Lebowitz

Men are better than cats because men pee only on the carpet in the loo.

Jo Brand

My wife thinks I should buy her a new dress just because she's fed up of treading on the veil of the one she's got.

Roy Brown

The difference between a man and a battery is that a battery has a plus side.

Jo Brand

Women are like banks, boy, breaking and entering is a serious business.

Joe Orton

Monogamy is the Western custom of one wife and hardly any mistresses.

Saki

God, why didn't you make women first – when you were fresh?

Yves Montand

Media and Films

Media and Films

There is more joy in the newspaper world over one sinner who cuts his sweetheart's throat than over the ninety-nine just men who marry and live happily ever after.

A. P. Herbert

Television is called a medium because it is neither rare nor well done.

Ernie Kovacs

Television is very educational – every time it comes on I go into another room and read a book.

Groucho Marx

I knew Doris Day before she was a virgin.

Groucho Marx

I have a television set in every room of the house but one. There has to be some place you can go when Bob Monkhouse is on.

Benny Hill

An editor is one who separates the wheat from the chaff and prints the chaff.

Adlai Stevenson

A starlet is any girl under thirty in Hollywood who is not regularly employed in a brothel.

Ben Hecht

Dead? With the newspaper strike on, I wouldn't even consider it.

Bette Davis

Everything you read in the newspapers is absolutely true, except for that rare story of which you happen to have first-hand knowledge, which is absolutely false.

Erwin Knoll

In a mere half-century, films have gone from silent to unspeakable.

Doug Larson

There is no bad publicity, except an obituary notice.

Brendan Behan

Television is a device that permits people who haven't anything to do to watch people who can't do anything.

Fred Allen

Hollywood is an asylum run by the inmates.

Laurence Stallings

He had been kicked in the head by a mule when young, and believed everything he read in the papers.

George Ade

'Hello', he lied.

Robert Maxwell

They shot too many pictures and not enough actors.

Walter Winchell

To give an accurate and exhaustive account of that period would need a far less brilliant pen than mine.

Max Beerbohm

The reason why so many people showed up at Louis B. Mayer's funeral was because they wanted to make sure he was dead.

Samuel Goldwyn

Accuracy to a newspaper is what virtue is to a lady, except that a newspaper can always print a retraction.

Adlai Stevenson

Media and Films

A publisher would prefer to see a burglar in his office to a poet.

Don Marquis

I was photographed on one occasion, sitting up in an over-elaborate bed looking like a heavily doped Chinese illusionist.

Noel Coward

One watches David Frost with the same mixture of fascination and disgust that one looks at one's turds floating in a toilet.

Patrick Murray

Sir, I have tested your gramophone machine. It adds a new terror to life and makes death a long-felt want.

Herbert Beerbohm Tree

Television is totally in the hands of semi-articulate barbarians who can barely read an autocue.

William Rushton

After being turned down by numerous publishers, he decided to write for posterity.

George Ade

If you cannot get a job as a pianist in a brothel, you become a royal reporter.

Max Hastings

We have all passed a lot of water since then.

Samuel Goldwyn

The essence of humour is surprise; that is why you laugh when you see a joke in *Punch*.

A. P. Herbert

Now Barabbas was a publisher.

Kenneth Tynan

Barbara Cartland's eyes were twin miracles of mascara and looked like two small crows that had crashed into a chalk cliff.

Clive James

What do you mean 'we' paleface?

Tonto

Television is for appearing on, not looking at.

Noel Coward

Films should have a beginning, a middle and an end – but not necessarily in that order.

Jean-Luc Godard

Glenda Jackson has a face to launch a thousand dredgers.

Jack de Manio

I don't write for pornographic magazines or swim in sewers.

Jerry Falwell

I am about to, or I am going to die. Either expression is used.

Noah Webster

Before television, people didn't even know what a headache looked like.

D. Fields

Never argue with a man who buys ink by the gallon.

Bill Greener

The current Hollywood outbreak of rabies is due to Hedda Hopper going round biting dogs.

Edith Sitwell

I have recently been broadcasting in the interests of a breakfast food whose name for the moment escapes me.

Alexander Woollcott

Media and Films

The only time I use women in films is when they're either naked or dead.

Joel Silver

Never let that son of a bitch in the studio again – until we need him.

Samuel Goldwyn

I love British cinema like a doctor loves his dying patient.

Ben Kingsley

Television is still in its infancy – that's why you have to get up and change it so often.

Michael Hynes

Hollywood is a trip through a sewer in a glass-bottomed boat.

Wilson Mizner

An epic is a movie with Charlton Heston in it.

James Agate

Otto Preminger couldn't direct his little nephew to the bathroom.

Dyan Cannon

No passion in the world, no love or hate, is equal to the passion to alter someone else's copy.

H. G. Wells

My films won't send people out into the streets with axes or anything. The Shirley Temple movies are more likely to do that. After listening to *The Good Ship Lollipop*, you just gotta go out and beat up somebody. Stands to reason.

Lee Marvin

Media and Films

What we want is a story that starts with an earthquake and works its way up to a climax.

Samuel Goldwyn

I don't want any yes-men around me. I want everyone to tell me the truth even if it costs them their jobs.

Samuel Goldwyn

We're overpaying him but he's worth it.

Samuel Goldwyn

You can fool all of the people all of the time if the advertising is right and the budget is big enough.

Joseph E. Levine

Some are born great, some achieve greatness, and some hire public relations officers.

Daniel J. Boorstin

Imagine the Lone Ranger's surprise when many years later he discovered that 'kemo sabay' means 'horse's ass'.

Garry Larsen

Beaverbrook is so pleased to be in Government that he is like the town tart who has finally married the Mayor.

Beverley Baxter

Having the critics praise you is like having the hangman say you've got a pretty neck.

Eli Wallach

Freedom of the press is limited to those who own a newspaper.

A.J. Liebling

Media and Films

Being published by the Oxford University Press is rather like being married to a duchess; the honour is greater than the pleasure.

G.M. Young

Most of the time Marlon Brando sounds as if he has a mouth full of wet toilet paper.

Rex Reed

Television is a twenty-one-inch prison. I'm delighted with it because it used to be that films were the lowest form of art. Now we have something to look down on.

Billy Wilder

David Frost is the bubonic plagiarist.

Jonathan Miller

No good will come of television. The word is half Greek and half Latin.

C.P. Scott

About once a month, after dinner, I gird up my loins such as they are, take as deep a breath as I can, throw my shoulders back as far as they will go, walk into the room with the television set, boldly turn it on, picking a channel at random, and then see how long I can stand it.

James Thurber

I have a face like an elephant's behind.

Charles Laughton

I saw the sequel to the movie *Clones* and you know what? It was the same movie!

Jim Samuels

Mr Mencken has just entered a Trappist monastery in Kentucky and left strict instructions that no mail was to be forwarded. The enclosed is returned, therefore, for your archives.

H.L. Mencken

Small earthquake in Chile – not many dead.

Claud Cockburn

My movies were the kind they show in prisons and aeroplanes, because nobody can leave.

Burt Reynolds

She would be a nymphomaniac if only they could calm her down a little.

Judy Garland

The longest word in the English language is the one which follows the phrase, 'And now, a word from our sponsor.'

Hal Eaton

Every time I sell 100,000 copies of *For Whom The Bell Tolls* I will forgive a son of a bitch, and when we sell a million I will forgive Max Eastman.

Ernest Hemingway

In Hollywood, writers are considered only the first drafts of human beings.

Frank Deford

You can take all the sincerity in Hollywood, place it in the navel of a fruitfly and still have room for three caraway seeds and a producer's heart.

Fred Allen

Paint eyeballs on my eyelids and I'll sleepwalk through any picture.

Robert Mitchum

Talent is sometimes forgiven in Hollywood, genius never.
Evelyn Waugh

The Antiques Roadshow now becomes the For God's Sake
Stop Telling me How Rare and Delightful This Heirloom Is
I just want to hear how much it's worth and even though I'll
tell you that I'll never sell it because it has sentimental value
as soon as the show finishes I'll shoot off to Sothebys and
flog it and blow the lot on a fortnight in Majorca Show.
Victor Lewis-Smith

Well if I dialled a wrong number, why did you answer the
phone?

James Thurber

Leonardo DiCaprio is patently the result of an unnatural act
of passion between William Hague and the piglet from Babe.
A.A. Gill

They used to shoot Shirley Temple through gauze. They
ought to shoot me through linoleum.

Tallulah Bankhead

It is part of the social mission of every great newspaper to
provide a refuge and a home for the largest possible number
of salaried eccentrics.

Roy Thomson

Whom is fooling whom?

Joan Crawford

The voice-over narration on this movie helps to explain
what is going on, and became necessary when the producers
lost the soundtrack.

Christopher Tookey

For those of you watching who haven't got TV sets, live
commentary is on Radio Two.

David Coleman

It's Norden, Speight and Sykes, back from the dead, for one
night only.

Spike Milligan

Lillian Hellman is deceased but in need of further
persecution.

Paul Kirchner

Find out what those people pushing an elephant along the
corridor of the twentieth floor of the New Yorker are doing,
but don't tell me.

Alexander Woollcott

Good news is no news.

Kirk Douglas

At the movie my tears stuck in their little ducts, refusing to
be jerked.

Peter Stack

Television has raised writing to a new low.

Samuel Goldwyn

I'm here to speak about Kirk Douglas's wit, his charm, his warmth, his talent – at last a real acting job!

Burt Lancaster

There are two continuity announcements guaranteed to make the viewer's blood run cold – 'and the programme is introduced by Ross King' along with 'This programme was originally transmitted by BBC East Midlands'.

Victor Lewis-Smith

Michael Jackson was a poor black boy who grew up to be a rich white woman.

Molly Ivins

I wonder if Steve McQueen made that movie before or after he died.

Yogi Berra

Blind Date tempts our voyeuristic appetites, although what everybody really wants to see would required infra-red cameras and a team from the BBC Badger Watch Unit.

Victor Lewis-Smith

The magician Joe Pasguale did something Paul Daniels can't do – he pulled at the roots of his hair.

Victor Lewis-Smith

I don't care if the movie doesn't make a nickel, I just want every man, woman, and child in America to see it.

Samuel Goldwyn

I had no idea that the Academy Awards were televised. Boy, is my face red.

David Letterman

An acquaintance of mine, who once spent several months in a psychiatric hospital, remembers a curious fact about the television set there. It was permanently turned to ITV, with tape stuck over the selection buttons and he had to apply for a special chit to watch any other channel.

Victor Lewis-Smith

In *Lawrence of Arabia* they got only two things right – the camels and the sand.

Lowell Thomas

Wilcox's film ended up like a convincing advertisement for euthanasia. Desmond Wilcox is married to Esther Rantzen and has been for a very long time.

A.A. Gill

The biggest hit movie in Russia is *Escape to Alcatraz*.

Leo Rosten

Hurry Sundown is perhaps the worst-reviewed film of all time. *At Long Last Love* must run it close, but the extra ingredients of racial offensiveness and juvenile smut give this one the edge.

Christopher Tookey

Media and Films

Teen Angel had all the usual ingredients: boy meets girl; girl stalls her car on railway tracks and picks this inopportune moment to search for her boyfriend's missing school ring; girl is crushed to death by a moving train.

Karl Shaw

The telephone is a good way to talk to people without having to offer them a drink.

Fran Lebowitz

So they are going to show a man die on television; after Barry Norman, I don't think I could sit through it again.

A.A. Gill

The human race is faced with a cruel choice – work or daytime television.

Dave Barry

The advertisements are the most truthful part of a newspaper.

Thomas Jefferson

The end of each commercial break was coming like the next wave of peristalsis during a night of vomiting, that Oh-God-it's-starting-again feeling.

Victor Lewis-Smith

To criticise Hurry Sundown would be like tripping a dwarf.

Wilfrid Sheed

Watching John Thaw is like being embalmed alive by an arthritic with halitosis.

A.A. Gill

For extra fun, play with the colour control until I turn green.

Dave Letterman

Television is a kind of radio which lets people at home see what the studio audience is not laughing at.

Fred Allen

Desk-top publishing is a system of software and hardware enabling users to create documents with a cornucopia of typefaces and graphics and the intellectual content of a Formica slab.

Stephen Manes

Even when James Stewart made a visible effort to play a love scene, he always gave the impression he was wearing only one shoe and looking for the other while he slowly droned his lines.

Marlene Dietrich

Gentlemen, listen to me slowly.

Samuel Goldwyn

Hollywood is a place where they place you under contract instead of under observation.

Walter Winchell

Media and Films

Marilyn Monroe has breasts of granite and a mind like Gruyere cheese.

Billy Wilder

Publishing is harder to get into than the inner rectum of the Vatican.

Gerard Kelly

When I was presenting *Cluedo* on television, we used to have to turn over the studio audience in case they got bed sores.

Chris Tarrant

Don't you wish there was a knob on the TV to turn up the intelligence? There's one called 'Brightness' but doesn't work.

Tom Gallagher

The fact that a man is a newspaper reporter is evidence of some flaw of character.

Lyndon B. Johnson

The ideal voice for radio may be defined as having no substance, no sex, no owner, and a message of importance for every housewife.

Harry Wade

For this scene let's get some Indians from the reservoir.

Samuel Goldwyn

Media and Films

Compared to Hale and Pace, everything on television deserves a BAFTA.

A.A. Gill

The ad in the paper said 'Big Sale. Last Week!' Why advertise? I already missed it. They're just rubbing it in.

Yakov Smirnoff

I won't believe in colour television until I see it in black and white.

Samuel Goldwyn

Arnold Schwarzenegger looks like a condom full of walnuts.

Clive James

I never go to movies where the hero's bust is bigger than the heroine's.

Groucho Marx

Clark Gable's ears made him look like a taxicab with both doors open.

Howard Hughes

I can't honestly say that Esther Williams ever acted in an Andy Hardy picture, but she swam in one.

Mickey Rooney

If Cubby Broccoli were on fire, I wouldn't piss on him to put out the flames.

Sean Connery

Media and Films

If it wasn't for Venetian blinds it would be curtains for all of us.
Billy Wilder

In every movie scene which includes a person carrying a bag of groceries, the bag will invariably contain a long, skinny, French baguette loaf, and exactly 8.5 inches will be exposed.
Michael J. Pilling

The title "Little Napoleon" in Hollywood is equivalent to the title "Mister" in any other community.
Alva Johnson

William Mannix had a sound journalistic sense of what makes a good story, but no idea that this should relate to something that is actually happening.
Norman Moss

It was a cute picture. They used the basic story of *Wuthering Heights* and worked in the surfriders.
Neil Simon

The language in prison was worse than Channel Four.
Sheila Bowler

Imagine how your bum feels after sitting on a motorbike for twenty-four hours. Now imagine that feeling all over your body and you get a fair idea of the appeal of this Mickey Rourke biker picture.
Simon Rose

Media and Films

A party was thrown in Hollywood in 1966 for the wrap up of the Marlon Brando film *A Countess from Hong Kong*. The party was such a success and the film such a flop, it was suggested they should dump the film and release the party.

Brian Behan

The special effects in the movie are the worst ever. It doesn't help that the anti-heroine's height varies noticeably from shot to shot, rarely reaching the requisite fifty feet.

Christopher Tookey

Several tons of dynamite are set off in the movie *Tycoon*; none of it under the right people.

Jame Agee

The only good acting you see nowadays is from the losing nominees on Oscar night.

Will Rogers

An epic is any film so unnecessarily long that one has to go out and urinate during it.

Mike Barfield

If you buy your husband or boyfriend a video camera, for the first few weeks he has it, lock the door when you go to the bathroom. Most of my husband's early films end with a scream and a flush.

Rita Rudner

Media and Films

My father carried around the picture of the kid who came with his wallet.

Rodney Dangerfield

The writers and editors of *Coronation Street* should be extradited to Spain and put on show trial for crimes against humanity and 3,000 disappeared character actors.

A.A. Gill

The third secret of Fatima, the Coca-Cola formula and the appeal of Ally McBeal: these are the three mysteries of our time.

Martin James

What I said to them at half-time would be unprintable on the radio.

Gerry Francis

If *Confidential Magazine* continues to publish slanderous pieces about me, I shall feel compelled to cancel my subscription.

Groucho Marx

I read in the newspapers that the German army had invaded France and was fighting the French, and that the English expeditionary force had crossed the Channel. "This," I said to myself, "means war." As usual, I was right.

Stephen Leacock

I'd like to think every director I've worked with has fallen a little in love with me. I know Dorothy Arzner did.

Joan Crawford

My show is always screened after nine o'clock at night: my face frightens children.

Jay Leno

If you want to keep a secret, tell it to the BBC Press Office.

John Cleese

The best time I ever had with Joan Crawford was when I pushed her down the stairs in *Whatever Happened to Baby Jane?*

Bette Davis

In the 1930s, bosoms came back in again, so I was in luck, but Carole Lombard required some artificial help. Before she would go before the camera, she was famous for yelling out to her costumers, "Bring me my breasts."

Joan Crawford

I was led to believe that the new TV series *Sex in the City* would involve lots of intimate physical contact. I've seen more intimate physical contact on *Match of the Day*.

A.A. Gill

Darryl Zanuck is the only man in Hollywood who can eat an apple through a tennis racquet.

David Norris

I flew to London on the Concorde. It goes faster than the speed of sound, which is fun. But it's a rip-off because you couldn't hear the movie until two hours after you got there.

Howie Mandel

Michael Redgrave and Dirk Bogarde in *The Sea Shall Not Have Them*: I don't see why not, everyone else has.

Noel Coward

For John Ford, nothing was impossible: for an actor.

John Wayne

Charlie Chaplin was the greatest ballet dancer who ever lived and if I had got the chance I would have killed him with my bare hands.

W. C. Fields

If the Y2K bug does kick in and all modern machinery reverts to 1900 mode, those good ol' boys at ITV won't feel a thing.

Danny Baker

Look at movie stars, they took their skin from their ass and stuck it on their face. The skin on the ass was the last to wrinkle. They all walked around in their later years with buttock faces.

Charles Bukowski

I've made so many movies playing a hooker that they don't pay me in the regular way any more. They leave it on the dresser.

Shirley MacLaine

The trouble with the movie business is the dearth of bad pictures.

Samuel Goldwyn

The BBC has no business buying sports rights: it ought to be doing programmes about sparrows in Serbia and the lower-crested rhubarb hunter.

Kelvin MacKenzie

Bo Derek does not understand the concept of Roman numerals. She thought we fought in World War Eleven.

Joan Rivers

I love the weight of American Sunday newspapers. Pulling them up off the floor is good for the figure.

Noel Coward

I don't care what you say, for me or against me, but for heaven's sake, say something about me.

Nellie Melba

Media and Films

John McCririck looks like a hedge dragged through a man backwards.

Clive James

She works at Paramount all day and Fox at night.

Mae West

Show business is worse than dog eat dog. It's dog doesn't return other dog's phone call.

Woody Allen

Oscar winners under "other categories" are defined as "films you would never pay to see, even if the only alternative was staying home and watching Demi Moore in *Striptease*".

Joe Joseph

An actress I knew: when I filmed with her, I was thirty-one and she was thirty-six. Today, I'm forty and she's still only thirty-seven.

Tony Curtis

In television police films, why do they always say "Attention all eunuchs"?

Sheila Huffman

Gerry and the Pacemakers movie *Ferry Cross the Mersey* was a little glimpse into hell.

Kenneth Tynan

Kirk Douglas would be the first to tell you that he's a difficult man. I would be the second.

Burt Lancaster

Keep an eye on that time: that will give you a good indication of how fast the athletes are running.

Ron Pickering

We all steal, but if we are smart, we steal from great directors. Then we can call it influence.

Krzystof Kieslowski

What do I look for in a script? Days off.

Spencer Tracy

Snakes: why does it always have to be snakes?

Harrison Ford

Joan Crawford would have made an ideal prison matron, possibly at Buchenwald.

Harriet van Horne

What do I think of Kierkegaard? What movies was he in?

Pamela Anderson

Some of my friends said they didn't think I behaved too badly on *Wogan*. Like Alex Higgins and Oliver Reed, for example.

George Best

Media and Films

I'm not handsome in the classical sense. My eyes droop, the mouth is crooked, the teeth aren't straight, the voice sounds like a Mafioso pallbearer, but somehow it all works.

Sylvester Stallone

To refuse awards is another way of accepting them with more noise than is normal.

Peter Ustinov

At the end, Schwarzenegger makes his ritual preparations for the climatic showdown, decking himself out in leather, packing up an arsenal of guns, and, as he leaves his apartment, copping a quick look of satisfaction in the mirror. It's his only love scene.

Pauline Kael

In Westerns you are permitted to kiss your horse, but never your girl.

Gary Cooper

Here's a good one to try: if you're ever on TV just beside the person being interviewed, mouth, but do not say, "I hope all you ******* lip readers are enjoying this."

George Carlin

People are always dying in *The Times* who don't seem to die in other papers, and they die at greater length and maybe even with a little more grace.

James Reston

274

All television is children's television.

Richard Adler

I don't care what you say about me as long as you say something about me, and as long as you spell my name right.

George M. Cohen

Johnny Depp puts the dire in director.

Edward Porter

The Daily Mail is written by office boys for office boys.

Lord Salisbury

Alistair Cooke had the idea for *Letter from America* so long ago that Marconi is credited with inventing radio in order to get the programme on the air.

Peter Bernard

There are just three certainties in life: death, taxes and television repeats.

Neil Hassett

If the world does end, we will of course bring you full coverage here on Radio Four. *The Archers* will continue on long wave.

Eddie Mair

Media and Films

They're doing things on television these days that I wouldn't do in bed: even if I could.

Bob Hope

The fact that I did not marry George Bernard Shaw is the only real disappointment I've had.

Jean Arthur

Jack Ford's idea of a love story is Ward Bond and John Wayne.

Philip Dunne

Pure drivel tends to drive ordinary drivel off the TV screen.

Marvin Kitman

Awards are like piles, sooner or later every bum gets one.

Maureen Lipman

When they made Carrie Crowley they threw away the mould, but some of the mould clearly grew back.

Liam Fay

Harry, we've got a little prize for you, a two-week all expenses paid trip on a torpedo.

Steve Allen

I will have you remember that a Goldwyn comedy is not to be laughed at.

Samuel Goldwyn

Mickey Rooney's favourite exercise is climbing tall people.

Phyllis Diller

Citizen Kane? Not one good car chase in the whole movie.

Simon Rose

Twenty stone and encrusted in warts, imagine a toad
wearing a dinner jacket, that was Dennis Shaw: the face that
closed a thousand cinemas.

Jeffrey Bernard

Rambo isn't violent. I see Rambo as a philanthropist.

Sylvester Stallone

Cleopatra was the biggest asp disaster in the world.

Pauline Kael

I am amazed at radio D.J.s today. I am firmly convinced that
AM on my radio stands for Absolute Moron. I will not
begin to tell you what FM stands for.

Jasper Carrot

I have come up with a sure-fire concept for a hit television
show, which would be called *A Live Celebrity Gets Eaten by a
Shark*.

Dave Barry

Media and Films

Of course I know that all the pages of our paperbacks fall out in the reading. You don't think we want the damn things to last for ever, do you?

Clarence Paget

You can always tell a detective on TV. He never takes his hat off.

Raymond Chandler

Little girls who wear glasses in movies tell the truth. Little boys who wear glasses in movies always lie.

Gene Siskel

In Hollywood a marriage is a success if it outlasts milk.

Rita Rudner

Michael Jackson is known as the carrier bag: white, plastic and best kept away from kids.

Angus Deayton

All those who think Mia Farrow should go back to making movies where the devil gets her pregnant and Woody Allen should go back to dressing up as a human sperm, please raise your hands.

Dave Barry

Warren Beatty is forty above the waist and fourteen below it.

Shirley MacLaine

I'll tell you what sort of guy I was. If you ordered a boxcar full of sons-of-bitches and opened the door and found only me inside, you could consider your order filled.

Robert Mitchum

If Arnold Schwarzenegger hadn't existed we would have had to build him.

John Milius

The way things are going, I'd be more interested in seeing Cleopatra play the life of Elizabeth Taylor.

Earl Wilson

It is very hard for anything to make it out of Hollywood these days without a lame-ass wimpout ending tacked on at the whining request of test audiences selected from the most puerile of the Nielsen families, who are, as we know, chosen on the basis of the number of cousin-cousin marriages in their family over the last ten generations.

Nix Thompson

Marlon Brando attracts women like faeces attract flies.

Anna Kashfi

Table for Five would be an ideal movie to watch on a plane; at least they provide free sick bags.

Simon Rose

Media and Films

One time I went to a drive-in movie in a cab. The movie cost me $500.

Steven Wright

Raquel Welch is silicone from the knees up.

George Masters

The correct relationship between the media and politicians ought to be that between a dog and a lamppost.

H.L.Mencken

Anybody who ever worked on any picture for the Marx Brothers said he would rather be chained to a galley and lashed at ten minute intervals until the blood spurted from his frame than ever work for those sons of bitches again.

S. J. Perelman

Michael Fish and his pals make John Peel look like a man who was expelled from the Hellfire Club for bad behaviour.

A.A. Gill

Our old mistakes do come back to haunt us. Especially with video.

Peter O'Toole

In this world there are two kinds of people, my friend: those with loaded guns and those who dig. You dig.

Clint Eastwood

My most recent movie was a disaster movie. I didn't plan it that way.

Mel Brooks

What kind of director is David Lean? He's a tall director.

Robert Mitchum

I keep Radio Three on all the time, just to deter burglars.

Joan O'Hara

In movies, humans are violently killed with impunity, but dogs are never killed. Thus, an alien race studying films would conclude that dogs are gods.

Paul Cassel

My girlfriend is a movie actress. I'd love to see her in 3D. That's my hotel bedroom.

Benny Hill

Clive James walks like a man who has just discovered there is no paper.

A.A. Gill

I come from a family of seven boys, and the only thing we all had in common was that none of us ever won an Academy Award.

Bob Hope

Media and Films

Clifford Makins was a legend in his own lunchtime.

Christopher Wordsworth

And here they are, Jayne Mansfield.

Jack Parr

Hillary Clinton could not pose nude in *Penthouse* because they don't have a page that broad.

Gennifer Flowers

Ask about our cup size or favourite position, but please – no personal questions.

Shane Barbi

If I've still got my pants on in the second scene, I think they've sent me the wrong script.

Mel Gibson

A new study reveals that guests on daytime talk shows are predominantly female. Of course most of them weren't born that way.

Conan O'Brien

Groucho Marx had the compassion of an icicle and the generosity of a pawnbroker.

S. J. Perelman

The 'g' in Camille Paglia's name is silent – about the only part of her that is.

Julie Burchill

Media and Films

My interest in the cinema has lapsed since women began to talk.

George J. Nathan

Making a film with Greta Garbo does not constitute an introduction.

Robert Montgomery

Jack Warner never bore a grudge against anyone he wronged.

Simone Signoret

Mr Myers misjudged the mood of the *Late Late Show* and went down like a cupful of warm Dettol with a hair in it.

Hugh Leonard

The right side of Claudette Colbert's face was called the other side of the moon because nobody ever saw it.

Mary Astor

When you want a man to play with you, wear a full-length black nightgown with buttons all over it. Sure it's uncomfortable, but it makes you look like his remote control.

Joan Rivers

Gilbert Harding was a take-away Dr Johnson.

John Osborne

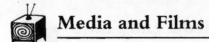

Media and Films

I am too short to play Oscar Wilde – except on radio, the last refuge of the physically disqualified.

Simon Callow

The biggest prize we ever gave away on *Blankety Blank* was a weekend in Reykjavik.

Terry Wogan

Quality newspaper journalism – interdepartmental memoranda for the elite.

A. J. P. Taylor

Giving your book to Hollywood is like turning your daughter over to a pimp.

Tom Clancy

If I had my life to live over I would do everything the exact same way – with the possible exception of seeing the movie remake of *Lost Horizon*.

Woody Allen

Nobody likes my acting except the public.

John Wayne

They are doing things on the screen now that the French don't even put on postcards.

Bob Hope

Media and Films

The invention of television can be compared to the introduction of indoor plumbing. Fundamentally it brought no change in the public's habits. It simply eliminated the necessity of leaving the house.

Alfred Hitchcock

I give hope to the hopeless. People look at me and say: 'If he can make it, I can be Queen of England.'

Robert Mitchum

Clark Gable – the best ears of our lives.

Milton Berle

I am the Ukrainian Cary Grant.

Walter Matthau

It is true that I am a low mean snake. But Ted Turner could walk beneath me wearing a top hat.

Rupert Murdoch

Then came *Easy Rider*, a disaster in the history of film to set beside the loss of Technicolour, the early death of Murnau, and the longevity of Richard Attenborough.

David Thomson

One of my pictures was so bad, they had to do retakes before they threw it in the bin.

King Vidor

Elizabeth Taylor has an unlisted dress size.

Joan Rivers

John Ford was a son of a bitch who also happened to be a genius.

Henry Fonda

As a simple reporter I decided that facts must never get in the way of the truth.

James Cameron

Rudolph Valentino had the acting talents of the average wardrobe.

Clyde Jeavons

I kept the same suit for six years – and the same dialogue. We just changed the title of the picture and the leading lady.

Robert Mitchum

Anyone who leaves De Mille for the armed forces is a coward.

Charlton Heston

Bad reviews of my pictures run off my back like a duck.

Samuel Goldwyn

In Ben Hur, Charlton Heston throws all his punches in the first ten minutes (three grimaces and two intonations) so that he has nothing left long before he stumbles to the end, four hours later, and has to react to the crucifixion. (He does make it clear, I must admit, that he disapproves of it.)

Dwight MacDonald

Media and Films

Some of my best leading men have been horses and dogs.

Elizabeth Taylor

You can quote me as saying that I was misquoted.

Groucho Marx

Camelot is the Platonic idea of boredom roughly comparable to reading a three-volume novel in a language of which one knows only the alphabet.

John Simon

I sometimes think I shall never view
A French film lacking Gerard Depardieu

John Updike

People think I have an interesting walk. Hell, I'm just trying to hold my gut in.

Robert Mitchum

Go into any major studio and shout 'Fill her up', and all the leading men in the place will instinctively come running.

Humphrey Bogart

Men don't care what's on TV. They only care what else is on TV.

Jerry Seinfeld

The other night I saw a *Road* picture on TV so cut to make room for 45 commercials that Bing and I weren't even in it.

Bob Hope

I was pretty – so pretty that actresses didn't want to work with me.

Roger Moore

Fred Astaire is the closest we are ever likely to get to a human Mickey Mouse.

Graham Greene

Did you know that the historic figures John Calvin and Thomas Hobbes were named after popular comic strip characters?

Paul Johnston

Billy Wilder at work is two people – Mr Hyde and Mr Hyde.

Harry Kurnitz

The making of a journalist: no ideas and the ability to express them.

Karl Kraus

My wife doesn't get jealous when she sees me in sex scenes on the screen. She knows I am only acting and that I can't last that long.

Jeremy Irons

Raise the Titanic? It would have been cheaper to lower the Atlantic.

Lew Grade

Media and Films

To have Mae Marsh display a surprised look, D. W. Griffith had a gun discharged behind her back. The effect lasted fifty years.

James Agate

The talkies made me sound as if I had been castrated.

Tallulah Bankhead

It's simple. PG means the hero gets the girl, 15 means that the villain gets the girl and 18 means that everybody gets the girl.

Michael Douglas

Star Spangled Rhythm is a variety show including everyone at Paramount who was not overseas, in hiding or out to lunch.

James Agee

Gary Cooper was one of the best loved illiterates this country has ever known.

Carl Sandburg

Many a good story has been ruined by over-verification.

James Bennett

On radio every Sunday, we have a stroke of culture, a symphony concert from New York or somewhere with a tooth-wash. That's the culture part, the tooth-wash.

Lincoln Steffens

Medicine and Doctors

Medicine and Doctors

I have the body of an eighteen year old. I keep it in the fridge.

Spike Milligan

I was under the care of a couple of medical students who couldn't diagnose a decapitation.

Jeffrey Bernard

The art of medicine consists in amusing the patient while Nature affects the cure.

Voltaire

Kilbarrack, over by Howth, my father always maintained, was the healthiest graveyard in the country, with the sea air.

Brendan Behan

Either this man is dead or my watch is stopped.

Groucho Marx

A sure cure for seasickness is to sit under a tree.

Spike Milligan

A shin is a device for finding furniture in the dark.

Colin Bowles

I'm not feeling very well – I need a doctor immediately. Ring the nearest golf course.

Groucho Marx

The operation was a complete success, but the patient died of something else.

John Chiene

Armpits lead lives of quiet perspiration.

Patrick Murray

Is there anything worn under the kilt? No, it's all in perfect working order.

Spike Milligan

My doctor gave me six months to live, but when I couldn't pay the bill he gave me six months more.

Walter Matthau

He wrote a doctor's hand – the hand which from the beginning of time has been so disastrous to the pharmacist and so profitable to the undertaker.

Mark Twain

Doctors think a lot of patients are cured who have simply quit in disgust.

Don Herold

One of the most difficult things to contend with in a hospital is the assumption on the part of the staff that because you have lost your gall bladder you have also lost your mind.

Jean Kerr

I make it a rule never to smoke more than one cigar at a time.

Mark Twain

Ordinarily he was insane, but he had lucid moments when he was merely stupid.

Heinrich Heine

My army medical consisted of two questions (i) Have you got piles? (ii) Any insanity in the family? I answered yes to both and was accepted A1.

Spike Milligan

Medicine and Doctors

His low opinion of medical students sprang largely from the days when he had been reading Theology at Cambridge and, on his attempt to break up a noisy party of medicals late one night, he had been forcibly administered an enema of Guinness stout.

Richard Gordon

Insanity doesn't just run in our family – it practically gallops.

Cary Grant

Condoms aren't completely safe. A friend of mine was wearing one and got hit by a bus.

Bob Rubin

My brain – that's my second favourite organ.

Woody Allen

One finger in the throat and one in the rectum make a good diagnostician.

William Osler

Anyone who goes to a psychiatrist should have his head examined.

Samuel Goldwyn

All those people with wooden legs – it's pathetic, they're not fooling anyone.

Michael Redmond

I refuse to endure months of expensive humiliation from a psychoanalyst only to be told that at the age of four I was in love with my rocking-horse.

Noel Coward

My piles bleed for you.

Herbert Beerbohm Tree

Every man catches himself in the zipper of his fly once, and only once in his lifetime.

Walt Giachini

Roses are red, violets are blue
I'm schizophrenic, and so am I.

Frank Crow

Henry the Fourth's feet and armpits enjoyed an international reputation.

Aldous Huxley

A woman went to a plastic surgeon and asked him to make her like Bo Derek. He gave her a lobotomy.

Joan Rivers

It is a poor doctor who cannot prescribe an expensive cure for a rich patient.

Sydney Tremayne

I woke up the other morning and found that everything in my room had been replaced by an exact replica. So I rang my best friend and told him that everything in my room had been replaced by an exact replica. He said 'Do I know you?'

Steven Wright

My father had a profound influence on me – he was a lunatic.

Spike Milligan

She got her looks from her father – he's a plastic surgeon.

Groucho Marx

I have just learnt about his illness; let us hope it is nothing trivial.

Irvin Cobb

Medicine and Doctors

Lassa Fever is so bad it makes spending one's entire life in
Bognor Regis look good.

George Thomas

When I was young I was so mixed up my parents sent me to
a child psychiatrist. But the boy was useless.

Rodney Dangerfield

Are you all right? You should have two of everything down
the sides and one of everything down the middle.

Ken Dodd

Jonathan Miller has put his finger on it – it's OK, he's a
doctor, he's allowed to put his finger on it.

Victor Lewis-Smith

I told my doctor I get very tired when I go on a diet, so he
gave me pep pills. Know what happened? I ate faster.

Joe E. Lewis

I've decided that perhaps I'm bulimic and just keep
forgetting to purge.

Paula Poundstone

Every man has a sane spot somewhere.

Robert Louis Stevenson

God heals, and the doctor takes the fee.

Benjamin Franklin

Medicine and Doctors

Here is a test to see if you are obese. Do people sometimes use you to show their home-movies on?

Lee Schreiner

Then Norm went and died. I could have given up and returned to Australia – that brown and pleasant land, but instead I founded the charity Friends of the Prostate, to increase knowledge of the Cinderella organ.

Edna Everage

To avoid dandruff falling on your shoulders, step nimbly to one side.

George Burns

When Charles II had a fit while shaving in 1685, he was lucky to be treated with the finest medical advice of the day. He was attended by 14 physicians who drew blood, forced him to vomit violently and gave him a strong laxative. Then they shaved his head, applied blistering agents to his scalp, put special plasters made from pigeon droppings onto the soles of this feet, fed him bezoar stones (much-prized gallstones from the bladder of a goat) and made him drink 40 drops of extract from a dead man's skull. He died two days later.

Karl Shaw

Akinesia is a medical term to denote the absence of kinesia.

Lee Schreiner

I'm going to Boston to see my doctor. He's a very sick man.

Fred Allen

Medicine and Doctors

Varicose veins are the result of an improper selection of grandparents.

William Osler

Dad always thought laughter was the best medicine, which I guess is why several of us died of tuberculosis.

Jack Handey

A reputable optometrist is one who does not make you remove your clothes for the examination.

George Thomas

In Govan, until something actually turns black and drops off, they think it's bad form to bother the doctor.

Rab. C. Nesbitt

The lungs are the largest organs in the body, and with good reason. They are essential to three of the hypochondriac's most vital bodily functions – coughing, wheezing and smoking.

George Thomas

Servants should not be ill. We have quite enough illnesses of our own without them adding to the symptoms.

Diana Cooper

In the middle ages, people took potions for their ailments. In the 19th century they took snake oil. Citizens of today's shiny technological age are too modern for that. They take antioxidants and extract of cactus instead.

Charles Krauthammer

Robert Lister, described as "the finest surgeon in Europe", had a personal best of 28 seconds for a leg amputation, although while achieving this record he accidentally cut off two of his assistant's fingers and the patient's left testicle.

Karl Shaw

After five days in hospital, I took a turn for the nurse.

Spike Milligan

Get your room full of good air, then shut up the windows and keep it. It will last for years. Anyway, don't keep using your lungs all the time. Let them rest.

Stephen Leacock

The true aim of medicine is to rescue men from the consequences of their vices.

H.L. Mencken

The cervix is an anatomical term referring to either the opening of the uterus or to the bones of the neck – an unfortunate ambiguity that has resulted in several famous operating theatre errors.

George Thomas

A hospital is no place to be sick.

Samuel Goldwyn

Medicine and Doctors

Have you ever had this tooth pulled before?

W. C. Fields

You can pick your friends and you can lead a horse to water, but you can't keep your eyes open when you sneeze.

Al Yankovic

L-I-M-P pronounced limp.

Spike Milligan

Medical care in Europe is excellent, and you may rest assured that if God forbid anything were to happen to you, the hospital personnel will use only the highest-quality stainless steel drill to bore a hole in your skull to let out the evil spirits.

Dave Barry

I haven't half put on a lot of weight: I used to be only seven pounds two ounces.

John Maloney

My husband, Mr. Merton, cannot travel. Once he gets outside of Stockport he can't call his bowels his own.

Mrs. Merton

The American Medical Association has stated that the leading cause of death among Americans returning from trips is being attacked by refrigerator mould.

Dave Barry

Two bats were hanging up in a cave and one said to the other, "When I'm older, I hope I don't become incontinent."

Mick Miller

He decided to commit suicide or die in the attempt.

Spike Milligan

When you get old, everything is hurting. When I get up in the morning, it sounds like I'm making popcorn.

Lawrence Taylor

The trouble with Viagra is that it can keep you stiff: permanently.

Dave Letterman

Doctor, feel my purse.

Jane Ace

How come you can always read a doctor's bill but never his prescription?

Finley Peter Dunne

The other day I got on a weighing machine that stamps out your weight on a card. When the card came out it read, "Come back in ten minutes: alone."

Jackie Gleason

How long have you had that birthmark?

W. C. Fields

I have gained and lost the same ten pounds so many times my cellulite must have déjà vu.

Jane Wagner

Tests on twenty students who thought they had fallen in love revealed a common pattern of brain cells similar to that of people suffering an obsessive–compulsive disorder.

John Follian

My biological clock is ticking so loudly I'm nearly deafened by it. They search me going into planes.

Marian Keyes

There is only one type of doctor who needs to wear a bow tie and that's a gynaecologist.

Martin Fischer

Good cheekbones are the brassière of old age.

Barbara De Portago

I've been on a diet for the last two decades. I've lost a total of 789 pounds. By all accounts I should be hanging from a charm bracelet.

Erma Bombeck

The hypothalamus controls the "four fs": fighting, fleeing, feeding and mating.

Martin Fischer

Aristotle was famous for knowing everything. He taught that the brain exists merely to cool the blood and is not involved in the process of thinking. This is true only of certain persons.

Will Cuppy

During the anatomy lesson the lecturer told us that the human male's testicles were about the size of a partridge's egg. A female student sitting next to me nudged me and said, "At least I know now how big a partridge's egg is."

Richard Gordon

Hypochondria is the imaginary complaint of indestructible old ladies.

E. B. White

On the other hand you have five fingers.

Steven Wright

I don't mind giving them a reasonable amount of blood, but a pint: why that's very nearly an armful.

Tony Hancock

If the patient isn't dead, you can always make him worse if you try hard enough.

Frank Vertosick

Once you start buying first-aid kits you start having accidents.

George Mikes

Medicine and Doctors

I will transcribe the conversations between the voices in my head and send them to you.

David Borenstein

I never go to a dentist who's had his office soundproofed.

Milton Berle

Mummy and I take so many pills, we rattle.

Raine Spencer

I have cancer: my veins are filled, once a week, with a Neapolitan carpet cleaner distilled from the Adriatic and I am as bald as an egg. However, I still get around and am mean to cats.

John Cheever

I have a left shoulder-blade that is a miracle of loveliness. People come miles to see it. My right elbow has a fascination that few can resist.

W. S. Gilbert

The most common error made in matters of appearance is the belief that one should disdain the superficial and let the true beauty of one's soul shine through. If there are places on your body where this is a possibility, you are not attractive, you are leaking.

Fran Lebowitz

Caution: living may be dangerous to your health.

Willard Espy

Medicine and Doctors

The medical profession wasn't always the highly organised racket that it is today.

Flann O'Brien

I'm fat and proud of it. If someone asks me how my diet is going, I say, "Fine, how was your lobotomy?"

Roseanne Barr

I have flabby thighs but fortunately my stomach covers them.

Joan Rivers

Every man who feels well is a sick man neglecting himself.

Jules Romains

The worst thing about a lung transplant is coughing up somebody else's phlegm.

Jackie Martling

A sure cure for toothache is to tickle a mule's heel.

Ken Alstad

My book *Venereal Disease and Its Prevention* is affectionately dedicated to my wife.

Felix Leblanc

She suffers badly from tinnitus: ringing in the ears, and they're wedding bells.

Richard Gordon

Medicine and Doctors

My husband Norm has invented a revolutionary heat-seeking bedpan.

Edna Everage

The Mayo Clinic was named after its founder, Dr. Ted Clinic.

Dave Barry

One of the most pleasing sounds of springtime to be heard all over the country is the contented cooing of osteopaths as Man picks up his garden spade.

Oliver Pritchett

Never drop dead around a specialist.

S.J. Perelman

I cannot abide the obstetrical anecdotes of ancient dames.

H.L. Mencken

Operating on the wrong patient or doing the wrong side of the body makes for a very bad day.

Frank Vertosick

I've got Parkinson's Disease. I can shake a Margarita in five seconds.

Michael J. Fox

After a certain age, if you don't wake up aching in every joint, you're probably dead.

Tommy Mein

Medicine and Doctors

He was a man of unbounded stomach.

William Shakespeare

Middle age is when anything new you feel is most likely a symptom.

Sidney Body

For every day you spend in hospital, you need a week to recuperate.

Esther Selsdon

I was once engaged when I was forty and I found it gave me very serious constipation. So I broke off the engagement and the lady quite understood.

Arthur Smith

When doctors in Los Angeles went on strike back in 1976, the local death rate fell by eighteen per cent.

Ross Bergman

My wife had but two topics of conversation: the Royal family and her bowels.

Alan Bennett

Tonsils and adenoids are lumps of lymphoid tissue that exist only to provide food, clothes and private education for the children of ear, nose and throat surgeons.

Michael O'Donnell

Medicine and Doctors

I've just got the bill for my operation. Now I know why those guys were wearing masks.

Jim Boren

I have a friend who died from a simple sneeze. Of course, he was standing in his neighbour's bedroom closet at the time.

Charles Jarvis

When I prepare to go to sleep, everything comes off or out.

Phyllis Diller

I think my kid is going to be a doctor. Nobody can read anything he writes.

Henny Youngman

My mother had morning sickness after I was born.

Rodney Dangerfield

My wife lost two stones swimming last year. I don't know how. I tied them around her neck tight enough.

Les Dawson

When the doctor asked me if I became breathless when taking exercise, I had to say no, as I never took exercise.

John Mortimer

I have been on a convalescent diet. If you come across nineteen or eighteen pounds of human flesh, they belong to me. I look as if a curate has been taken out of me.

Sydney Smith

I've examined your son's head, Mr Glum, and there's nothing there.

Frank Muir

Does your epileptic fit, or do you have to take him in a bit at the sides?

Jason Byrne

The placenta is very useful because it is so very hideous that by comparison, the baby is quite attractive.

Jenny Eclair

In some ways, cramp is worse than having a broken leg. But leukaemia is worse still. Probably.

Kevin Keegan

When I was pregnant my breasts were so huge they needed their own postcode.

Kathy Lette

During one of his many bouts of insanity King George the Third insisted on ending every sentence with the word 'peacock'.

Geoff Tibballs

Nancy Reagan has agreed to be the first artificial heart donor.

Andrea Michaels

No man is a hero to his wife's psychiatrist.

Eric Berne

Medicine and Doctors

I had examined myself pretty thoroughly and discovered that I was unfit for military service.

Joseph Heller

Nothing is dearer to a woman than a nice long obstetrical chat.

Cornelia Otis Skinner

I went to the doctor the other day and told him my arm was broken in three places. He told me to stay out of those places.

Tommy Cooper

They say men can never experience the pain of childbirth; they can if you hit them in the goolies with a cricket bat for fourteen hours.

Jo Brand

A cough is something that you yourself can't help, but everybody else does on purpose just to torment you.

Ogden Nash

He cured his sciatica by boiling his buttock.

John Aubrey

My friend George is weird. He has false teeth – with braces on them.

Steven Wright

Medicine and Doctors

A natural death is where you die by yourself without the aid of a doctor.

Mark Twain

I went to the doctor and he told me I had acute paranoia. I reminded him that I had come to be examined, not to be admired.

Gracie Allen

Physicians of all men are most happy; what good success soever they have, the world proclaimeth and what faults they commit the earth covereth.

Francis Quarles

The first need in the reform of hospital management is the death of all dietitians and the resurrection of the French chef.

Martin Fischer

I'm not saying my body is a wreck, but my gynaecologist wears a hard hat.

Joan Rivers

The doctor told me I should buy day-returns from now on instead of season tickets.

Hugh Leonard

It is a known medical fact, and it has been so since the dawn of time, that a man asking directions will hear just the first word and then break down.

Jeremy Clarkson

Music

 **Music**

The music teacher came twice a week to bridge the awful
gap between Dorothy and Chopin.

George Ade

The bagpipes are an instrument of torture consisting of a
leaky bag and punctured pipes, played by blowing up the bag
and placing the fingers over the wrong holes.

Dick Diabolus

Most rock journalism is people who cannot write
interviewing people who cannot talk for people who cannot
read.

Frank Zappa

Jazz is music invented for the torture of imbeciles.

Henry Van Dyke

I could eat alphabet soup and shit better lyrics than that.

Johnny Mercer

A violin is the revenge exacted by the intestines of a dead
cat.

Ambrose Bierce

The Mafia once moved in and took over the New York
Ballet. During a performance of 'Swan Lake', there was a lot
of money on the swan to live.

Woody Allen

Brass bands are all very well in their place – outdoors and
several miles away.

Thomas Beecham

Swans sing before they die – 'twere no bad thing did certain
persons die before they sing.

S. T. Coleridge

Classical music is the kind you keep thinking will turn into a tune.

Kin Hubbard

I have never heard any Stockhausen, but I do believe I have stepped in some.

Thomas Beecham

Wagner has some lovely moments but some terrible quarters of an hour.

Gioacchino Rossini

The harpsichord sounds like two skeletons copulating on a corrugated tin roof.

Thomas Beecham

She was a town-and-country soprano of the kind often used for augmenting grief at a funeral.

George Ade

The Sydney Opera House looks as if it were something that had crawled out of the sea and was up to no good.

Beverley Nichols

One cannot judge Wagner's opera Lohengrin after a first hearing and I have no intention of sitting through it a second time.

Gioacchino Rossini

Wagner's music is better than it sounds.

Mark Twain

Having adapted Beethoven's Ninth Symphony for *Fantasia*, Walt Disney commented 'Gee, this'll make Beethoven'.

Marshall McLuhan

 **Music**

The third movement of Bartok's Fourth Quartet began with a dog howling at midnight, proceeded to imitate the regurgitations of the less refined type of water-closet and concluded with the cello reproducing the screech of an ungreased wheelbarrow.

Alan Dent

I find that distance lends enchantment to bagpipes.

William Blezard

Please do not shoot the pianist – he's doing his best.

Oscar Wilde

I liked your opera. I think I will set it to music.

Ludwig van Beethoven

I write music as a sow piddles.

W.A. Mozart

I'm a concert pianist. That's a pretentious way of saying I'm unemployed at the moment.

Oscar Levant

A highbrow is anyone who can listen to the William Tell Overture and not think of The Lone Ranger.

Jack Perlis

We will now have the Second Dance Rhapsody of Frederick Delius, a work which was given some years ago and of which we shall now hear the first performance.

Thomas Beecham

Wagner is the Puccini of music.

J.B. Morton

Why do we in England engage at our concerts so many third-rate continental conductors when we have so many second-rate ones of our own?

Thomas Beecham

It is sobering to consider that when Mozart was my age he had already been dead for a year.

Tom Lehrer

Bagpipes are the missing link between music and noise.

E.K. Kruger

Others, when the bagpipe sings i' the nose, cannot contain their urine.

William Shakespeare

If that's what the top twenty records sound like, I shudder to think what the bottom fifty must sound like.

C. Street

The third movement of Beethoven's Seventh Symphony is like a lot of yaks jumping about.

Thomas Beecham

Sleep is an excellent way of listening to an opera.

James Stephens

Crooning is a reprehensible form of singing that established itself in light entertainment mainly about the 1930s. It recommended itself at first to would-be singers without voices who were unable to acquire an adequate technique. The principle of crooning is to use as little voice as possible and instead to make a sentimental appeal by prolonged moaning somewhere near the written notes.

Eric Blom

 **Music**

I was not able to detect in the vocal parts of Parsifal anything
that might with confidence be called rhythm or tune or
melody.

Mark Twain

I believe that the kidnapping of Frank Sinatra Jr. was carried
out by music critics.

Oscar Levant

Claude Debussy played the piano with the lid down.

Robert Bresson

The darting eyes of James Galway give the impression of a
man permanently watching tennis at Wimbledon; his
haunted expression may well be divine retribution for his
appalling recording of 'Annie's Song' he made in the 1970s, a
rendition that inspired a million tone-deaf kids to take up
the flute.

Victor Lewis-Smith

Daughters, lock up your mothers, Daniel O'Donnell is in
town.

Patrick Murray

As a sex symbol Tom Jones is nothing short of inexplicable.

Sheridan Morley

Music-hall songs provide the dull with wit, just as proverbs
provide them with wisdom.

Somerset Maugham

Signor Tamberlik sings in a doubtful falsetto and his movements are unmeaning and frequently absurd. For the C sharp in the celebrated duet he substituted a strange description of shriek at about that pitch. The audience, ever appreciative of vocal curiosities, eagerly redemanded it.

George Bernard Shaw

Music makes a nation's disposition more gentle – for example 'The Marseillaise'.

Gustave Flaubert

You want something by Bach? Which one – Johann Sebastian or Jacques Offen?

Victor Borge

The most expensive solution would be to blow up all the opera houses.

Pierre Boulez

No one should be allowed to play the violin until he has mastered it.

Jim Fiebig

A guy who hangs around with musicians is called a drummer.

Lisa Fuglie

Miss Marcia Devin sang 'I Will Not Pass This Way Again', giving obvious pleasure to the entire congregation.

Leo Rosten

 **Music**

George Gershwin played us a medley of his hit.

Oscar Levant

The opera was pretty good. Even the music was nice.

Yogi Berra

I have witnessed and greatly enjoyed the first act of everything which Wagner created, but the effect on me has always been so powerful that one act was quite sufficient; whenever I have witnessed two acts I have gone away physically exhausted; and whenever I have ventured an entire opera the result has been the next thing to suicide.

Mark Twain

Listening to Vaughan William's Fifth Symphony is like staring at a cow for forty-five minutes.

Aaron Copland

To test the acoustics at his new Bayrueth theatre, soldiers from the local garrison were brought in to squat on the floor and Wagner was moved to describe them as the ideal audience on three counts:
1. They were all in their places before the music began.
2. They did not talk or fidget while it was being played.
3. When it was over they made no pretence of having understood anything of what they had seen or heard and so refrained from airing their opinions about it.

Robert Hartford

When something is not worth saying, sing it.

Gioacchino Rossini

Music

If the Almighty himself played the violin, the credits would still read Rubenstein, God, and Piatigorsky, in that order.

Jascha Heifetz

It takes four jazz trumpeters to change a lightbulb. One to actually change it and the other three to discuss how Dizzy Gillespie would have done it.

Geoff Boardwell

I'd like to see a nude opera, because when they hit those high notes, I bet you can really see it in those genitals.

Jack Handey

Paul, George, and Ringo are recording a song using the last of John's unreleased tapes. It goes 'Hello, this is the Lennon residence, I can't come to the phone right now…'

Chris Cox

Now, ladies and contraltos, if you will look to your parts, you will see where the gentlemen and tenors come in.

Thomas Beecham

The best way to confuse a drummer is to put a sheet of music in front of him.

Lizzi Davenport

I couldn't warm to Chuck Berry even if I was cremated next to him.

Keith Richards

 **Music**

God dammit! Jimmy Hendrix beat me to dying.

Janis Joplin

I must shut my ears. The man of sin rubbeth the hair of the horse to the bowels of the cat.

John O'Keeffe

I once worked in a circus beside a drum so loud that in a short time I was able to hear only disturbances like thunder, explosions and collapsing buildings.

W. C. Fields

Lloyd Webber's music is everywhere but so is AIDS.

Malcolm Williamson

There are few moments during her recital when one can relax and feel confident that she will make her goal, which is the end of the song.

Paul Hume

A new survey shows that one out of every four drivers has fallen asleep at the wheel while on the road. And for half of those the last thing they remember hearing is "And now here's a new one from John Tesh."

Dennis Miller

I prefer flying on Concorde because I cannot get in and out of aircraft toilets but on a three and a half hour flight I can hold out.

Luciano Pavarotti

Music

The worst feature of a new child is its mother's singing.

Kin Hubbard

I know only two tunes. One of them is "Yankee Doodle".
The other isn't.

Ulysses S. Grant

Abstain from wine, women and song; mostly song.

Brad Templeton

Composers should not think too much: it interferes with
their plagiarism.

Howard Dietz

There won't be a Beatles reunion as long as John Lennon
remains dead.

George Harrison

Did you write the words or the lyrics?

Bruce Forsyth

The purpose of jazz is the destruction of music.

Thomas Beecham

Mothers used to breastfeed their babies while I played the
piano: I guess they used to find it soothing. I played the odd
very sudden loud note because I loved to watch the nipples
shooting out of their mouths.

Harpo Marx

 **Music**

Dudley Moore is such a clever little pianist. He can play on the white keys and the black.

Noel Coward

The Queen's distaste for dreary repetition fills me with admiration. Sent a rare invitation from the Royal Opera House to see *The Marriage of Figaro*, she politely sent her regrets because she had already seen it.

Jasper Gerard

Luciano Pavarotti is only slightly smaller than Vermont.

Norman Lebrecht

The music is in German. You would not understand it.

Oscar Wilde

Twentieth-century music is like paedophilia. No matter how persuasively and persistently its champions urge their cause, it will never be accepted by the public at large, who will continue to regard it with incomprehension, outrage and repugnance.

Kingsley Amis

The Spice Girls is a five-member girl group with the talent of one bad actress between them.

David Hutcheon

My girlfriend, she was thin. Two more navels and she would have been a flute.

Stu Francis

Music

Men who listen to classical music tend not to spit.

Rita Rudner

People are wrong when they say that opera is not what it used to be. It is what it used to be. That is what is wrong with it.

Noel Coward

Members of the orchestra, we cannot expect you to be with us all the time, but perhaps you could be good enough to keep in touch now and again.

Thomas Beecham

He's my favourite kind of musician. He knows how to play the ukulele, but he doesn't.

Will Rogers

Dana International looked as if she had smeared herself with superglue before colliding with a flock of crows.

Paul Hoggart

Offenbach's music is wicked. It is abandoned stuff: every accent in it is a snap of the fingers in the face of moral responsibility; every ripple and sparkle on its surface twits me for my teetotalism, and mocks at the early rising of which I fully intend to make a habit some day.

George Bernard Shaw

I hate music: especially when it is played.

Jimmy Durante

Undeterred, his weekend now in ruins, the young Wolfgang answered the by now more insistent Prince Leopold's entreaties and proceeded to speedily pen his fifty-second symphony, which he finished by the following Tuesday.

Peter Bruce

My Fair Lady: I must say Bernard Shaw is greatly improved by music.

T. S. Eliot

If Rock 'n' Roll is here to stay I might commit suicide.

Sammy Davis Jr.

This is a very old English folksong. I know it is a very old English folksong because I wrote it myself when I was very young.

Paddy Roberts

A bodhran is a large, round, thick-skinned object, usually tight, which you have to hit with a stick to get anything out of. Elsewhere in the world this is known as a husband.

Terry Eagleton

If I had a hammer, I'd use it on Peter, Paul and Mary.

Howard Rosenberg

Adolf Hitler was one of the first rock stars. Look at some of his films and see how he moved. I think he was quite as good as Mick Jagger.

David Bowie

Music

Once after Caruso had sung a duet with a celebrated soprano, more noted for her beauty than her voice, he was asked how he liked her singing. "I don't know," he replied, "I never heard her."

Dorothy Caruso

At the rehearsals I let the orchestra play as they like. At the concert I make them play as I like.

Thomas Beecham

Let's face it, we became ingrown, clannish and retarded. Cut off from the mainstream of humanity, we came to believe that pink is "flesh-colour", that mayonnaise is a nutrient and that Barry Manilow is a musician.

Barbara Ehrenreich

An "orchestra" in radio circles is any ensemble comprising more than three players, while a "symphony" programme is one that includes Liszt's Liebenstraum.

Deems Taylor

The problem with Lloyd Webber's music is not that it sounds as if it were written by other composers, but that it sounds as if it were written by Lloyd Webber.

Gerald Kaufman

Dear Mr. Edison, I am astonished at the wonderful form you have developed and terrified at the thought that so much hideous and bad music will be put on records for ever.

Arthur Sullivan

 **Music**

At Gloucestershire Airport we used to broadcast cassette tapes with birds' distress sounds on them to keep the runway clear of seagulls, blackbirds and rooks. They didn't work very well so now we use Tina Turner records: the birds really hate her, especially "Simply the Best".

Ron Johnson

Italian singing: bestial howling and entirely frantic vomiting up of damned souls through their still carnal throats.

John Ruskin

Listen, kid, take my advice. Never hate a song that has sold half a million copies.

Irving Berlin

I don't like my music, but what is my opinion against that of millions of others?

Frederick Loewe

King's College Chapel: it's the building. That acoustic would make a fart sound like a sevenfold amen.

David Willcocks

Irving Berlin had a voice that sounded like a hoarse tomcat with its tail in a clothes wringer.

Bob Hope

I hope Harry Secombe dies before me because I don't want him singing at my funeral.

Spike Milligan

When we couldn't get a seat in the pub, we used to play "O Superman" by Laurie Anderson on the jukebox. It worked every time.

Alan James

The best thing I can say about bagpipes is that they don't smell, too.

Brendan Behan

I wrote a song, but I can't read music. Every time I hear a new song on the radio, I think, "Hey, maybe I wrote that."

Steven Wright

A manager of a cinema in South Korea decided that the *Sound of Music* was too long to show so he edited out all the songs.

Ross Bergman

The only thing a bassoon is good for is kindling an accordion fire.

Ross Bergman

Have you heard about the fellow who played "Flight of the Bumble Bee" on the tuba? He blew his liver out.

Tommy Boyd

Stravinsky looks like a man who was potty-trained too early and his music proves it as far as I am concerned.

Russell Hoban

 **Music**

Being music director of the Berlin Philharmonic is like being the Pope – except for the celibacy.

Simon Rattle

I've just been listening to a sonata written by Chopin in a flat; you'd think with the sort of money he was earning he could afford a house.

Alastair McGowan

The opera always loses money. That's as it should be. Opera has no business making money.

Rudolf Bing

We live in a country where John Lennon takes six bullets to the chest. Yoko Ono is standing next to him. Not one ******* bullet. Explain that to me! Explain that to me.

Denis Leary

Movie music is noise. It's more painful than even my sciatica.

Thomas Beecham

The soloist tonight reminded me very much of Paderewski. Paderewski was no violinist, and neither was the soloist tonight.

George Bernard Shaw

Bing Crosby sings like everybody thinks they sing in the shower.

Dinah Shore

Lionel Bart's musical *Blitz* was very close to the real thing but it seemed to last twice as long and be just as noisy.

Noël Coward

I would have given my right arm to be a pianist.

Bobby Robson

Greig's music is like a pink bon-bon filled with snow.

Claude Debussy

In the Sixties I played lead guitar in a band called the Federal Duck and we made an album which sounds like a group of people who have been given powerful but unfamiliar instruments as a therapy for a degenerative nerve disease.

Dave Barry

A musical is a series of catastrophes ending with a floor show.

Oscar Levant

It was the most fun I've had since I've been black.

Dizzy Gillespie

I know the acoustics in the hall are terrible. But we've done everything to remedy the situation – we've put down traps, we've put down poison and we still can't shift them.

Jon Kenny

Last night I played a blank tape at full blast. The mime living next door went nuts.

Steven Wright

If Yoko Ono's singing voice was a fight, they'd stop it.

Robert Wuhl

Mick Jagger told me his wrinkles were due to laughter and not age. I told him that nothing was that funny.

George Melly

For the score of a movie, I like music like Wagner, only louder.

Samuel Goldwyn

Most bands don't think about the future. Most musicians can't even spell future. Lunch is how far we think ahead.

David Roth

The problem with reality is the lack of background music.

Steven Wright

Mozart composed symphonies at eight, but they weren't very good.

Steven Pinker

The people of Halifax invented the harmonium, a device for castrating pigs during the Sunday service.

Mike Harding

Can she sing? Why, she's practically a Florence Nightingale.

Samuel Goldwyn

I do not accept floral wreaths at the end of a performance. Floral wreaths are for prima donnas or corpses. I am neither.

Arturo Toscanini

I don't normally sing and when I sing I don't sing normally.

Danny Cummins

Chopin was a composer for the right hand.

Richard Wagner

My address? I think 'Italy' will be sufficient.

Giuseppe Verdi

I have heard Liszt and I have heard Paderewski, but neither of them perspired as much as Liebling does.

W. S. Gilbert

Leonard Bernstein is an educator who has been disclosing musical secrets which have been well-known for years.

Oscar Levant

A quartet is a singing group in which all four think the other three cannot sing.

Doris Maloney

Nationalities and Places

In England there are a hundred religions and only one sauce which is melted butter.

Francesco Caracciolo

Note the tower, which is said to be the sixth highest in East Anglia.

Stephen Potter

Canada could have enjoyed English government, French culture and American know-how. Instead it ended up with English know-how, French government and American culture.

John Robert Colombo

The Irish gave the bagpipes to the Scots as a joke, but the Scots haven't seen the joke yet.

Oliver Herford

I am willing to love all mankind, except an American.

Samuel Johnson

People don't actually swim in Dublin Bay – they are merely going through the motions.

Brendan Behan

I would like to live in Manchester, England. The transition between Manchester and death would be unnoticeable.

Mark Twain

Always remember that you are an Englishman and therefore have drawn first prize in the lottery of life.

Cecil Rhodes

The first item on the agenda of every Irish organisation is 'The Split'.

Brendan Behan

It is no longer true that Continentals have a sex life whereas the English have hot-water bottles – the English now have electric blankets.

George Mikes

In Pierre Trudeau Canada has at last produced a political leader worthy of assassination.

Irving Layton

America is the only nation in history which miraculously has gone from barbarism to degeneracy without the usual interval of civilisation.

Georges Clemenceau

The bars in Dublin are shut from 2.30 to 3.30. We call it the Holy Hour. The politician who introduced it was shot an hour afterwards.

Brendan Behan

Once you've been on a plane full of drunken Australians doing wallaby imitations up and down the aisles, you'll never make fun of Americans again.

P.J. O'Rourke

The main difference between Los Angeles and yogurt is that yogurt has an active living culture.

Tom Taussik

There are still parts of Wales where the only concession to gaiety is a striped shroud.

Gwyn Thomas

Of course America had often been discovered before Columbus, but it had always been hushed up.

Oscar Wilde

Nationalities and Places

For breakfast, the first morning I was in France, I had a
steaming bidet of coffee, followed by porridge and frogs.

Spike Milligan

The English have sex on the brain – which is a frightfully
uncomfortable place to have it.

Malcolm Muggeridge

In Paris they simply stared when I spoke to them in French; I
never did succeed in making those idiots understand their
own language.

Mark Twain

I have a great admiration for Mussolini, who has welded a
nation out of a collection of touts, blackmailers, ice-cream
vendors and gangsters.

Michael Bateman

The war situation has developed not necessarily to Japan's
advantage.

Emperor Hirohito (1945)

Much may be made of a Scotchman, if he be caught young.

Samuel Johnson

A great many people in Los Angeles are on strict diets that
restrict their intake of food. The reason for this appears to be
a widely-held belief that organically grown fruit and
vegetables make the cocaine work faster.

Fran Lebowitz

We must keep America whole and safe and unspoiled.

Al Capone

She lived in France – that country to which lesbianism is
what cricket is to England.

Quentin Crisp

Nationalities and Places

America is the land of permanent waves and impermanent wives.

Brendan Behan

I know only two words of American slang; 'swell' and 'lousy'. I think 'swell' is lousy, but 'lousy' is swell.

J.B. Priestley

The high standards of Australians are due to the fact that their ancestors were all hand-picked by the best English judges.

Douglas Copland

I don't hold with abroad and think that foreigners speak English when our backs are turned.

Quentin Crisp

Those comfortably padded lunatic asylums which are known, euphemistically, as the stately homes of England.

Virginia Woolf

The noblest prospect which a Scotchman ever sees is the high road that leads him to England.

Samuel Johnson

There are over thirty words in the Irish language which are equivalent to the Spanish 'manana'. But somehow none of them conveys the same sense of urgency.

Patrick Kavanagh

When St Patrick drove the snakes out of Ireland, they swam to New York and joined the police force.

Eugene O'Neill

I have been trying all my life to like Scotchmen, and am obligated to desist from the experiment in despair.

Charles Lamb

Nationalities and Places

Canada is useful only to provide me with furs.

Madame de Pompadour

Americans are a race of convicts and ought to be thankful for anything we allow them short of hanging.

Samuel Johnson

No man is thoroughly miserable unless he is condemned to live in Ireland.

Jonathan Swift

The English winter – ending in July, to recommence in August.

George Gordon

In Ireland a girl has the choice between perpetual virginity and perpetual pregnancy.

George Moore

The French invented the only known cure for dandruff. It is called the guillotine.

P.G. Wodehouse

Your proper child of Caledonia is the bandy-legged lout from Tullietudlesleugh, who, after a childhood of intimacy with the cesspool and the crablouse, and twelve months at 'the college' on moneys wrung from the diet of his family, drops his threadbare kilt and comes south in a slop suit to instruct the English in the arts of civilisation and in the English language

T.W. Crosland

He was so depressed, he tried to commit suicide by inhaling next to an Armenian.

Woody Allen

How about the raffle where the first prize was a week in Belfast and the second prize was a fortnight in Belfast.

Brendan Behan

Nationalities and Places

Australia is a country whose industrial and commercial development has been unspeakably retarded by an unfortunate dispute among geographers as to whether it is a continent or an island.

Ambrose Bierce

The ignorance of French society gives one a rough sense of the infinite.

Joseph Ernest Renan

The sun never sets on the British Empire because God wouldn't trust an Englishman in the dark.

Duncan Spaeth

The softer the currency in a foreign country, the harder the toilet paper.

John Fountain

The Irish climate is wonderful, but the weather ruins it.

Tony Butler

To be a Frenchman abroad is to be miserable; to be an American abroad is to make other people miserable.

Ambrose Bierce

We had a very successful trip to Russia – we got back.

Bob Hope

A gesticulation is any movement made by a foreigner.

J.B. Morton

I can never forgive God for creating the French.

Peter Ustinov

What do I think of Western civilisation? I think it would be a very good idea.

Mahatma Gandhi

Nationalities and Places

When the missionaries came to Africa they had the Bible and
we had the land. They said 'Let us pray.' We closed our eyes.
When we opened them we had the Bible and they had the
land.

Desmond Tutu

Nebraska is proof that hell is full and the dead walk the earth.

Liz Winston

Black Englishmen and women who win Olympic medals are
described as English while those who riot and throw petrol
bombs are invariably West Indian.

Edward Hughes

The English find ill-health not only interesting but respectable,
and often experience death in the effort to avoid a fuss.

Pamela Frankau

It must be marvellous to be a man and just cheerfully assume
I was superior. Better still, I could be an Irishman and have
all the privileges of being male without giving up the right
to be wayward, temperamental and an appealing minority.

Katharine Whitehorn

The English never smash in a face. They merely refrain from
asking it to dinner.

Margaret Halsey

I have to choose between this world, the next world and
Australia.

Oscar Wilde

Dutch is not so much a language as a disease of the throat

Mark Twain

In the Soviet Union a writer who is critical is taken to a lunatic
asylum. In the United States, he is taken to a talk show.

Carlos Fuentes

Nationalities and Places

When in Paris, I always eat at the Eiffel Tower restaurant because it's the only place where I can avoid seeing the damned thing.

William Morris

It is unthinkable for a Frenchman to arrive at middle age without having both syphilis and the Cross of the Legion of Honour.

André Gide

The US embassy in Moscow is nothing but an eight-storey microphone plugged into the Politburo.

Richard Armey

It is peculiar that all the sights in Rome are called after London cinemas.

Nancy Mitford

I never met anyone in Ireland who understood the Irish question, except one Englishman who had only been there a week.

Kenneth Fraser

One of the girls in my swimming squad complained that there were men in the women's changing room, only to discover on investigation that she had merely overheard East German girls in the next cubicle.

Charles Wilson

Going to the loo in a yacht in a French harbour is not so much goodbye as au revoir.

Noel Coward

An Iranian moderate is one who believes that the firing squad should be democratically elected.

Henry Kissinger

The English are good at forgiving their enemies; it releases them from the obligation of liking their friends.

P.D. James

German ought to be gently and reverently set aside among the dead languages, for only the dead have time to learn it.

Mark Twain

My father was from Donegal – he didn't metabolise ethanol very well.

George Carlin

From the earliest times the Welsh have been looked upon as an unclean people. It is thus that they have preserved their racial integrity. Their sons and daughters mate freely with sheep but not with human kind, except their own blood relations.

Evelyn Waugh

The Todas of Southern India are of the opinion that if a girl is still a virgin at her wedding, her maternal uncle will be taken ill and die.

Mark Fowler

If you do somebody in Ireland a favour, you make an enemy for life.

Hugh Leonard

When in Turkey, do as the turkeys do.

Honoré De Balzac

Nationalities and Places

Japanese Prime Ministers are just glorified transistor salesmen.

Charles De Gaulle

Whenever the literary German dives into a sentence, that is the last you are going to see of him till he emerges on the other side of the Atlantic with his verb in his mouth.

Mark Twain

My club is world famous – we get coaches from as far away as Sheffield.

Bernard Manning

Arrival-Angst is closely connected with guilt, with the dread of something terrible having happened during our absence. Death of parents. Entry of bailiffs. Flight of loved one. Sensations worse at arriving in the evening than in the morning, and much worse at Victoria and Waterloo, than at Paddington.

Cyril Connolly

Everybody has a right to pronounce foreign names as he chooses.

Winston Churchill

The best empire-builder is the colonist who has good reasons for not coming home again.

David Somervell

The Israelis are now what we call 'enemy-friends'.

Yasser Arafat

Nationalities and Places

Since Finland first entered the Eurovision fray in 1961 they have appeared in the competition 34 times, finishing last on an unequalled nine occasions with songs which sounded as though they were originally designed to frighten elks.

Karl Shaw

The first commandment of life in Ireland would appear to be, thou shalt never under any circumstances wash a car.

Rowan Atkinson

The FA are optimistic about England's bid to stage the World Cup in twenty thousand and six.

Peter Snow

German is the most extravagantly ugly language. It sounds like someone using a sick bag on a 747.

Willy Rushton

New York now leads the world's great cities in the number of people around whom you shouldn't make a sudden move.

David Letterman

A nation is a people who share a common misconception as to their origins and a common antipathy towards their neighbours.

Eric Hobsbawm

Don't worry about the world coming to an end today. It's already tomorrow in Australia.

Charles Schultz

He was shouting in a sort of Franglais – 'I will frappez votre teeth so far down votre gorge, you'll be able to manger avec your derriere'.

Victor Lewis-Smith

The English may not be the best writers in the world; but they are incomparably the best dull writers.

Raymond Chandler

Sign in a Paris restaurant:
A ten percent discount is cheerfully given to customers who do not attempt to order in French.

Leo Rosten

Bernie Slevin was half Scottish and half Irish. Half of him wanted to get drunk while the other half didn't want to pay for it.

Jack Charlton

Traditionally, most of Australia's exports come from overseas.

Keppel Enderbery

I love Americans, but not when they try to speak French. What a blessing it is that they never try to speak English.

H.H. Munro

Blackpool is a town which looks like as if it's helping police with their enquiries.

Victor Lewis-Smith

Nationalities and Places

American husbands are the best in the world; no other husbands are so generous to their wives, or can be so easily divorced.

Elinor Glyn

Holland lies so low it is saved only by being dammed.

Thomas Hood

In Russia everything is forbidden. In Germany, everything is forbidden unless it is permitted. In Britain, everything is permitted unless it is forbidden. And in Italy, everything is permitted whether it is forbidden or not.

P.J. O'Rourke

People say New Yorkers can't get along. Not true. I saw two New Yorkers, complete strangers, sharing a cab. One guy took the tyres and the radio; the other guy took the engine.

David Letterman

At first the dive-bombing was impressive, but after half an hour deadly monotonous. It was like everything German – overdone.

Evelyn Waugh

Tip the world over on its side and everything loose will land in Los Angeles.

Frank Lloyd Wright

To Americans, English manners are far more frightening than none at all.

George Mikes

The tourist in Ireland has only to ask and he will be directed
to something; whether or not it is what he thinks he is
looking for is another matter.

Ciarán Carson

For God's sake, madam, do not say in England that the
quality of air in Ireland is good, or they will surely tax it.

Jonathan Swift

On a clear day, from the terrace, you can't see Luxembourg
at all. This is because a tree is in the way.

Alan Coren

Melbourne is a ghost town. You couldn't even get a
parachute to open here after 10pm.

Max Bygraves

The definition of an American virgin is any girl that can run
faster than Bill Clinton.

Iain Dale

After a day smiling like insane persons and talking about
how they would very much like to help handicapped
animals, the Miss America contestants go back to their hotel
rooms and unwind by smoking enormous cigars and spitting
out the window onto elderly pedestrians.

Dave Barry

We should export all of our toxic waste to third world
countries because underpopulated countries in Africa are
vastly underpolluted.

Lawrence Summers

Nationalities and Places

Americans have different ways of saying things. They say 'elevator', we say 'lift'; they say 'President', we say 'stupid psychopathic git'.

Alexei Sayle

The reason there is so little crime in Germany is that it's against the law.

Alex Levin

Like so many Americans, she was trying to construct a life that made sense from things she found in gift shops.

Kurt Vonnegut Jr.

I don't have a problem with parking in San Francisco. I drive a forklift.

Jim Samuels

Am I to understand that an overweight Italian singing in his own language is part of my English heritage?

Terence Dicks

Speculation is that the Swedes are slowly boring themselves to death. This is certainly the case if their cars and movies are any indication.

P.J. O'Rourke

In English history the king always turned out to be a syphilitic hunchbacked lunatic dwarf whose basic solution to virtually all problems, including humidity, was to have somebody's head cut off. Henry VIII could barely get through a day without beheading a wife.

Dave Barry

Nationalities and Places

Dublin, though a place much worse than London, is not so bad as Iceland.

Samuel Johnson

Edna Everage is Australia's revenge for penal colonisation.

Michael Parkinson

Arkansas is very proud of Bill Clinton – all those women coming forward and none of them is his sister!

John Simmons

It is all very well to call Ned Kelly a white-livered cur, a bully, a coward, a liar and a psychotic murderer, but to actually name him as a queer is going too far.

Keith Dunstan

Life is very important to many Americans.

Bob Dole

In a British hotel, the words 'Can I help you sir?' mean roughly 'What the hell do you want?'

Kingsley Amis

Organised crime in America takes in forty billion dollars a year and spends very little on office supplies.

Woody Allen

No matter how many times I visit New York City, I am always struck by the same thing: a yellow taxi cab.

Scott Adams

Anyone found smiling after curfew on the streets of Philadelphia was liable to get arrested. If a woman dropped her glove on the street she was liable to be arrested and hauled before a judge on a charge of strip-teasing.

W.C. Fields

All Englishmen talk as if they've got a bushel of plums stuck in their throats and then after swallowing them get constipated from the pits.

W.C. Fields

The American male does not mature until he has exhausted all other possibilities.

Wilfred Sheed

A German film-goer was beaten to death in a Bonn cinema by ushers because he had brought his own popcorn.

Karl Shaw

During the potato famine, how come the Irish couldn't afford the cost of a square meal but could still afford to go to America?

Steve Coogan

It is easy to understand why the most beautiful poems about England were written by poets living in Italy at the time.

George Sanders

I would love to speak Italian but I can't, so I grew underarm hair instead.

Sue Kolinsky

I gave him a Dublin uppercut – a kick in the groin.

Brendan Behan

Finding out your sister is black is fine; finding out that your sister is Welsh is another thing.

A.A. Gill

Wales is the land of song: but no music.

David Wulstan

Give me your tired, your poor, your huddled masses yearning to be free, provided they have satisfactorily filled-out forms 3584-A through 3597-Q.

Dwight McDonald

Philadelphia is the greatest cemetery in the world.

W.C. Fields

Knocking down a house in Dublin recently, the workmen found a skeleton with a medal on a ribbon around its neck. The inscription was: Irish Hide and Seek Champion 1910.

Frank Carson

On stage I often ask the audience if they would like to hear an Irish joke. If they say "yes", I tell them one: in Gaelic.

Ian McPherson

A group of innocent American tourists was taken on a tour bus through a country the members later described as "either France or Sweden", and subjected to three days of looking at old dirty buildings where it was not possible to get a cheeseburger.

Dave Barry

Chief amongst the mysteries of India is how the natives keep those little loin cloths up.

Robert Benchley

The colour slides we took of our trip to the Virgin Islands featured nearly two dozen shots of the airplane wing alone.

Dave Barry

In England, if you are a Duchess, you don't need to be well dressed: it would be thought quite eccentric.

Nancy Mitford

Imagine the Lord speaking French! Aside from a few odd words in Hebrew, I took it completely for granted that God had never spoken anything but the most dignified English.

Clarence Day

Pittsburg is Hell with the lid taken off.

James Parton

Irish weather consists of rain: lots of it. It has been known for the rain to cease, sometimes for as much as two weeks at a time. But when this happens, the Irish complain of drought, pestilence and imminent bankruptcy.

Stan Gebler Davies

There are no more thefts in New York: there's nothing left to steal.

Henny Youngman

I do not know the American gentleman. God forgive me for putting two such words together.

Charles Dickens

They should never have shared the Nobel Peace Prize between two people from Northern Ireland. They will only fight over it.

Graham Norton

The Welsh are such good singers because they have no locks on their bathroom doors.

Harry Secombe

The sex urge in Ireland is either sublimated by religion, dissipated in sport or drowned in drink, or in the case of Paddy Kavanagh, all three.

Niall Toibin

The population of England is thirty million, mostly fools.

Thomas Carlyle

Nationalities and Places

The French are tremendous snobs, despite that rather showy
and ostentatious Revolution.

Arthur Marshall

Belgium is just a country invented by the British to annoy
the French.

Charles De Gaulle

I do not know the location of the Virgin Islands but at least I
know that they are on the other side of the world from
Maidenhead.

Winston Churchill

You have to know a man awfully well in Canada to know his
surname.

John Buchan

The trouble with America is that there are far too many
wide open spaces surrounded by teeth.

Charles Luckman

The Greeks: dirty and impoverished descendants of a bunch
of la–de–da fruit salads who invented democracy and then
forgot to use it while walking around like girls.

P. J. O'Rourke

The archives of the Turkish Foreign Office were kept in
saddlebags: so much more convenient if you have to move
quickly.

G. M. Young

Nationalities and Places

To many, no doubt, he will seem blatant and bumptious, but we prefer to regard him as simply British.

Oscar Wilde

The real people of Ireland are the people who have their dinner in the middle of the day.

Jackie Healy-Rae

It should have been written into the armistice treaty that the Germans would be required to lay down their accordions along with their arms.

Bill Bryson

Ivan was coming with us only as far as Minsk where he was attending a village idiots' conference. The banners read "Welcome Idiots".

Woody Allen

England is the only country in the world where the food is more dangerous than the sex.

Jackie Mason

The Italians' technological contribution to mankind stopped with the pizza oven.

Bill Bryson

A naturally free, familiar, good-natured, precipitate, Irish manner had been schooled and schooled late in life into a sober, cold, stiff, deportment, which she mistook for English.

Maria Edgeworth

Nationalities and Places

To learn English you must begin by thrusting the jaw forward, almost clenching the teeth, and practically immobilising the lips. In this way the English produce the series of unpleasant little mews of which their language consists.

Jose Ortega y Gasset

Brighton Pavilion looks as if St. Paul's had come down and littered.

Sydney Smith

They say the situation in Northern Ireland is not as bad as they say it is.

Denis Taylor

My French stinks. It seems that when I asked somebody for a light I asked them to set me on fire.

Jeffrey Bernard

There are only three things against living in Britain: the place, the climate and the people.

Jimmy Edwards

England will fight to the last American.

Will Rogers

The Welsh are a nation of male voice choir lovers whose only hobbies are rugby and romantic involvement with sheep.

Lenny Henry

In the game there were at least five instances of people being grabbed by the testicles. Neath is the bag-snatching capital of Wales.

Dylan Thomas

I think it possible that all Scots are illegitimate, Scotsmen being so mean and Scotswomen so generous.

Edwin Muir

During World War Two, Ireland was neutral on the Allied side.

John A. Murphy

Had Cain been a Scot, God would have changed his doom. Not forced him to wander, but confined him home.

John Cleveland

The Vicar of St. Ives says that the smell of fish there is sometimes so terrific as to stop the church clock.

Francis Kilvert

"Down there", is a polite phrase used by schoolgirls who learn it from nuns. Do not confuse it with Australia which is called "Down under".

Sterling Johnson

In the world of the British nanny there are three sorts of sin: little sins, bigger sins and taking off your shoes without undoing the laces.

Jonathan Gathorne-Hardy

Liverpool is at the moment the centre of the consciousness of the human universe.

Allen Ginsberg

The actual Irish weather report is really a recording made in 1922, which no one has had occasion to change. "Scattered showers, periods of sunshine."

Wilfrid Sheed

It is difficult to describe Norwegian charisma precisely because it is somewhere between a Presbyterian minister and a tree.

Johnny Carson

A French screwdriver is a hammer.

Reinhold Aman

I am an Englishman. I was born in Ireland: but if a racehorse is born in a pigsty, that does not make him a pig.

Arthur Wellesley

The British must be gluttons for satire: even the weather forecast seemed to be some kind of spoof, predicting every possible combination of weather for the next twenty-four hours without actually committing itself to anything.

David Lodge

The English think that incompetence is the same thing as sincerity.

Quentin Crisp

Nationalities and Places

I've been under a lot of pressure recently because I originally came from the Moon.

Boothby Graffoe

Scotland is renowned for its peace and solitude. In fact, crowds from all over the world flock here to enjoy the solitude.

Stuart Collinson

I said, "It is most extraordinary weather for this time of year!" He replied, "Ah, it isn't this time of year at all."

Oliver St. John Gogarty

Rome reminds me of a man who lives by exhibiting to travellers his grandmother's corpse.

James Joyce

By midday the heat is so unbearable that the streets are empty except for thousands of Englishmen taking mad dogs for walks.

Spike Milligan

It was not until I went back to Ireland as a tourist, that I perceived the charm of my country was quite independent of the accident of my having been born in it.

George Bernard Shaw

There are so many ways to die here.

Denis Leary

Addis Ababa looks as if it has been dragged piecemeal from an aeroplance carrying rubbish.

John Gunther

It is disconcerting to be naked in a Japanese bath and to be massaged by a young girl who has picked up a few English phrases, and remarks as she is walking up and down your spine, "Changeable weather we are having lately."

Peter Ustinov

China is a big country, inhabited by many Chinese.

Charles de Gaulle

House names are cabalistic phrases carved on pieces of wood that the English middle class place in obscure corners of their property to ward off GPs seeking them by torchlight on rainy nights.

Michael O'Donnell

New York City is the most exciting place in the world. Nothing could discredit capitalism more than a decision of the Russians to try it.

Jack Tanner

New York is the only city in the world where you can get deliberately run over on the sidewalk by a pedestrian.

Russell Baker

Nationalities and Places

I don't like Norway at all. The sun never sets, the bar never opens and the whole country smells of kippers.

Evelyn Waugh

I asked him, "Are you a pole vaulter?" He said, "No, I'm a German and how did you know my name was Walter?"

Billy Connolly

Signor Angeli, Professor of Italian at Trinity College, Dublin, was asked to translate the proceedings of the opening of Queen's College Cork into Italian and forward them to the Pope. He reported the fact that the ceremony was attended by both men and women as "There were present men of both sexes" which led a cardinal to observe that Cork must be a very queer city.

Robert Kane

For a marriage to be valid in Scotland it is absolutely necessary that it should be consummated in the presence of two policemen.

Samuel Butler

America is the only country in the world where a housewife hires a woman to do her cleaning so she can do volunteer work at the day-care centre where the cleaning woman leaves her child.

Milton Berle

If you hear anyone saying "Begorrah" during your stay in Ireland, you can be sure he's an undercover agent for the Irish Tourist Board pandering to your false expectations.

Terry Eagleton

The French hate anything that is ugly. If they see an animal that is ugly, they immediately eat it.

Jeremy Clarkson

It's easy enough to get to Ireland. It's just a straight walk across the Irish Sea as far as I'm concerned.

Brian Clough

When it is three o'clock in New York, it's still 1938 in London.

Bette Midler

Washington, D.C. is a little too small to be a state, but too large to be an asylum for the mentally deranged.

Anne Burford

If the French were really intelligent they would speak English.

Wilfred Sheed

"Du ye think the Almighty would be understanin' siccan gibberish?" said the old Scotch lady, when, during the Napoleonic war, she was reminded that maybe a French mother was praying as fervently for victory as she was herself.

F.A. Steel

Foreigners may pretend otherwise but if English is spoken loudly enough, anyone can understand it, the British included.

P.J. O'Rourke

Where else in the world but Australia is a generous man defined as one who would give you his arsehole and shit through his ribs?

Germaine Greer

Europe is a place teeming with ill-intentioned persons.

Margaret Thatcher

In the Soviet Union there is no mystical or obscure treatment of love, such as decadent Western poets use. We sing of how a young man falls in love with a girl because of her industrial output.

Stephan Petroviv

Nobody knows what the original people of Scotland were: cold is probably the best informed guess, and wet.

A. A. Gill

I genuinely believe that one of the reasons Britain is such a steady and gracious place is the calming influence of the football results and shipping forecasts.

Bill Bryson

In Mexico a bachelor is a man who cannot play the guitar.

Lillian Day

Every time I see a picture of those people in Somalia it brings a tear to my eye. I mean I'd love to be that thin but not with all those flies and everything.

Mariah Carey

Nationalities and Places

Belief in progress is a doctrine of idlers and Belgians.

Charles Baudelaire

I am inconsolable at the death of King Hussein of Jordan. I was a very good friend of Jordan: he was the greatest basketball player this country has ever seen or will see again.

Mariah Carey

In a hotel in County Mayo I saw a notice displayed over the barometer: Don't hit me. I am doing my best.

M.F. Watson

Ireland is a modern nation but it is modernised only recently and at the moment it is behaving rather like a lavatory attendant who has just won the lottery.

Terry Eagleton

I took one look at Madame Chiang Kai-Shek and thought to myself "Holy Smoke, I forgot to collect my laundry."

Jack Warner

Those who survived the San Francisco earthquake said, "Thank God, I'm still alive." But of course those who died, their lives will never be the same again.

Barbara Boxer

It's a scientific fact that if you live in California you lose one point of your I.Q. every year.

Truman Capote

I wrote to a Tyrolean landlord in search of accommodation and received the following reply :"Do not distress yourself that I am poor in bath; I am excellent in bed."

Gerard Hoffnung

The Welsh are not meant to go out in the sun. They start to photosynthesise.

Rhys Ifans

Have you heard about the Irishman who had a leg transplant? His welly rejected it.

Frank Carson

I plan to buy the Millennium Dome, turn it upside down, float it out into the Mediterranean and rename it the Wok of Gibraltar.

Brian Conley

America is a country that doesn't know where it is going but is determined to set a speed record getting there.

Laurence J. Peter

Ask any man what nationality he would prefer to be and ninety-nine out of a hundred will tell you that they would prefer to be Englishmen.

Cecil Rhodes

When President Reagan came to Ireland, he was greeted with a beautifully ambiguous banner which read "Welcome to the Ould Sod".

Dominic Cleary

In Yorkshire folk will occasionally smile, usually when they are about to pass wind.

> Simon Henry

In the Romanian army no one beneath the rank of major is permitted to wear lipstick.

> Evelyn Waugh

In all my long experience as Her Majesty's hangman only one of my customers ever put up a struggle – and he wasn't British.

> Albert Pierrepoint

My birthplace was near the monkey cage in Regent's Park Zoo – it was pure luck I was outside the cage.

> Donald McGill

The Americans have a proud and noble tradition of being utterly hopeless in warfare. They lost in Vietnam, they lost in Somalia, they lost in the Bay of Pigs and though they won the Gulf War, they managed to kill more British soldiers than the Iraqis.

> Jeremy Clarkson

People say to me things like 'You're Irish – you must be stupid.' I'm stumped.

> Jimeoin McKeown

American men seem to be interested in only two things – money and breasts.

> Hedy Lamarr

Nationalities and Places

The difference between a French kiss and a Belgian kiss is that a Belgian kiss is half Flemish.

Roy Mason

I don't despair about the cultural scene in Australia because there isn't one here to despair about.

Robert Helpman

French films follow a basic formula: husband sleeps with Jeanne because Bernadette cuckolded him by sleeping with Christophe, and in the end they all go off to a restaurant.

Sophie Marceau

In England only uneducated people show off their knowledge; nobody quotes Latin or Greek authors in the course of conversation, unless he has never read them.

George Mikes

I love Morocco – it's a combination of the Bible and Hollywood.

George Patton

I was once criticised for swearing on television. The word I used was 'bloody' which, where I come from in Yorkshire, is practically the only surviving adjective.

Maureen Lipman

If you ever see two people on a boat on the Clyde in Glasgow, you know one of them is not coming back.

Danny Bhoy

Nationalities and Places

There's an Ethiopian in the fuel supply.

W. C. Fields

I have recently been all round the world and have formed a very poor opinion of it.

Thomas Beecham

The shortest way out of Manchester is notoriously a bottle of Gordon's gin.

William Bolitho

As a means of shortening your life-span I heartily recommend London.

Kingsley Amis

We produced *Brigadoon* on the MGM lot because I went to Scotland and found nothing there that looked like Scotland.

Arthur Freed

The Italian flag is a white cross on a white background.

P. J. O'Rourke

You know you are Canadian when you know which leaves make good toilet paper.

Heather Turnbull

In a museum in Havana there are two skulls of Christopher Columbus – one when he was a boy and one when he was a man.

Mark Twain

Denial ain't just a river in Egypt.

> Mark Twain

Los Angeles is where you've got to go to be an actor. You go there or New York. I flipped a coin – it came up New York. So I flipped it again.

> Harrison Ford

It is because of their sins and more particularly the wicked and detestable vice of homosexuality, that the Welsh were punished by God and so first lost Troy and then Britain.

> Girald DeBarri

Please God, let there be victory – before the Americans arrive.

> Douglas Haig

For years the Soviet Union has stood on the edge of an abyss. Now, fellow countrymen, we must take a great step forward.

> Boris Yeltsin

Where I grew up in Brooklyn, nobody committed suicide. Everyone was too unhappy.

> Woody Allen

At birth when a Welshman is slapped on the behind, he does not cry; he sings Men of Harlech in perfect pitch.

> Alan Jay Lerner

Nationalities and Places

Tourists – have some fun with New York's cabbies. When you get to your destination, say to your driver, 'Pay? I was only hitchhiking.'

Dave Letterman

Anytime four New Yorkers get into a cab together without arguing, a bank robbery has just taken place.

Johnny Carson

We should have the Queen for reigning, the Duke of Edinburgh for putting his foot in it, Prince Charles for pursuing his eccentric hobbyhorses, Prince William for waiting in the wings, and the Queen Mother for waving from balconies. That's enough Royals.

Keith Waterhouse

In Canada we have enough to do keeping up with two spoken languages without trying to invent slang, so we just go right ahead and use English for literature, Scotch for sermons and American for conversations.

Stephen Leacock

I would not however, push the case for a sense of history quite so far as the History Fellow of an Oxford College who criticised the reasoning behind the Bursar's investment policy on the grounds that the last two hundred years had been exceptional.

Donald MacDougall

In England you will find people so desirous of titles that, if they cannot acquire them, they will stick two surnames together with a hyphen.

Oliver St John Gogarty

The shortage of parking spaces in Boston is like an alcatraz around my neck.

Thomas Menino

My favourite British weather forecast, culled from a newspaper, reads in toto, 'Dry and warm, but cooler with some rain.'

Bill Bryson

The only idea of wit that the Scots have is laughing immoderately at stated intervals.

Sydney Smith

The American GIs are overpaid, overfed, oversexed and over here.

Tommy Trinder

Nothing is more narrow-minded than chauvinism or race hatred. To me all men are equal; they are jackasses everywhere and I have the same contempt for all. No petty prejudices.

Karl Kraus

Rome is a very loony city in every respect. One needs to spend only an hour or two there to realise that Fellini made documentaries.

Fran Lebowitz

Nationalities and Places

What depresses me about this country is the way more and more money is being given to the working classes to spend on their unpleasant enthusiasms, such as transistor radios, sweets, caravans, frozen food, plastic flowers, souvenir spoons from dreadful places, which can only make England a nastier country.

Auberon Waugh

I know of only four languages – Latin, Irish, Greek and Chinese. These are languages because they are instruments of integral civilisation. English and French are not languages: they are mercantile codes.

Flann O'Brien

The British national anthem belongs to the eighteenth century. In it you find us ordering God about to do our political work.

George Bernard Shaw

In Chicago not only your vote counts, but all kinds of other votes – kids, dead folks and so on.

Dick Gregory

Any multimillionaire can grow up to become President of the United States.

Richard Wallis

To Naples for a few days, for a bracing glimpse of the poor.

Auberon Waugh

A Scotchman must be a very sturdy moralist who does not love Scotland more than the truth.

Samuel Johnson

I wouldn't mind seeing China if I could come back the same night. I hate being abroad.

Philip Larkin

Very little is known of the Canadian country since it is rarely visited by anyone but the Queen and illiterate sports fishermen.

P. J. O'Rourke

'We must have lunch sometime,' in the hypocritical code of English manners means, 'I do not care if I ever see you again.'

Philip Howard

Manhattan is a narrow island off the coast of New Jersey devoted to the pursuit of lunch.

Raymond Sokolov

In Spain a society for the protection of animals was once founded but they were short of money. So they put on some spectacular bullfights.

Kurt Tucholsky

Italy has managed to create a society that combines a number of the least appealing aspects of socialism with practically all of the vices of capitalism.

Gore Vidal

Politics

Politics

The ideal form of government is democracy tempered with
assassination.

Voltaire

Democracy is a pathetic belief in the collective wisdom of
individual ignorance.

H.L. Mencken

I never trust a man unless I've got his pecker in my pocket.

Lyndon B. Johnson

Sure let him join our campaign. I'd prefer to have him inside
our tent pissing out than outside our tent pissing in.

Lyndon B. Johnson

It is true that liberty is precious – so precious it must be
carefully rationed.

V.I. Lenin

The cardinal rule of politics – never get caught in bed with a
live man or a dead woman.

Larry Hagman

I do not belong to any organised political party – I am a
Democrat.

Will Rogers

The main difference for the history of the world if I had
been shot rather than Kennedy, is that Onassis probably
wouldn't have married Mrs Khrushchev.

Nikita Khrushchev

It is now known that men enter local politics solely as a
result of being unhappily married.

C.N. Parkinson

Politics

The Tories are nothing else but a load of kippers, two-faced with no guts.

Eric Heffer

The draft is white people sending black people to fight yellow people to protect the country they stole from red people.

James Rado

I never vote for anyone – I always vote against.

W.C. Fields

Watergate was the only brothel where the madam remained a virgin.

Mort Sahl

A fool and his money are soon elected.

Will Rogers

An honest politician is one who when he is bought, stays bought.

Simon Cameron

I don't make jokes. I just observe the government and report the facts.

Will Rogers

No comment, but don't quote me.

Dan Quayle

My family was in Irish politics while De Valera's was still bartering budgerigars on the back streets of Barcelona.

James Dillon

Politics

A statesman is a dead politician. We need more statesmen.

Bob Edwards

Stanley Baldwin is dead – the light in that great turnip has at last gone out.

Winston Churchill

A debate without the honourable member would be like Hamlet without the third grave digger.

Winston Churchill

Reader suppose you were an idiot; and suppose you were a member of Congress; but I repeat myself.

Mark Twain

I do not see the EEC as a great love affair. It is more like nine middle-aged couples with failing marriages meeting at a Brussels hotel for a group grope.

Kenneth Tynan

The government has been faced with an orchestrated campaign of pressure by the newspapers. They even had the gargantuan intellect of Bernard Levin squeaking away in the undergrowth like a demented vole.

Denis Healey

If you don't say anything you won't be called on to repeat it.

Calvin Coolidge

One of the things that being in politics has taught me is that men are not a reasoned or a reasonable sex.

Margaret Thatcher

Politics

Sir Robert Peel's smile is like the silver fittings on a coffin.
The Right Honourable Gentleman is reminiscent of a
poker. The only difference is that a poker gives off occasional
signs of warmth.

Benjamin Disraeli

The difference between a misfortune and a calamity is this: if
Gladstone fell into the Thames, it would be a misfortune. But
if someone dragged him out again, that would be a calamity.

Benjamin Disraeli

All political parties die at last of swallowing their own lies.

John Arbuthnot

I'm glad I'm not Brezhnev. Being the Russian leader in the
Kremlin, you never know if someone's tape-recording what
you say.

Richard M. Nixon

Richard Nixon told us he was going to take crime off the
streets. He did. He took it into the White House.

Ralph Abernathy

The speeches of Warren Harding left the impression of an
army of pompous phrases moving over the landscape in
search of an idea. Sometimes these meandering words would
actually capture a straggling thought and bear it
triumphantly a prisoner in their midst, until it died of
servitude and overwork.

William McAdoo

During Stalin's speeches to the Praesidium, the first delegate
to stop clapping was routinely hauled off to be shot.

Clive James

Politics

The purpose of the Presidential Office is not power, or leadership of the Western World, but reminiscence, bestselling reminiscence.

Roger Jellinek

Sometimes I look at Billy and Jimmy and I say to myself 'Lillian, you should have stayed a virgin.'

Lillian Carter

Actually, I vote Labour – but my butler's Tory.

Louis Mountbatten

Chamberlain seemed such a nice old gentleman that I thought I would give him my autograph.

Adolf Hitler

He has all the characteristics of a dog except loyalty.

Sam Houston

You'll notice that Nancy Reagan never drinks water when Ronnie speaks.

Robin Williams

Some Republicans are so ignorant they wouldn't know how to pour piss out of a boot – even if the instructions were printed on the heel.

Lyndon B. Johnson

When the President does it, that means it's not illegal.

Richard M. Nixon

Tony Benn is the Bertie Wooster of Marxism.

Malcolm Bradbury

Gerald Ford looks like the guy in a science fiction movie who is first to see the Creature.

David Frye

Politics

The Vice-Presidency isn't worth a pitcher of warm spit.

J.N. Garner

A politician is any citizen with influence enough to get his old mother a job as a charwoman in the City Hall.

H.L. Mencken

It's easy being a humorist when you've got the whole government working for you.

Will Rogers

I like Republicans, and I would trust them with anything in the world except public office.

Adlai Stevenson

I am sorry that I cannot address the people of Latin America in their own language which is Latin.

Dan Quayle

Stanley Baldwin occasionally stumbled over the truth, but hastily picked himself up and hurried on as if nothing had happened.

Winston Churchill

Richard Nixon is a no-good, lying bastard. He can lie out of both sides of his mouth at the same time, and if he ever caught himself telling the truth, he'd lie just to keep his hand in.

Harry S. Truman

An aristocracy in a republic is like a chicken whose head has been cut off: it may run about in a lively way, but in fact it is dead.

Nancy Mitford

He who throws mud loses ground.

Adlai Stevenson

Politics

Deep down I am quite conservative, so I vote Labour.

Christopher Logue

Goebbels wore lifts in his shoes yet still qualified as a midget.

Victor Lewis-Smith

I am a more virtuous man than President Kennedy or President Bush, two notorious philanderers.

Saddam Hussein

I never vote for the best candidate, I vote for the one who will do the least harm.

Franklin Dane

I disapprove of what you say and I will defend to the death my right to prevent you from saying it.

Dominic Cleary

He couldn't find his ass with both hands.

Lyndon B. Johnson

Bill Clinton should remember that goats don't talk.

Yasser Arafat

There is a winter you know in Russia. Hitler forgot about this. He must have been very loosely educated. We all hear about it at school, but he forgot it. I have never made such a bad mistake as that.

Winston Churchill

Politics

The new definition of silence: Dan Quayle and Bill Clinton telling their Vietnam war stories to each other.

Iain Dale

Montgomery was in defeat unbeatable; in victory, unbearable.

Winston Churchill

There are too many politicians who believe, with a conviction based on experience, that you can fool all of the people all of the time.

Franklin P. Adams

To an MP's wife nobody is common, provided he's on the register.

George Bernard Shaw

If I were two-faced, would I be using this one?

Abraham Lincoln

The man with the best job in the country is the Vice President. All he has to do is to get up every morning and say, 'How's the President?'

Will Rogers

Democracy becomes a government of bullies tempered by editors.

Ralph Waldo Emerson

 **Politics**

My opponents have done a full 360° turn on this issue.

Mary McAleese

What makes Clint Eastwood, a middle aged actor who has played with a chimp, think he could have a future in politics?

Ronald Reagan

Democracy is the art and science of running the circus from the monkey cage.

H.L. Mencken

Pat Buchanan is racist, homophobic, xenophobic and sexist. In a word, he's the perfect Republican candidate.

Bill Press

When Bob Dole does smile, he looks as if he's just evicted a widow.

Mike Royko

Crime does not pay – as well as politics.

Alfred E. Neumann

Dan Quayle is more stupid than Ronald Reagan put together.

Matt Groening

The House of Peers, throughout the war, did nothing in particular, and did it very well.

W.S. Gilbert

If elected, I will win.

Pat Paulsen

I've been married to one Marxist and one Fascist, and neither one would take the garbage out.

Lee Grant

It is useless to hold a person to anything he says while he's in love, drunk, or running for office.

Shirley MacLaine

Calvin Coolidge's perpetual expression was that of someone smelling something burning on a stove.

Sherwin Cook

Anyone who is capable of getting themselves elected President should on no account be allowed to do the job.

Douglas Adams

Richard Nixon inherited some good instincts from his Quaker forebears, but by diligent hard work, he overcame them.

James Reston

Calvin Coolidge didn't say much and when he did, he didn't say much.

Will Rogers

Politics

The year 1908 saw the election of the first US president to successfully weigh more than three hundred pounds, William Howard Taft, who ran on a platform of reinforced concrete and who, in a stirring inauguration speech, called for 'a bacon cheeseburger and a side order of fries'.

Dave Barry

I believe that Ronald Reagan can make this country what it once was – an Arctic region covered with ice.

Steve Martin

In those days he was wiser than he is now – he used frequently to take my advice.

Winston Churchill

A citizen of America will cross the ocean to fight for democracy, but won't cross the street to vote in a national election.

Bill Vaughan

Bill Clinton thinks international affairs means dating girls from out of town.

Tom Clancy

Nobody believes the unofficial spokesman, but everybody trusts an unidentified source.

Ron Nesen

The word 'politics' is derived from the word 'poly', meaning 'many', and the word, 'ticks', meaning 'blood-sucking parasites'.

Larry Hardiman

We hang the petty thieves and appoint the great ones to public office.

Aesop

A child can go only so far in life without potty training. It is not mere coincidence that six of the last presidents were potty trained, not to mention half of the nation's state legislators.

Dave Barry

We are ready for any unforeseen event that may or may not occur.

Dan Quayle

The House of Lords must be the only institution in the world which is kept efficient by the persistent absenteeism of most of its members.

Herbert Samuel

If you want to trace your family tree, all you have to do is to run for public office.

Patricia Vance

Watergate was worse than a crime – it was a blunder.

Richard Nixon

Politics

A group of politicians deciding to ditch the President because his morals are bad is like the Mafia getting together to bump off the Godfather for not going to church on Sunday.

Russell Baker

The authorities were at their wits' end, nor had it taken them long to get there.

Desmond McCarthy

Congress is so strange. A man gets up to speak and says nothing. Nobody listens. Then everybody disagrees with him.

Will Rogers

It is hard to argue with the government. Remember, they run the Bureau of Alcohol, Tobacco and Firearms, so they must know a thing or two about satisfying women.

Scott Adams

I think it is absolutely tantamount.

Edward McCarthy

You can fool some of the people all of the time, and you can fool all of the people some of the time, but you can't fool some of the people some of the time.

Stan Laurel

Even Napoleon had his Watergate.

Danny Ozark

The Conservative Establishment has always treated women as nannies, grannies and fannies.

Teresa Gorman

I tried to tell the French Prime Minister in French that I admired the various positions he had taken on so many matters. What I actually said was that I desired the French Prime Minister in many different positions.

Tony Blair

Tony Blair is just Bill Clinton's toyboy.

Saddam Hussein

Clinton has kept all of the promises that he intended to keep.

George Stephanopolous

Campaigning for governor, there have been a couple of times when I yearned for the serenity I knew as a Marine Corps tank commander in Korea.

Adlai Stevenson

Ask not what you can do for your country, ask what your country can do for you.

Teddy Kennedy

Politics

I think it's about time we voted for senators with breasts.
We've been voting for boobs long enough.

Claire Sargent

If the Lord's Prayer was introduced in Congress, Senators
would propose a large number of amendments to it.

Henry Wilson

Politics is the art of preventing people from taking part in
affairs that properly concern them.

Paul Valèry

It is exciting to have a real crisis like the Falklands on your
hands, when you have spent half your political life dealing
with humdrum issues like the environment.

Margaret Thatcher

Michael Foot is a kind of walking obituary for the Labour
Party.

Chris Patten

The Lord Privy Seal is neither a lord, a privy or a seal.

Sydney D. Bailey

Politicians are people who, when they see light at the end of
the tunnel, go out and buy some more tunnel.

John Quinton

Politics

The House of Lords is a body of five hundred men chosen at random from amongst the unemployed.

David Lloyd-George

An official denial is a de facto confirmation.

John Kifner

Nothing beats Reaganomics: though herpes runs it close.

Art Buchwald

The F.B.I. is filled with Fordham graduates keeping tabs on Harvard men in the State Department.

Daniel P. Moynihan

Even Al Gore has won an award and he has less star quality than head lice.

Joe Joseph

These people like Ben Elton suddenly criticising New Labour. It's the first ever recorded case of rats leaving a floating ship.

Alexei Sayle

John Prescott has been to Hull and back.

Roland Watson

The Reformed Parliament: I never saw so many shocking bad hats in my life.

Arthur Wellesley

Politics

I don't mind how much my ministers talk: as long as they do what I say.

Margaret Thatcher

The Treasury in 1850 kept a half-wit to make a nominal field against the official candidates. On one occasion he was successful.

G. M. Young

There is nothing in Socialism that a little age or a little money will not cure.

Will Durant

David Lloyd-George is a goat-footed bard, a half-human visitor to our age from the hag-ridden magic and enchanted woods of Celtic antiquity.

John Maynard Keynes

You won the elections. But I won the count.

Anastasio Somoza

Malcolm Fraser looks like an Easter Island statue with an arse full of razor blades.

Paul Keating

Bill Clinton cannot seriously oppose the gun lobby because it is part of the phallocentric culture which he has done so much to promote.

Patrick Murray

Politics

There is a simple and practical method of putting this long-suffering government out of its misery. Since sex scandals seem to be the only method of dislodging a politician from his post, it is the duty of every patriotic woman to bear a love child by a Tory M.P.

Margarette Driscoll

Government is like a baby: a huge appetite at one end and no sense of responsibility at the other.

Ronald Reagan

My wife has a very major cause and a very major interest that is a very complex and consuming issue with her. And that's me.

Dan Quayle

Never underestimate the hypocrisy of politicians.

James Herbert

There are few ironclad rules of diplomacy but to one there is an exception. When an official reports that talks were useful, it can safely be concluded that nothing was accomplished.

J.K. Galbraith

Seventy-six would not be an old age to leave office. Andrew Jackson left the White House at the age of seventy-five and he was still quite vigorous. I know because he told me.

Ronald Reagan

As a politician my only known vice is chocolate.

Carlo Ciampi

She is the lady of the mansion, she is the wife of a peer of the realm, the daughter of a marquis, has five Christian names; and hardly ever speaks to a commoner except for political purposes.

Thomas Hardy

My first qualification for the great job of being mayor of New York is my monumental personal ingratitude.

Fiorello la Guardia

The really neat thing about Dan Quayle, as you realise from the first moment you look into those lovely blue eyes, is impeachment insurance.

Barbara Ehrenreich

Robin Cook's misfortune is to sound as if his voice never broke but his behaviour encourages this view.

Jacob Rees-Mogg

Democracy is the art of running the circus from the monkey cage.

H. L. Mencken

A good politician is quite as unthinkable as an honest burglar.

H. L. Mencken

I couldn't possibly vote Conservative while William Hague still leads the party. There is nothing personal in this, it's purely on class grounds.

Auberon Waugh

Vote for insanity, you know it makes sense.

Lord Sutch

The time has come for all good men to rise above principles.

Huey Long

Words cannot express my regret at the news that Anthony Wedgewood Benn has decided to retire from parliament. My regret is that he has left it twenty years too late.

Gerald Kaufman

Kings are not born; they are made by artificial hallucination.

George Bernard Shaw

The Left does not have a monopoly on ecology. We at the National Front respect life and love animals. I myself have a white rat whom I kiss every day on the mouth.

Jean-Marie le Pen

I have tried all sorts of excitement, from tip cat to tiger shooting, all degrees of gambling from beggar-my-neighbour to Monte Carlo, but have found no gambling like politics, and no excitement like a big division in the House of Commons.

Randolph Churchill

Politics

Anything any politician did with a woman other than his wife prior to May 5th 1987 ought to be allowed to go unrevealed.

Gary Hart

No country which has cricket as one of its national games has yet gone Communist.

Woodrow Wyatt

I never became a politician because I could not stand the strain of being right all the time.

Peter Ustinov

All of these black people are screwing up my democracy.

Ian Smith

The Berlin Wall was the defining achievement of Socialism.

George Will

There should have been a last line of defence during the war. It would have been made up entirely of the more officious breed of cricket stewards. If Hitler had tried to invade these shores he would have been met by a short stout man in a white coat who would have said, "I don't care who you are, you're not coming in here unless you are a member."

Ray East

The American Communist Party was notoriously infiltrated by informers. It used to be said that spies practically kept the Party going with their dues and contributions.

Helen Lawrenson

Terry Dicks is living proof that a pig's bladder on a stick can be elected as a member of parliament.

Tony Brooks

Democracy is the recurrent suspicion that more than half the people are right more than half of the time.

E.B. White

In this world of sin and sorrow, there is always something to be thankful for; as for me, I rejoice that I am not a Republican.

H.L. Mencken

Experts are saying that President Bush's goal now is to politically humiliate Saddam Hussein. Why not just make him the next Democratic presidential nominee?

Jay Leno

Roosevelt proved a man could be President for life; Truman proved anybody could be President; and Eisenhower proved you don't need to have a President.

Kenneth Keating

When they call the roll in the Senate, the Senators do not know whether to answer "Present" or "Not guilty".

Theodore Roosevelt

I never called Richard Nixon a son of a bitch; after all, he claims to be a self-made man.

Harry S. Truman

Politics

Politics has always been the systematic organisation of hatreds.

Henry Adams

Politics: a strife of interests masquerading as a contest of principles.

Ambrose Bierce

Support your local politician: with a rope.

Steve Jackson

Whatever happens will be for the worse, and therefore it is in our interest that as little as possible should happen.

Lord Salisbury

Margaret Thatcher adds the diplomacy of Alf Garnett to the economics of Arthur Daley.

Denis Healey

Edwina Curry is the female Margaret Thatcher.

Mrs. Merton

People must not do things for fun. We are not here for fun. There is no reference to fun in any Act of Parliament.

A. P. Herbert

I have had more women by accident than JFK had on purpose.

Lyndon B. Johnson

Hereditary peers sit independently, weigh arguments independently, think independently. Then they independently vote Conservative.

Lord Richards

Party Political Conferences are gatherings of the walking undead.

John Green

A politician is a statesman who approaches every question with an open mouth.

Adlai Stevenson

The difference between golf and government is that in golf you can't improve your lie.

George Deukmejian

Anthony Eden is the original banana man: yellow outside and a softer yellow inside.

Reginald Paget

The policies of the Monster Raving Loony Party include putting crocodiles in the Thames, jogging machines to make electricity for pensioners, banning January and February to make winter shorter, and the introduction of a Scottish Olympics to include caber-tossing and haggis-lifting.

Lord Sutch

If you want to succeed in politics, you must keep your conscience well under control.

Frank McNally

Politics

The punishment for those who are too smart to engage in politics is to be governed by those who are dumber.

Plato

We women politicians have got the men out there worrying that we'll all have PMS on the same day and blow up the town.

Barbara Carr

The Marxist law of distribution of wealth is that shortages will be divided equally among the peasants.

John Guftason

Joseph Chamberlain was dangerous as an enemy, untrustworthy as a friend, but fatal as a colleague.

Hercules Robinson

Joseph McCarthy is the only major politician in the country who can be labeled 'liar' without fear of libel.

Joseph Alsop

How can I vote Liberal? I just hold my nose and mark the ballot paper.

Frank Underhill

Mr Chamberlain loves the working man; he loves to see him work.

Winston Churchill

Italian communists are slightly to the right of English Liberals.

John Mortimer

Half of those who attended De Valera's funeral came to confirm that he dead. The other half came to ensure that he was buried.

Barry Desmond

The House of Lords is a refuge for cattle robbers, land thieves and court prostitutes.

Jack Jones

Russian democracy is vastly superior to American democracy. In Russia we know the result of the elections a week before they take place. In America they don't know the result of the election a week after it takes place.

Vladimir Putin

Margaret Thatcher should be hung up by the bollocks.

Jo Brand

There is only one party in this coalition.

Henry McLeish

Politics

If you open that Pandora's box you never know what Trojan horses will jump out.

Ernest Bevin

It was not a lie. I was merely being economical with the truth.

Robert Armstrong

Welcome to President Bush, Mrs Bush and my fellow astronauts.

Dan Quayle

Most Conservatives believe that a creche is something that happens between two Range Rovers in Tunbridge Wells.

Caroline Shorten

If Gandhi were alive today he would approve of the SDP.

Richard Attenborough

When the Berlin Wall fell and Germany was reunited, the Stasi, the former East German secret police, made wonderful taxi-drivers. All you had to do was tell them your name and they immediately knew where you lived.

Paul Merton

I apologise for the intelligence of my remarks, Sir Thomas. I had forgotten that you are a Member of Parliament.

George Sanders

Politics

A chill ran along the Labour back benches looking for a
spine to run up.

Winnie Ewing

The ship follows Soviet custom: it is riddled with class
distinctions so subtle it takes a trained Marxist to appreciate
them.

Paul Theroux

Edward the Eighth was far to the right of my husband.

Diana Mosley

I am always on the job.

Margaret Thatcher

What this country needs is more unemployed politicians.

Angela Davis

These are trying moments, and it seems to me a defect in
our much-famed constitution to have to part with an
admirable government like Lord Salisbury's for no question
of any importance, or any particular reason, merely on
account of the number of votes.

Queen Victoria

The election isn't very far off when a candidate can
recognise you across the street.

Kin Hubbard

 **Politics**

Mrs Thatcher can be compared with Florence Nightingale. She walks through the hospitals as a lady with a lamp — unfortunately, in her case it is a blowlamp.

Denis Healey

Where Caligula made his horse a consul, Long's constituents have made the posterior of a horse a US senator.

Senator Glass

I think the voters misunderestimate me.

George W. Bush

The mystery of government is not how Washington works but how to make it stop.

P. J. O'Rourke

It doesn't matter if Margaret Thatcher or Michael Heseltine is Tory leader. They are both millionaires and both peroxide blondes.

Dennis Skinner

When I am abroad I always make it a rule never to criticise or attack the government of my country. I make up for lost time when I am at home.

Winston Churchill

If John Major was drowning, his whole life would pass in front of him and he wouldn't be in it.

Dave Allen

The difference between a New Labour back-bench MP and a supermarket trolley is that a supermarket trolley has a mind of its own.

Peter Lilley

The vice-president is just a spare tyre on the automobile of government.

John Garner

Corruption is the most infallible symptom of constitutional liberty.

Edward Gibbon

Paddy Ashdown is the only party leader to be a trained killer. Although to be fair Mrs Thatcher was self-taught.

Charles Kennedy

You suddenly realise you are no longer in government when you get into the back of your car and it doesn't go anywhere.

Malcolm Rifkind

We've got a carrot and stick policy on Saddam Hussein. And the carrot is, if he pulls out, he doesn't get the stick.

James Baker

Religion

✝ Religion

Not only is there no God, but try getting a plumber at weekends.

Woody Allen

God made everything out of nothing. But the nothingness shows through.

Paul Valéry

The men who really believe in themselves are all in lunatic asylums.

G.K. Chesterton

A good sermon should be like a woman's skirt: short enough to rouse the interest, but long enough to cover the essentials.

Ronald Knox

Peter remained on friendly terms with Christ even though Christ had healed his mother-in-law.

Samuel Butler

How can I believe in God when only last week I got my tongue caught in the roller of an electric typewriter?

Woody Allen

The trouble with most of us is that we have been inoculated with small doses of Christianity in childhood which keeps us from catching the real thing.

Bob Phillips

He was of the faith chiefly in the sense that the church he currently did not attend was Catholic.

Kingsley Amis

I don't believe in astrology because I'm a Gemini, and Geminis never believe in astrology.

Raymond Smullyan

Millions long for immortality who do not know what to do with themselves on a rainy Sunday afternoon.

Susan Ertz

Woman was God's second mistake.

Friedrich Nietzsche

As God once said, and I think rightly ...

Margaret Thatcher

I'm astounded by people who want to 'know' the universe when it's so hard to find your way around Chinatown.

Woody Allen

I do benefits for all religions – I'd hate to blow the hereafter on a technicality.

Bob Hope

Some people say there is a God; others say there is no God. The truth probably lies somewhere in between.

W.B. Yeats

Philosophy is unintelligible answers to insoluble problems.

Henry B. Adams

I have spent a lot of time searching through the Bible for loopholes.

W.C. Fields

The Bible tells us to love our neighbours, and also to love our enemies; probably because they are generally the same people.

G.K. Chesterton

I'm really a timid person – I was beaten up by Quakers.

Woody Allen

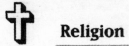

Religion

Sir, a woman preaching is like a dog walking on its hind legs. You don't expect it to be done well – you are surprised to find it done at all.

Samuel Johnson

An atheist is a guy who watches a Notre Dame versus SMU football game and doesn't care who wins.

Dwight D. Eisenhower

On the question of eternal punishment, the word 'eternal' did not appear to the elders of St Osoph's to designate a sufficiently long period of time.

Stephen Leacock

Hearing nuns' confessions is like being stoned to death with popcorn.

Fulton J. Sheen

I have tried in my time to be a philosopher, but cheerfulness always kept breaking in.

Oliver Edwards

The word *good* has many meanings. For example, if a man were to shoot his grandmother at a range of five hundred yards, I should call him a good shot, but not necessarily a good man.

G.K. Chesterton

Thank God I'm an atheist.

Luis Buñuel

The Bible was a consolation to a fellow alone in the old cell. The lovely thin paper with a bit of mattress stuffing in it, if you could get a match, was as good a smoke as ever I tasted.

Brendan Behan

Become a Protestant? Certainly not. Just because I've lost my faith doesn't mean I've lost my reason.

James Joyce

If you want to make God laugh, tell him your future plans.

Woody Allen

Why do born again people so often make you wish they had never been born the first time?

Katharine Whitehorn

I do not believe in an after life, although I am bringing a change of underwear.

Woody Allen

The Anglo-Saxon conscience doesn't stop you from sinning; it just stops you from enjoying it.

Salvador de Madariaga

How was I to know that the Pope was a Catholic? Nobody's infallible.

George Brown

Only one man ever understood me – and he didn't understand me.

G. W. Hegel

They say that Joseph Smith did not receive from the hands of an angel the written revelation that we obey. Let them prove it!

Brigham Young

I desire to go to hell and not to heaven. In the former place I shall enjoy the company of Popes, Kings and Princes, while in the latter are only beggars, monks and apostles.

Niccolo Machiavelli

I'm not really a practising Jew but I keep a kosher kitchen just to spite Hitler.

Miriam Margolyes

Put down enthusiasm – the Church of England in a nutshell.

Mary Augusta Ward

The sacrament of confirmation in the Church of England tends to be a sort of spiritual sheep dip.

Lord Altrincham

'We need more money', said the vicar, 'for our organ repair fund – and if we can't get it by fair means, we'll have to organise another sale of work'.

J.B. Morton

It is much easier to repent of sins that we have committed that to repent of those we intend to commit.

Josh Billings

When you convert someone to an idea, you lose your faith in it.

Oscar Wilde

I read the bible – every goddamn day.

George Patton

Never take a reference from a clergyman. They always want to give someone a second chance.

Lady Selborne

Forgive your enemies – if you can't get back at them any other way.

Franklin P. Jones

Dear God, you help total strangers – so why not me?

Leo Rosten

The Puritans were an extremely religious group who lived in England and did not believe in drinking or dancing or having sex with hooved animals.

Dave Barry

When I get over to the other side, I shall use my influence to have the human race drowned again, and this time drowned good, no omissions, no Ark.

Mark Twain

If there is no God, who pops up the next Kleenex?

Art Hoppe

First secure an independent income. Then practise virtue.

Aristotle

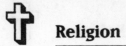 **Religion**

There can hardly be a town in the South of England where you could throw a brick without hitting the niece of a bishop.

George Orwell

The better sort of Ishmaelites have been Christian for many centuries and will not publicly eat human flesh uncooked in Lent, without special and costly dispensation from their bishop.

Evelyn Waugh

Many people think they have religion when they merely have dyspepsia.

Robert G. Ingersoll

We must respect the other fellow's religion, but only in the sense and to the extent that we respect his theory that his wife is beautiful and his children are smart.

H.L. Mencken

I think that it can fairly be said that everything in the Holy Land is cursed.

P.J. O'Rourke

Frisbeetarianism is the belief that when you die, your soul goes up on the roof and gets stuck.

George Carlin

There is no original sin – it's all been done before.

Louis Dudek

Religion

If there is no God, who opens the doors in supermarkets?
Patrick Murray

The universe is merely a fleeting idea in God's mind – a
pretty uncomfortable thought, particularly if you've just
make a down payment on a house.
Woody Allen

Our dourest parsons always seemed to me to be bent on
bullying God. After a few 'beseech thees' as a mere
politeness, they adopted a sterner tone and told Him what
they expected from Him and more than hinted He must
attend to His work.
J.B. Priestley

Lead me not into temptation – I can find it for myself.
John Bernal

The only thing wrong with immortality is that it tends to go
on forever.
Herb Caen

Finally, it emerged that Alan Clark, of all people, may cross
the Tiber, presumably after a record-breaking session in the
confessional.
Damian Thompson

The game of golf is an intensely Presbyterian activity.
Clifford Hanley

✞ Religion

We owe a lot to the Y.M.C.A: the invention of the triangular trouser button for example.

Spike Milligan

This is not mentioned by the Synoptists, and is passed over by St. John: but full details may be found in Farrar's Life of Christ.

Geoffrey Madan

Confirmation at Eton was like a huge garden party, faintly overshadowed by a sense of religion.

A. C. Benson

I'm going to marry a Jewish woman because I like the idea of getting up on a Sunday morning and going to the deli.

Michael J. Fox

The Church of England is the best church to live in but the Catholic Church is the best church to die in.

Oscar Wilde

The bishop had forty bedrooms in his palace, but only thirty-nine articles to put in them.

Winston Churchill

There is one passage in the Scripture to which all the potentates of Europe seem to have given their unanimous assent and approbation: "There went out a decree in the days of Caesar Augustus that all the world should be taxed."

Charles Colton

Never invoke the gods unless you really want them to appear. It annoys them very much.

G. K. Chesterton

A couple of Sundays ago I was watching *Songs of Praise* on television, which was coming from Maidstone Prison of all places, when I spotted to my amazement a man who owes me fifty pounds. He was standing there and had the gall to be singing "Abide With Me".

Jeffrey Bernard

It is ungentlemanly to include more than one foreign coin in contributions to the church collection.

George Moor

It is as hard for a rich man to enter the kingdom of Heaven as it is for a poor man to get out of Purgatory.

Finley Peter Dunne

From time to time I like to pay tribute to my four scriptwriters, Matthew, Mark, Luke and John.

Fulton J. Sheen

Sin is a dangerous toy in the hands of the virtuous. It should be left to the congenitally sinful, who know when to play with it and when to let it alone.

H. L. Mencken

My religion is that I'm an alcoholic.

Brendan Behan

✝ Religion

By 1879 there was little left of religion in Ruskin except an adolescent horror of fornication.

G. M. Young

The organs of human utterance are too frail to describe my lack of interest in papal affairs.

George Lyttelton

Since we have to speak well of the dead, let's knock them while they're still alive.

John Sloan

Like most Irish people, I was born a Catholic. This came as a big shock to my parents, who were Jewish.

Michael Redmond

About a year ago, I disturbed a burglar. I said, "There is no God."

Paul Merton

First I turned one cheek, then the other cheek. Now that the scriptures have been fulfilled, I intend to beat the hell out of thee.

William Penn

She had once been a Catholic, but discovering that priests were infinitely more attentive when she was in process of losing or regaining faith in Mother Church, she maintained an enchantingly wavering attitude.

F. Scott Fitzgerald

The followers of Ian Paisley threw a rosary and a Bible at me, which I felt was at least an ecumenical gesture.

Lord Soper

Charity creates a multitude of sins.

Oscar Wilde

It is far easier to forgive an enemy after you've got even with him.

Olin Miller

The only thing that stops God sending a second flood is that the first one was useless.

Sébastien Roch Nicolas Chamfort

Punch is very much like the Church of England. It is doctrinally inexplicable but it goes on.

Malcolm Muggeridge

We know that we must return good for evil: but that may just be a mistake in translation.

John Vanbrugh

What is my opinion of the hereafter? One world at a time.

Henry Thoreau

I know I ought not to yield to temptation, but somebody must or the thing becomes ridiculous.

Anthony Hawkins

✝ Religion

Catholics claim to be infallible, Anglicans to be always right.

Richard Steele

Zangwill's teeth are like the Ten Commandments: all broken.

Herbert Beerbohm Tree

If English was good enough for Jesus Christ, it's good enough for me.

David Edwards

Men don't get cellulite. God might just be a man.

Rita Rudner

I believe everything the Catholic Church teaches is true but I let my wife go to mass for me.

Brendan Behan

What do you say to God when He sneezes?

Steven Wright

By virtue we merely mean the avoidance of the vices that do not attract us.

Robert Lynd

I love my neighbour as myself, and to avoid coveting my neighbour's wife, I desire to be coveted by her: which you know is another thing.

William Congreve

God must love airline fares. He made so many of them.

Milton Berle

Heaven doesn't want me and Hell is scared I am going to take over.

Elizabeth Taylor

I was the child who always got picked to play Bethlehem in the school nativity play. And even then Mary and Joseph used to keep mistaking me for Greater Manchester.

Jo Brand

I always say beauty is only sin deep.

H.H.Munro

Old-fashioned vicar (Tractarian) seeks colleague; fine church; good musical tradition. Parish residential and farming. Good golf handicap an asset but not essential. Left-handed fast bowler preferred.

David Hopps

Many people believe they are attracted by God, or by Nature, when they are only repelled by man.

W.R. Inge

They used to have religious texts on the walls of the condemned cell in Durham. One of them read, "Today is the tomorrow you worried about yesterday." It was the last thing a bloke saw as he went out to be hanged.

Brendan Behan

Little is known about St. Valentine except that he was born in a wood and his twin brother was carried off by a bear. Hence the tradition, begun by greeting-card moguls in the fifteenth century, of the rest of us sending expensive unsigned messages to each other.

Mel Smith

Fundamentalists are to Christianity what painting by numbers is to art.

Robin Tyler

Puritanism is no religion for a gentleman and Anglicanism is no religion for a Christian.

G.K. Chesterton

People talk of their seats in Heaven with as much confidence as if they had booked them at the box office.

Leigh Hunt

I am determined my children shall be brought up in their father's religion, if they can find out what it is.

Charles Lamb

The only thing I would not wish on my worst enemy is eternal life.

Quentin Crisp

There are terrible temptations that it requires strength, strength and courage to yield to.

Oscar Wilde

Religion

The most important things to a Southern girl are God, family, and hair, almost never in that order.

Lucinda Ebersole

I knew an eighty-five-year-old man who married a girl of eighteen. He needed someone to answer the Rosary for him.

Eamon Kelly

If you are sufficiently irascible, God might just decide to wait.

Godfrey Just

It rains only straight down. God doesn't do windows.

Steven Wright

Poor Chesterton, his day is past
Now God will know the truth at last.

E. V. Lucas

A cult becomes a religion when it progresses from killing its members to killing non-members.

David Lewin

There are no atheists on turbulent airplanes.

Erica Jong

A clever theft was praiseworthy among the Spartans; and it is equally so among Christians, provided it be on a sufficiently large scale.

Herbert Spencer

✝ Religion

Evelyn Waugh was the nastiest-tempered man in England, Catholic or Protestant.

James Lees-Milne

He could never make up his mind between suicide and an equally drastic course of action known as Father D'Arcy.

Muriel Spark

My ambition is to rescue God from religion.

Sinead O'Connor

Moss Hart's country garden looks like what God would have done if He'd had the money.

Alexander Woollcott

I am told that printers' readers no longer exist because clergymen are no longer unfrocked for sodomy.

Evelyn Waugh

There may have been disillusionments in the lives of the mediaeval saints, but they would scarcely have been better pleased if they could have foreseen that their names would be associated nowadays chiefly with racehorses and the cheaper clarets.

Saki

My father was not at all devout. But he saw Jesus as quite a good chap, as the honorable member for Galilee South.

Malcolm Muggeridge

What would happen if Moses were alive today? He'd go up Mount Sinai, come back with the Ten Commandments, and spend the next eight years trying to get published.

Robert Orben

The prison warder asked me my religion and I replied 'agnostic'. He remarked with a sigh: 'Well, there are many religions, but I suppose we all worship the same God.'

Bertrand Russell

I want to play the role of Jesus. I'm a logical choice. I look the part. I'm a Jew and I'm a comedian. And I'm an atheist, so I'd be able to look at the character objectively.

Charlie Chaplin

I love gentiles. In fact, one of my favourite activities is Protestant spotting.

Mel Brooks

What some preachers lack in depth they make up for in length.

Mark Twain

As far as religion is concerned, I'm a Baptist and a good friend of the Pope, and I always wear a Jewish star for luck.

Louis Armstrong

I do not fast during Lent because although I have a Catholic soul, I have a Lutheran stomach.

> Desiderius Erasmus

God created Eve because when He had finished creating Adam, He stepped back, scratched His head and said, 'I think I can do better than that.'

> Phyllis Diller

We need a new cosmology. New Gods. New Sacraments. Another drink.

> Patti Smith

If God wanted me to touch my toes, he would have put them on my knees.

> Roseanne Barr

They say altar wine contains Glauber's salts so as priests won't get the taste and break their pledges.

> Dominic Behan

What a hell of a heaven it will be, when they get all those hypocrites assembled there.

> Mark Twain

When Frank Sinatra goes to heaven, he's going to give God a hard time for making him bald.

> Marlon Brando

Becoming an Anglo-Catholic must surely be a sad business –
rather like becoming an amateur conjurer.

John Strachey

Is there an afterlife? Well there's an afterbirth, so why
shouldn't there be an afterlife?

Kevin MacAleer

After his long fast, the toad has a very spiritual look, like a
strict Anglo-Catholic towards the end of Lent.

George Orwell

I would have more respect for the Pope if he wore a white
cotton teeshirt emblazoned in red with the legend:
INFALLIBLE BUT NOT INFLEXIBLE.

Fran Lebowitz

God never shut one door but He closed another.

James Plunkett

To steal from the rich is a sacred and religious act.

Jerry Rubin

I am an unbeliever but I sometimes have doubts.

George Bernard Shaw

Science and Technology

Science and Technology

Ouch!

Isaac Newton

In ancient times they had no statistics so they had to fall back on lies.

Stephen Leacock

The speed at which boiling milk rises from the bottom of the pan to any point beyond the top is greater than the speed at which the human brain and hand can combine to snatch the confounded thing off.

H. F. Ellis

Statistics are like loose women; once you get your hands on them you can do anything you like with them.

Walt Michaels

An expert is someone who has made all the mistakes that can be made, but in a very narrow field.

Niels Bohr

Everybody talks about the weather, but nobody does anything about it.

Charles D. Warner

It is impossible to combine the heating of milk with any other pursuit whatever.

H. F. Ellis

How does the little busy bee improve each shining hour and gather honey all the day from every opening flower? Well, he does not. He spends most of the day in buzzing and aimless acrobatics, and gets about a fifth of the honey he would collect if he organised himself.

Heneage Ogilvie

He uses statistics as a drunken man uses a lamp post – more for support than illumination.

Andrew Lang

To pray is to ask that the laws of the universe be annulled on behalf of a single petitioner confessedly unworthy.

Ambrose Bierce

Descended from the apes? Let us hope that is not true. But if it is, let us pray that it may not become generally known.

F.A. Montagu

Living on Earth may be expensive, but it includes an annual free trip around the sun.

Ashleigh Brilliant

Ketchup left overnight on dinner plates has a longer half-life than radioactive waste.

Wes Smith

How do they get that non-stick stuff to stick to the frying pan?

Steven Wright

Why don't they make the whole plane out of that black box stuff?

Steven Wright

Computer dating is fine – if you're a computer.

Rita May Brown

Get your facts right first and then you can distort them as much as you please.

Mark Twain

Time wasted only when sprinkling perfume on goat farm.
Charlie Chan

Scientists have invented something for getting chewing gum off the pavement. It is called a shoe.
Nick Percival

An intellectual is a man who doesn't know how to park a bike.
Spiro T. Agnew

We said zero, and I think any statistician will tell you that when you're dealing with very big numbers, zero must mean plus or minus a few.
William Waldegrave

Nuclear winter is the most important scientific theory since phlogiston, phrenology and Piltdown Man.
Tim Curry

Given apples and motion, the English produced Isaac Newton, the Swiss William Tell.
Malcolm Scott

My inclination to go by Air Express is confirmed by the crash they had yesterday, which will make them careful in the immediate future.
A. E. Housman

Science and Technology

Should human beings ever step on Europa, one of Jupiter's moons, they need not fear constipation. The surface is littered with Epsom Salts, a potent laxative.

Nigel Hawkes

Error is part of the overhead of doing research.

Michael Ghiselin

Astrology proves one scientific fact, and one only; there's one born every minute.

Patrick Moore

Man is the missing link between apes and human beings.

Konrad Lorenz

Time flies like an arrow. Fruit flies like a banana. So just what are time flies, and why do they like an arrow?

Groucho Marx

They've just found a gene for shyness. They would have found it earlier but it was hiding behind a couple of other genes.

Jonathan Katz

Immediately after Orville Wright's historic 12-second flight, his luggage could not be located.

Sydney Harris

I spilled spot remover on my dog. He's gone now.

Steven Wright

I think animal testing is a terrible idea. They get all nervous and give the wrong answers.

Hugh Laurie

I am always on the lookout to replace my current computer when it becomes obsolete: usually before I get it all the way out of the box.

Dave Barry

The most difficult book I have ever read was a manual on the use of iron mangles by A. J. Thompson.

Spike Milligan

Ladies and gentlemen: the world's greatest novelty: the twins Redwood and Brentwood. Redwood is the smallest giant in the world, while his brother Brentwood is the tallest midget in the world. They baffle science.

W. C. Fields

If it wasn't for burnt toast, entire species of birds in Britain would disappear.

Jeremy Noakes

A computer lets you make more mistakes faster than any invention in human history: with the possible exceptions of handguns and tequila.

Mitch Ratliffe

If the effort that went in research on the female bosom had gone into our space program, we would now be running hot-dog stands on the moon.

Robert Murphy

The sooner all the animals are extinct, the sooner we'll find where they've hidden their money.

Mikael Pawlo

The surest sign that intelligent life exists elsewhere in the Universe is that it has never tried to contact us.

Bill Watterson

The inside diameter of all pipes must not exceed the outside diameter, otherwise the hole will be on the outside.

Michael Stillwell

Baldrick, you wouldn't recognise a cunning plan if it painted itself purple and danced naked on top of a harpsichord singing, "Cunning plans are here again."

Rowan Atkinson

Have you ever noticed that when you blow in a dog's face he gets mad, but when you take him out in a car, he sticks his head out the window?

Steve Bluestein

I offer the modest proposal that our Universe is simply one of those things which happen from time to time.

Edward Tyron

Science and Technology

Okay: what's the speed of dark?

Wright Stevens

The Universe is a big place, perhaps the biggest.

Kilgore Trout

It's a good thing there's gravity or else when birds died, they'd stay where they were.

Steven Wright

Tell a man that there are three hundred billion stars in the Universe and he'll believe you. Tell him a bench has wet paint on it and he'll have to touch it to be sure.

Ed Jarger

Perennials are the ones that grow like weeds, biennials are the ones that die this year instead of next and hardy annuals are the ones that never come up at all.

Katharine Whitehorn

They will never really crack down on air pollution until it begins to interfere with television reception.

Francis Capelini

I know a man who has a device for converting solar energy into food. He's been doing it for years: it's called a farm.

David Stenhouse

I can only assume that God wanted penicillin and that was His reason for creating Alexander Fleming.

Alexander Fleming

My dog is glad to see me every minute of my life. I come home, he jumps around. I go in the closet, I come out, he jumps around and wags his tail. I turn my face away, I turn it back, he wags his tail. Either he loves me passionately or he has absolutely no short-term memory.

Harry Weston

They say the dog is man's best friend. I don't believe that. How many of your friends have you had neutered?

Larry Reels

I don't know why they keep complaining about this greenhouse effect. If they know what's causing the problem, why don't they just stop giving people permission to build them?

Joe Lavin

Most earthquakes are caused by sudden movements of Roseanne Barr.

Joan Rivers

Programming today is a race between software engineers striving to build bigger and better idiot-proof programs and the Universe trying to produce bigger and better idiots. So far the Universe is winning.

Rich Cook

The computer world has a language all of its own, just like Hungary. The difference is, if you hang around Hungarians long enough, you start to understand what they're talking about.

Dave Barry

Science and Technology

Birthdays are good for you. Statistics show that people who have the most birthdays live longest.

John Paulos

The genitals themselves have not undergone the development of the rest of the human form in the direction of beauty.

Sigmund Freud

Neil Armstrong was the first man to walk on the moon. I was the first man to piss his pants on the moon.

Buzz Aldrin

When decorating I always use a step-ladder. I don't really get on with my real ladder.

Harry Hill

Artificial Intelligence is the study of how to make real computers act like the ones in the movies.

David Arnold

Autumn wasps are the most dangerous, delirious and resentful that all the children have gone back to school.

Dylan Moran

If it looks like an elephant, sounds like an elephant, and there's half a ton of steaming manure on the floor, it's probably an elephant.

A.A. Gill

Science and Technology

The terrorist who mailed a letter bomb with insufficient postage wins a Darwin Award when he opens the returned package.

Wendy Northcutt

You know when you step on a mat in the supermarket and the door opens? For years, I thought it was a coincidence.

Richard Jeni

I think the aardvark just made up that name when he heard that Noah was taking the animals onto the Ark in alphabetical order.

Matt King

The marvels of modern technology include the development of a soda can which, when discarded, will last forever, and a $7000 car which, when properly cared for, will rust out in two or three years.

Paul Harwitz

The human brain is merely a device to prevent the ears grating on one another.

Peter DeVries

The only thing that continues to give us more for our money is the weighing machine.

George Clark

In relation to computers I am firmly of the opinion that Macintosh is Catholic and that MS-DOS is Protestant.

Umberto Eco

Social Behaviour and Manners

In my experience, if you have to keep the lavatory door shut by extending your left leg, it's modern architecture.

Nancy Banks-Smith

The general advertiser's attitude would seem to be: if you are a lousy, smelly, idle, under-privileged, overweight and over-sexed status-seeking neurotic moron, give me your money.

Kenneth Bromfield

Style is when they're running you out of town and you make it look like you're leading a parade.

William Battie

An acquaintance is someone we know well enough to borrow from but not well enough to lend to.

Ambrose Bierce

There are many who dare not kill themselves for fear of what the neighbours will say.

Cyril Connolly

As far as I'm concerned there are only two kinds of people in the world – those who are kind to their servants and those who are not.

Duke of Argyll

I told the traffic warden to go forth and multiply, though not exactly in those words.

Woody Allen

As yet, Bernard Shaw hasn't become prominent enough to have any enemies; but none of his friends like him.

Oscar Wilde

There is only one immutable law in life – in a gentleman's toilet, incoming traffic has the right of way.

Hugh Leonard

Social Behaviour and Manners

It is illegal to make liquor privately or water publicly.

Lord Birkett

Know him? I know him so well that I haven't spoken to him for ten years.

Oscar Wilde

The full potentialities of human fury cannot be reached until a friend of both parties tactfully intervenes.

G.K. Chesterton

He was a great patriot, a humanitarian, a loyal friend – provided of course he really is dead.

Voltaire

Don't touch a woman's knee at the dinner table; she has an instinctive knowledge whether a man who touches her knee is caressing her or only wiping his greasy fingers on her stocking.

George Moore

Always forgive your enemies. Nothing annoys them so much.

Oscar Wilde

The only thing I really mind about going to prison is the thought of Lord Longford coming to visit me.

Richard Ingrams

Whatever you have read I have said is almost certainly untrue, except if it is funny in which case I *definitely* said it.

Tallulah Bankhead

Social Behaviour and Manners

If any reader of this book is in the grip of some habit of
which he is deeply ashamed, I advise him not to give way to
it in secret but to do it on television. No one will pass him
with averted gaze on the other side of the street. People will
cross the road at the risk of losing their own lives in order to
say 'We saw you on the telly.'

Denis Pratt

I once sent a dozen of my friends a telegram saying FLEE
AT ONCE – ALL IS DISCOVERED.
They all left town immediately.

Mark Twain

Anyone can do any amount of work provided it isn't the
work he is supposed to be doing at the moment.

Robert Benchley

A pessimist is a man who, when he smells flowers, looks
around for the coffin.

H.L. Mencken

When you have to kill a man it costs nothing to be polite.

Winston Churchill

When little men cast long shadows, the sun is about to set.

Michael Seymour

There is nothing like the sight of an old enemy down on his
luck.

Euripides

If you cannot say anything good about someone, sit right
here by me.

Alice Roosevelt

Those who give up smoking aren't the heroes. The real heroes are the rest of us – who have to listen to them.

Hal Boyle

I do not have to forgive my enemies – I have had them all shot.

Ramon Narvaez

Wit is like caviar. It should be served in small elegant portions and not splashed about like marmalade.

Noel Coward

One should never be unnecessarily rude to a lady except in street cars.

O. Henry

Blown his brains out you say? He must have been an incredibly good shot.

Noel Coward

I have a most peaceable disposition. My desires are for a modest hut, a thatched roof, a good bed, good food, very fresh milk and butter, flowers in front of my window and a few pretty trees by my door. And should the good Lord wish to make me really happy, he will allow me the pleasure of seeing about six or seven of my enemies hanged upon those trees.

Heinrich Heine

I regret very much my inability to attend your banquet. It is the baby's night out and I must stay at home with the nurse.

Ring Lardner

If this is the way that Queen Victoria treats her prisoners, she doesn't deserve to have any.

Oscar Wilde

Social Behaviour and Manners

I have never liked working. To me a job is an invasion of privacy.

Danny McGoorty

Annie never changes. In fact she never even changes her clothes.

Flann O'Brien

Dear boy, it isn't that your manners are bad – it's simply that you have no manners at all.

Margot Asquith

You can never rival a millionaire if he has even the faintest inclination towards smartness. His valet wears his suits for the first three days so that they never look new, and confiscates them after three months so that they never look old.

Evelyn Waugh

A good listener is not someone who has nothing to say. A good listener is a good talker with a sore throat.

Katharine Whitehorn

There are just two classes in good society in England. The equestrian classes and the neurotic classes.

George Bernard Shaw

The dinner party was so dull that if I hadn't been there myself, I should have been bored to death.

Alexandre Dumas

Social Behaviour and Manners

My sartorial appearance was that of an unmade bed.

Dylan Thomas

Mass murderers are simply people who have had enough.

Quentin Crisp

The louder he talked of his honour, the faster we counted our spoons.

Ralph Waldo Emerson

Tact is the art of making guests feel at home when that's really where you wish they were.

George Bergman

Courtesy is opening a door for a woman you would not wish to open a bedroom door for.

Thomas Kyne

To be natural is such a very difficult pose to keep up.

Oscar Wilde

They say you shouldn't say anything about the dead unless it's good. He's dead. Good.

Moms Mabley

Actually, there is no way of making vomiting courteous. You have to do the next best thing, which is to vomit in such a way that the story you tell about it later will be amusing.

P.J. O'Rourke

I am, sir, your humble and obedient servant, which you
know, and I know, is a damn lie.

Duke of Wellington

I don't at all like knowing what people say of me behind my
back. It makes me far too conceited.

Oscar Wilde

A lady is someone who wants to punch another person in
the mouth, but doesn't.

Judith Martin

A bore is someone who persists in holding his own views
after we have enlightened him with ours.

Malcolm S. Forbes

I believe I have no prejudices whatsoever. All I need to
know is that a man is a member of the human race. That's
bad enough for me.

Mark Twain

I thoroughly disapprove of duels. If a man should challenge
me, I would take him kindly and forgivingly by the hand and
lead him to a quiet place and kill him.

Mark Twain

It was impossible to get a conversation going because
everyone was talking too much.

Yogi Berra

Class consciousness, particularly in England, has been so much inflamed that to mention a nobleman is like mentioning a prostitute sixty years ago. The new prudes say, 'No doubt such people do exist but we would sooner not hear about them.'

Evelyn Waugh

I am not eccentric. It's just that I am more alive than most people. I am an unpopular electric eel set in a pond of goldfish.

Edith Sitwell

Nobody can be exactly like me. Even I have trouble doing it.

Tallulah Bankhead

Always acknowledge a fault frankly. This will throw those in authority off their guard and give you opportunity to commit more.

Mark Twain

It is a terrible thing for a man to find out suddenly that all his life he has been speaking nothing but the truth.

Oscar Wilde

Sainthood is when you can listen to someone's tale of woe and not respond with a description of your own.

Andrew Mason

There's no pleasing some people. The trick is to stop trying.

Joel Rosenberg

Social Behaviour and Manners

The nineteenth-century Shah of Persia never quite got the hang of English high-society etiquette. On one state visit he was introduced to the Marchioness of Londonderry: and made an offer to buy her.

Graham Nown

It is conduct unbecoming to a lady or gentleman when being treated at the V.D. clinic to name as contacts those who spurned your advances.

George Moor

Even the best-intentioned of great men need a few scoundrels around them; there are some things you cannot ask an honest man to do.

La Bruyère

A man usually has no idea what is being said about him. The entire town may be slandering him, but if he has no friends he will never hear of it.

Honoré de Balzac

Do unto the other fellow the way he'd like to do unto you, but do it first.

Edward Westcott

She has a charming fresh colour, when it is fresh put on.

Richard Brinsley Sheridan

It was embarrassing. I felt like a figure skater who had forgotten to put on her knickers.

Hugh Leonard

I hate to spread rumours: but what else can one do with them?

Amanda Lear

As universal a practice as lying is, and as easy as it seems, I do not remember to have heard three good lies in any conversation, even from those who were most celebrated in that faculty.

Jonathan Swift

The ruffian pretended to mistake me for a commissionaire outside the theatre and said, "Would you call me a cab?" I replied, "Yes, but not a hansom one."

James Agate

On those summer evenings a radio playing loudly can be a great source of annoyance to your neighbours. Another good way to annoy them is to set fire to their dustbins.

Marty Feldman

My motto is "My rights or I bite."

Clarinda Breujere

I stuck up for her. Someone said she wasn't fit to live with pigs and I said she was.

Brendan Behan

Social Behaviour and Manners

Duty is what one expects from others, it is not what one does oneself.

Oscar Wilde

The only thing that sustains one through life is the consciousness of the immense inferiority of everybody else and this is a feeling I have always cultivated.

Oscar Wilde

The "t" is silent, as in Harlow.

Margot Asquith

He was so mean that if he owned the Alps, he wouldn't give you a slide.

Brendan Behan

If one hides one's talent under a bushel, one must be careful to point out the exact bushel under which it is hidden.

H. H. Munro

When you ascend the hill of prosperity, may you not meet a friend.

Mark Twain

If you bed people of below-stairs class, they will go to the papers.

Jane Clark

There is nothing so annoying as to have two people go right on talking when you're interrupting.

Mark Twain

"Yes, but not in the South", with slight adjustments will do for any argument about any place, if not about any person.

Stephen Potter

Do you suppose I could buy back my introduction to you?

Groucho Marx

That poor man. He's completely unspoiled by failure.

Noel Coward

Lord Glasgow, having flung a waiter through the window of his club, brusquely ordered, "Put him on the bill."

Guy Phillips

A Merry Christmas to all my friends except two.

W. C. Fields

What a lovely hat! But if I may make one teensy suggestion? If it blows off, don't chase it.

Miss Piggy

Hats divide generally into three classes. Offensive hats, defensive hats and shrapnel.

Katharine Whitehorn

I am loath to interrupt the rapture of mourning for Queen Victoria in which the nation is now enjoying its favourite festive: a funeral: but in a country like ours the total suspension of common sense and sincere human feeling for a whole fortnight is an impossibility.

George Bernard Shaw

All decent people live beyond their incomes nowadays, and those who aren't respectable live beyond other people's. A few gifted individuals manage to do both.

H. H. Munro

His smile explained everything; he always carried it with him as a leper carried his bell; it was a perpetual warning that he was not to be trusted.

Graham Greene

Dress simply. If you wear a dinner jacket, don't wear anything else on it: like lunch or dinner.

George Burns

The hatchet is buried but a bit of its handle may still be seen protruding from the ground.

Rhoda Broughton

Social Behaviour and Manners

It is always painful to part from people whom one has known for a very brief space of time. The absence of old friends one can endure with equanimity.

Oscar Wilde

The advantage of doing one's praising for oneself is that one can lay it on so thick and exactly in the right places.

Samuel Butler

Talk to a man about himself and he will listen for hours.

Benjamin Disraeli

If you are foolish enough to be contented, don't show it, but grumble with the rest.

Jerome K. Jerome

Yes, I am exactly like the characters in my books. I am very tough and have been known to break a Vienna roll with my bare hands. I am very handsome, have a powerful physique and change my shirt every Monday.

Raymond Chandler

I have stopped swearing. I now just say Zsa Zsa Gabor!

Noel Coward

Somebody must listen and I like to do all the talking myself. It saves time and prevents arguments.

Oscar Wilde

The bride usually has one friend who wanted to marry the groom. This girl should be maid of honour so the bride can rub it in.

P. J. O'Rourke

I belong to the most exclusive club in London. I am a friend of Randolph Churchill.

Bernard Levin

One should never make one's debut with a scandal. One should reserve that to give an interest to one's old age.

Oscar Wilde

She was a great prude, having but two lovers at a time.

Mary Montagu

Christopher Martin-Jenkins and Neil Durden-Smith were standing next to the bar, playing with each other's hyphens.

Peter Tinniswood

The depressing thing about an Englishman's traditional love of animals is the dishonesty thereof: get a barbed hook into the upper lip of a salmon, drag him endlessly around the water until he loses his strength, pull him to the bank, hit him on the head with a stone, and you may well become fisherman of the year. Shoot the salmon and you'll never be asked again.

Clement Freud

Eccentricity, to be socially acceptable, still has to have at least four or five generations of inbreeding behind it.

Osbert Lancaster

I must go home and do that which no one else can do for me.

Jonathan Swift

Dean Westcott's letter of condolence to Charles Kingsley on a bereavement: fourteen pages; only one phrase could be deciphered, apparently "ungrateful devil".

Geoffrey Madan

I expect to pass through this world but once and therefore if there is anybody that I want to kick in the crotch I had better kick them in the crotch now, for I do not expect to pass this way again.

Maurice Bowra

His aunt was a bit of a social climber, although very much on the lower slopes. I was once on a tram with her going past the gas works in Wellington Road and she said, "Alan, this is one of the biggest gas works in England. And I know the manager."

Alan Bennett

Few of us can stand prosperity. Another man's I mean.

Mark Twain

When I want your opinion I'll give it to you.

Laurence J. Peter

Social Behaviour and Manners

For the last twenty years Elsie de Wolfe's age has been legendary.

> Janet Flanner

Henry Ward Beecher is a remarkably handsome man when he is in the full tide of sermonising, and his face is lit up with animation, but he is as homely as a singed cat when he isn't doing anything.

> Mark Twain

I could have wept, parting with him, but I could not get at my handkerchief without unbuttoning my boatcloak and that was inconvenient.

> Jane Carlyle

Within minutes, several eyewitnesses were on the scene.

> Adam Boulton

Bores can be divided into two classes; those who have their own particular subject, and those who do not need a subject.

> A.A. Milne

If you want to be a leader with a large following, just obey the speed limit on a winding, two-lane road.

> Charles Farr

You'd be hoarse listening to her.

> Maureen Potter

There is nothing more dangerous than a resourceful idiot.

> Scott Adams

During a communal crisis, keep looking shocked and move slowly towards the cakes.

Homer Simpson

I don't get angry and I don't hate people. If something bad happens, I forget it right away. Or at least ten minutes later.

George Burns

The most important thing when you are going to do something brave is to have someone on hand to witness it.

Michael Howard

Never trust a man who combs his hair from his left armpit.

Theodore Roosevelt

He was the sort of man that Spooner would have referred to as a shining wit.

Hugh Leonard

The quotation of two or three lines of a stanza from Spenser's *Faerie Queene* is probably as good an all-round silencer as anything.

Stephen Potter

If you do your job right, only two people show up at your funeral.

Lewis Lapham

I managed capitally at dinner but I had a knife and two forks left at the end.

William Ridge

Gentlemen, Ravanelli may look like an idiot, he may behave like an idiot, but don't let that fool you; he really is an idiot.

Groucho Marx

To ensure peace of mind, ignore the rules and regulations.

George Ade

Weddings are sadder than funerals because they remind you of your own wedding. You can't be reminded of your own funeral because it hasn't happened. But weddings always make me cry.

Brendan Behan

In the tenth century, the Grand Vizier of Persia took his entire library with him wherever he went. The 117,000-volume library was carried by camels trained to walk in alphabetical order.

Geoff Tibbals

The sweetest words in the English language are: I told you so.

Gore Vidal

Knowledge is power if you know it about the right person.

Ethel Mumford

You could tell the sort of club it was. The bouncers were outside throwing the drunks in.

Les Dawson

For 'You really must come and see us soon' read 'If you call us we'll pretend we're out'.

Stephen Burgen

No man goes before his time – unless the boss leaves early.

Groucho Marx

It's not nice to joke about fat people – but they can't catch you.

Marsha Warfield

I'm a controversial figure. My friends either dislike me or hate me.

Oscar Levant

Give him an evasive answer. Tell him to go **** himself.

W. C. Fields

Come again when you can't stay so long.

Walter Sickert

Sport

Sport

Football is all very well. A good game for rough girls, but not for delicate boys.

Oscar Wilde

Much as bookmakers are opposed to law-breaking they are not bigoted about it.

Damon Runyon

When Nicklaus plays well he wins; when he plays badly he comes second. When he plays terribly he's third.

Johnny Miller

If there is a thunderstorm on a golf course, walk down the middle of the fairway holding a one-iron over your head. Even God can't hit a one-iron.

Lee Trevino

He hit me among my face.

Henny Youngman

If the people don't want to come out to the ball park, nobody's gonna stop 'em.

Yogi Berra

There are fools, damn fools, and jockeys who remount in a steeplechase.

John Oaksey

This city has two great football teams – Liverpool and Liverpool reserves.

Bill Shankly

I've seen better swings than Bob Hope's in a condemned playground.

Arnold Palmer

Sport

Of course I have played outdoor games. I once played dominoes in an open air cafe in Paris.

Oscar Wilde

Never play cards with a man named Doc.

Nelson Algren

Some people think football is a matter of life and death. I don't like that attitude. I can assure them it is much more serious than that.

Bill Shankly

Women playing cricket should treat it as a matter between consenting females in private.

Michael Parkinson

Go jogging? What, and get hit by a meteor?

Robert Benchley

My grandfather couldn't prescribe a pill to make a greyhound run faster, but he could produce one to make the other five go slower.

Benny Green

When I got into the boxing ring women used to scream with delight because usually I'd left my shorts in the locker.

Roy Brown

That's what I call an airport shot. You hit one of those, you miss the cut and you're heading off for the airport.

Lee Trevino

The hardest thing about boxing is picking up your teeth with a boxing glove on.

Kin Hubbard

Sport

Anybody can win, unless there happens to be a second entry.

George Ade

The only exercise I ever get is taking the cuff-links out of one shirt and putting them in another.

Ring Lardner

Trust everybody – but cut the cards.

Finley Peter Dunne

You don't know what pressure is in golf until you play for five bucks with only two in your pocket.

Lee Trevino

Wales didn't even have enough imagination to thump someone in the line-out when the ref wasn't looking.

J.P.R. Williams

It is frequently asserted in bookmaking circles that my mother and father met only once and then for a very brief period.

Lord Wigg

Although he is a bad fielder, he is also a very poor hitter.

Ring Lardner

I have hunted deer on occasions, but they were not aware of it.

Felix Gear

The rules of soccer are basically simple – if it moves, kick it; if it doesn't move, kick it until it does.

Phil Woosnam

I failed to make the chess team because of my height.

Woody Allen

Losing the Super Bowl is worse than death. With death you don't have to get up next morning.

George Allen

A fishing rod is a stick with a worm at one end and a fool at the other.

Samuel Johnson

A proper definition of an amateur sportsman today is one who accepts cash, not cheques.

Jack Kelly

Life is just an elaborate metaphor for cricket.

Marvin Cohen

I cannot see who is leading in the Boat Race, but it's either Oxford or Cambridge.

John Snagge

I went to a fight the other night and a hockey game broke out.

Rodney Dangerfield

The race is not always to the swift, nor the battle to the strong – but that's the way to bet.

Damon Runyon

I want to thank all the people who made this meeting necessary.

Yogi Berra

Never play tennis for money against a grey-haired player.

Tom Robinson

When I was a coach at Rochester they called me in and said 'We're making a change in your department.' I was the only guy in my department.

Don Cherry

Sport

Footballers are miry gladiators whose sole purpose in life is to position a surrogate human head between two poles.

Elizabeth Hogg

Winning isn't everything – it's the only thing.

Vince Lombardi

There is plenty of time to win this game, and to trash the Spaniards too – my bowels cannot wait.

Francis Drake

My horse was in the lead, coming down the home stretch, but the caddie fell off.

Samuel Goldwyn

Herbert Strudwick used to recommend to wicket-keepers 'Rinse your hands in the chamber pot every day. The urine hardens them wonderfully.'

David Lemmon

Skiing combines outdoor fun with knocking down trees with your face.

Dave Barry

You can observe a lot just by watching.

Yogi Berra

If you want a track team to win the high jump, you find one person who can jump seven feet, not seven people who can each jump one foot.

Frederick E. Terman

I'd give my right arm to get back into the England team.

Peter Shilton

Remember, postcards only, please. The winner will be the first one opened.

Brian Moore

A computer once beat me at chess, but it was no match for me at kick boxing.

Emo Philips

The British Board of Censors will not pass any seduction scene unless the seducer has one foot on the floor. Apparently sex in England is something like snooker.

Fred Allen

What a terrible round. I only hit two good balls all day and that was when I stepped on a rake in a bunker.

Lee Trevino

Pro basketball coaching is when you wake up in the morning and wish your parents had never met.

Bill Fitch

Remember, it doesn't matter whether you win or lose; what matters is whether I win or lose.

Darrin Weinberg

I'm going to win so much money this year that my caddie will make the top twenty money-winners list.

Lee Trevino

I promised I would take Rotherham out of the second division. I did – into the third division.

Tommy Docherty

I'd like to borrow Muhammad Ali's body for just forty-eight hours. There are three guys I'd like to beat up and four women I'd like to make love to.

Jim Murray

Sport

In Rugby you kick the ball; in Soccer you kick the man if you cannot kick the ball; and in Gaelic Football you kick the ball if you cannot kick the man.

J.J. MacCarthy

You aren't out of it until you're out of it.

Yogi Berra

To be an Olympic champion, first choose your parents carefully.

Per-Olaf Astrand

Offside, the referee suggests.

Bill McLaren

Mother always told me my day was coming, but I never realised I'd end up being the shortest knight of the year.

Gordon Richards

I'm only a prawn in this game.

Brian London

The Liverpool theme song is 'You'll Never Walk Alone' – the Wimbledon theme song is 'You'll Never Walk Again'.

Tommy Docherty

I considered filing a missing persons report on Leighton James in the second half.

Bobby Gould

I can see the carrot at the end of the tunnel.

Stuart Pearce

The only sport totally without style is football. It is for many reasons an unsatisfactory game. There is something faintly idiotic about a sport the rules of which forbid a player to use his hands which are the most adaptable and efficient parts of the human body.

Quentin Crisp

I find that if you keep throwing bogeys and double bogeys at your opponents, sooner or later they will crack from the sheer pressure.

Ring Lardner

I made a two-fingered gesture towards the fans to show that I had scored twice. It must have been misinterpreted.

Paul Peschisolido

On the golf course nobody really cares what happens to you except you and your caddy. And if he's bet against you, he doesn't care either.

Lee Trevino

I became a great runner because if you're a kid in Leeds and your name is Sebastian you've got to become a great runner.

Sebastian Coe

When Ilie Nastase plays John McEnroe, it's the only time the crowd call for silence.

Jerry Girard

 **Sport**

Always tell the truth. You may make a hole in one when you're alone on the golf course some day.

Franklin P. Jones

Ally McCoist is like dog shit in the penalty box. You don't know he's there until the damage is done.

John Hughes

For the Brazilian team in the World Cup there is only one rule: Do not change girlfriends on a Monday night.

Joao Saldanha

Why they call a fellow who keeps losing all the time a good sport beats me.

Kin Hubbard

Not only is he ambidextrous but he can throw the ball with either hand.

Duffy Daugherty

And now, as the evening wears on, the shadows cast by the floodlights get longer.

David Coleman

You can tell when Kirk Stevens is thinking. When he is not thinking, he looks like an Easter Island statue with a sinus problem. When he is thinking, he still looks like that, but licks his lips.

Clive James

We need the players, because without the players we wouldn't have a team.

Howard Wilkinson

The doctors X-rayed my head and found nothing.

Dizzy Dean

I never did say that you can't be a nice guy and win. I said that if I was playing third base and my mother rounded third with a winning run I'd trip her up.

Leo Durocker

Accrington Stanley's legendary centre forward had to be turned round by his colleagues at half-time and pointed towards the opponents' goal.

Victor Lewis-Smith

I wanted to be an Olympic swimmer, but I had some problems with buoyancy.

Woody Allen

The spirit at Sheffield United is the worst I've ever known, and the tea's not much better either.

Dave Bassett

 **Sport**

Where there's smoke there's usually a lot more smoke.

George Foreman

If a man watches three football games in a row, he should be declared legally dead.

Erma Bombeck

In a match, even when you're dead, you must never allow yourself to lie down and be buried.

Gordon Lee

Billiards is very similar to snooker, except there are only three balls and no one watches it.

Steve Davis

It's just a job. Grass grows, birds fly, waves pound the sand. I just beat people up.

Mohammed Ali

I joined as an apprentice at £25 a week. That's a bit like Ravanelli but without the noughts.

Jamie Hewitt

John McCririck looks like Worzel Gummidge after an incident with a letter bomb.

Victor Lewis-Smith

Watching Manchester City is probably the best laxative you can take.

Phil Neal

That has capped a superb season. It was an emotional night
and I have one small complaint: both of the streakers were
men.

Colin Todd

Golf may be played on a Sunday, not being a game within
the view of the law, but being a form of moral effort.

Stephen Leacock

The only way to beat Martina Navratilova is to run over her
foot in the car park.

Pam Shriver

The meek will inherit the earth, but they won't make the
green in two.

Lee Trevino

Monday, in Christian countries, is the day after the baseball
game.

Ambrose Bierce

My toughest fight was with my first wife.

Mohammad Ali

I got some girl's pants through the post the other day, but I
didn't like them; well, they didn't fit, to be honest.

Jamie Redknapp

I don't have any prematch superstitions or habits, but I
always have my packet of chocolate buttons.

Peter Beardsley

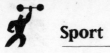

Sport

The problem with hunting, as a sport, is that it is not competitive. A guy with a shotgun squats in a swamp. An unarmed duck with an I.Q. of maybe four flies overhead; the guy blasts the duck into individual duck molecules. Where is the challenge here?

Dave Barry

Women want to be loved, to be listened to, to be desired, to be respected, to be needed, to be trusted, and sometimes, just to be held. Men just want tickets for the World Series.

Dave Barry

They've nicknamed me Ena Sharples because my head was never out of the net.

Ian Thain

Contrary to popular belief, I have always had a wonderful repertoire with my players.

Danny Ozark

Water polo is terribly dangerous. I had two horses drowned under me.

Tony Curtis

What James Dalton lacks in intelligence, he makes up for in stupidity.

Neil Francis

What a game! The referee was wearing glasses over his contact lenses.

Mike Harding

In the opening twenty minutes at Murrayfield, Portugal bought more dummies than a nurse on a maternity ward.

Alasdair Reid

Even though I've retired from boxing, I still go to the gym to spar every day. I miss being hit on the head.

Frank Bruno

Southampton football team is a very well-run outfit from Monday to Friday. It's Saturdays we've got a problem with.

Lawrie McMenemy

In my house in Houston I still have that putter with which I missed that two and a half foot to win the Open. It's in two pieces.

Doug Sanders

Do you know what I love most about baseball? The pine tar, the resin, the grass, the dirt: and that's just in the hot-dogs.

David Letterman

I don't know if the marriage of Joe DiMaggio and Marilyn Monroe is good for baseball but it sure beats the hell out of rooming with Phil Rizzuto.

Yogi Berra

There are only two inevitable things in life: people die and football managers get sacked.

Eoin Hand

Alan Hansen looks like a pissed vampire.

Chris Donald

Our shot–putters are in better condition than Gazza.

Linford Christie

I'm not a believer in luck, although I believe you need it.

Alan Ball

Glen Hoddle has nothing against the disabled. After all, he picked eleven of them to play for England.

Ian Hislop

In Wales's last attack, Scott Quinnell brushed aside three Irish players as if they were mannequins.

Denis Walsh

Football is just a fertility festival. Eleven sperm trying to get into the egg. I feel sorry for the goalkeeper.

Björk

No, of course I haven't been betting on horses Sybil dear. That's just another little avenue of pleasure you've closed off.

Basil Fawlty

Being hit by Victor Costello is like being hit by a cement mixer travelling at forty miles an hour.

George Hook

Women are around all the time but the World Cup comes only once every four years.

Peter Osgood

Kenny Dalglish wasn't that big but he had a huge arse. It came down below his knees and that's where he got his strength from.

Brian Clough

Do my eyes deceive me or is Senna's car sounding a bit rough?

Murray Walker

People seem to think that Jack Charlton and I are exactly the same. But I was a forthright, blunt, arrogant bastard long before I ever got involved with him.

Mick McCarthy

I was watching Germany and I got up to make a cup of tea. I bumped into the telly and Klinsmann fell over.

Frank Skinner

Joe Dimaggio is one of the loneliest guys I ever knew. He leads the league in room service.

Joe E. Brown

I know soccer stories so succulent you would feast on them like Pavarotti at a chophouse after the three-minute warning went off.

Danny Baker

Sport

Bolton Wanderers are doing well aren't they? Last season we got a corner.

Stu Francis

We will definitely improve this year. Last year we lost ten games. This year we play only nine.

Ray Jenkins

The entire contents of the Manchester City trophy room have been stolen. Police are looking for a man carrying a light blue carpet.

Bernard Manning

When I toured with the Irish rugby team I found social contact with other members of the squad very difficult. They were always using big words like "galvanise" and "marmalade".

Phil O'Callaghan

Football is football; if that weren't the case, it wouldn't be the game it is.

Garth Crooks

The Sheffield United strip looks as if it was designed by Julian Cleary when he had a migraine.

Sean Bean

Quit fouling like a wimp. If you're gonna foul, knock the crap outta him.

Norm Stewart

The sport of skiing consists of wearing three thousand dollars' worth of clothes and equipment and driving for two hundred miles in the snow in order to stand around at a bar and get drunk.

P. J. O'Rourke

I'm a great fan of baseball: I watch a lot of games on the radio.

Gerald Ford

Pressure is no excuse for Cantona's behaviour. I would take any amount of personal abuse for £10,000 a week.

Stanley Matthews

If Roger Chase wants to become popular it's easy: he should quit as chairman.

Jimmy Jones

If a woman has to choose between catching a fly ball and saving an infant's life, she will choose to save the infant's life without even considering if there are men on base.

Dave Barry

The most effective way of getting rid of vermin is hunting: provided that a sufficient number of them fall off their horses and break their necks.

Hugh Leonard

If you can't imitate him, don't copy him.

Yogi Berra

 **Sport**

Since retiring from riding, eating is going to be a whole new ball game. I may even have to buy a new pair of trousers.

Lester Piggot

Every Monday Stan Collymore would ask me to give him a good boot on the ankle so that he's be injured for Tuesday's training.

Darren Reilly

This is a football. It's an elongated spheroid, inflated with air and covered with an outer layer of coarsely grained leather. Heaven help the first man who fumbles it.

John Heisman

Welcome back to BBC2. While you were away we had a bit of excitement: the batsman asked the umpire if the sightscreen could be moved a few inches to the left and the umpire refused.

Richie Benaud

Golf scores are directly proportional to the number of witnesses.

Robin Wilson

It was grand playing for Nottingham Forest. Brian Clough told me just to go out, get the ball, and give it to my Nigel.

Roy Keane

At one stage I gave up golf and took up ten-pin bowling for a while. At least I didn't lose so many balls.

Bob Hope

It's a pleasure to be standing up here. In fact it's a pleasure to be standing up.

George Best

Boxing got me started on philosophy. You bash them, they bash you and you think, what's it all for?

Arthur Mullard

Football is a very simple game. For ninety minutes, twenty-two men go running after the ball and at the end the Germans win.

Gary Lineker

My favourite event at the Wimbledon Tennis Championships is the mixed singles.

Des MacHale

The other advantage England have got when Phil Tufnell is bowling is that he isn't fielding.

Ian Chappell

My skill at slip is due to the fact that when I was quite young I made a boy, when out for a walk, throw stones into the hedge, and as the sparrows flew out, I caught them.

F. R. Spofforth

As the race wore on, his oar was dipping into the water nearly twice as often as any other.

Desmond Coke

Sport

We don't mind sitting around Wimbledon in the rain waiting for play, but the moment we see Cliff Richard, we're off.

David Stoneball

You can't stay married in a situation where you're afraid to go to sleep in case your wife might cut your throat.

Mike Tyson

A loving wife is better than making fifty at cricket or even ninety-nine; beyond that I will not go.

J. M. Barrie

Who needs the N.F.L. and their stupid "No Taunting" rule? You can hit a guy at full speed and put him in the hospital, but you can't say "Nah, nah! Quarterback has a big butt."

Drew Carey

Professional cricket coaching for women is a man trying to get you to keep your legs close together when other men had spent a lifetime trying to get them apart.

Rachel Heyhoe-Flint

They call it golf because all the other good four-letter words were already taken.

Lewis Grizzard

I've been writing a book for years. It's called *Horses That Owe Me Money*, and I haven't come to the end of it yet.

Sophie Tucker

Whatever you say to the referee, leave his mother out of it.

Jim Davis

The uglier a man's legs are, the better he plays golf. It's almost a law.

H. G. Wells

When you see a cricket coach, run off as fast as you can.

Bill O'Reilly

The last bowler to be knighted was Sir Francis Drake.

Alec Bedser

The Republic of Ireland have just one game plan. If Plan A fails, resort to Plan A.

Mark Lawrenson

Never put superglue in a bowling ball.

Fred Flintstone

Terry Venables has a choice of Gascoigne, Platt, Beardsley and Ince. Any of those would be in the Swiss side. I've got to pick between Sforza, Sforza and Sforza. I usually pick Sforza.

Roy Hodgson

I can bowl so slowly that if I don't like a ball I can run after it and bring it back.

J. M. Barrie

Sport

Ballet has always looked to me like football for girls. Both sports exist in a prolonged artificial prepubescence that gives the audience permission to exercise simple primary-playground emotions. Their practitioners remain in a neotenised childhood where bodies are artificially manipulated and the physical, moral and spiritual casualty rate is so high that in any other sphere of life they'd be banned as cruel.

A.A. Gill

As ducks go, that of Such was up there with the best.

Richard Hobson

Sex is a nicer activity than watching football: no nil–nil draws, no offside trap, no cup upsets and you're warm.

Nick Hornby

Derek Randall bats like an octopus with piles.

Matthew Engel

Alexi Lalas resembles the love child of Rasputin and Phyllis Diller.

Simon Ingram

The Bolivian football team leave me as baffled as Adam on Mother's Day.

Xavier Azkargorta

Ian Botham couldn't bowl a hoop downhill.

Fred Trueman

Wimbledon have changed their style. They are now kicking the ball fifty yards instead of sixty.

Mike Walker

When I lost the decathlon record, I took it like a man. I cried for a week.

Daley Thompson

The Duke of York got on very badly at Wimbledon. He was left-handed and the crowd tried to encourage him by calling out, "Try the other hand, sir."

Frank Pakenham

The mincing run-up of Merv Hughes resembles someone in high heels and a panty girdle chasing after a bus.

Martin Johnson

The only thing Ian Botham knows about dawn runs is coming back from parties.

Graham Gooch

Real golfers don't cry when they line up their fourth putt.

Karen Hurwitz

Confidence builds with successive putts. The putter, then, is a club designed to hit the ball partway to the hole.

Ring Lardner

Real golfers tape the Masters so they can go play themselves.

George Roope

Sport

With Ron Yeats at centre-half, we could play Arthur Askey in goal.

> Bill Shankly

I'm hitting the woods just great, but I'm having a terrible time getting out of them.

> Harry Toscano

The only advice my caddy gave me was to keep my putts low.

> Lee Trevino

Just as the Wimbledon umpire called 'New balls please', a male streaker dived over the net and did a forward roll on the court.

> Elizabeth Judge

Are there bunkers in St Andrew's?

> Tiger Woods

All professional athletes are bilingual. They speak English and profanity.

> Gordie Howe

I love women – my mother is a woman.

> Mike Tyson

A lot of horses get distracted – it's just human nature.

> Nick Zito

Sport

Football is not a contact sport; it is a collision sport. Dancing is a contact sport.

Vince Lombardi

I've read my husband David Beckham's autobiography from cover to cover. It's got some nice pictures.

'Posh Spice'

I have to exercise in the morning before my brain figures out what I'm doing.

Marsha Doble

After the Royal Command Performance, I asked the Queen if she was keen on football. When she replied that she was not very keen, I asked her if I could have her cup final tickets.

Tommy Cooper

He waltzed through the defence like a magician and shot like Tommy Cooper.

Len Shackleton

I think I was the best baseball player I ever saw.

Willie Mays

The racecourse is as level as a billiard ball.

John Francombe

Strangely, in the slow-motion replay the ball seemed to hang in the air for even longer.

David Acfield

Sport

With half the race gone, there is still half the race to go.

Murray Walker

Rugby League is the best sport in the world. It's got everything – speed and tough ugly men.

Terry O'Connor

Cycling is not a sport. It is sado-masochism on a major level.

David Miller

David Beckham cannot kick with his left foot, he cannot head a ball, he cannot tackle and he doesn't score many goals. Apart from that, he's all right.

George Best

Mansell can see him on his earphone.

Murray Walker

I like my baseball players to be married and in debt. That's the way you motivate them.

Ernie Banks

An oxymoron is when two contradictory concepts are juxtaposed such as in 'footballing brain'.

Patrick Murray

I bought a greyhound the other day. I'm going to race it. And by the look of it, I think I'd beat it.

Tommy Cooper

Sport

The new sliding roof on Wembley Stadium is designed to keep Gareth Southgate penalties in.

Angus Deayton

Well, either side could win it, or it could be a draw.

Ron Atkinson

The lead car is absolutely unique, except for the one behind it which is identical.

Murray Walker

If it doesn't fart or eat hay, my daughter isn't interested in it.

The Duke of Edinburgh

Apart from their three goals to our one, I thought we were the better team.

Jimmy Quinn

So many English football players go abroad and spend all their time in hotel rooms booking airline tickets and mainlining Marmite.

Simon Barnes

If you can't be an athlete, be an athletic supporter.

Eve Arden

I have been told I am the Nureyev of American football. Who the hell is Nureyev?

Jack Lambert

Sport

I can't imagine what kind of problem Senna has. I imagine it must be some sort of grip problem.

Murray Walker

Am I scared? Of course I'm scared. I'm scared I might kill Schmelling.

Joe Louis

We are going to turn this team around 360 degrees.

Jason Kidd

I was putting like a blind lobotomised baboon.

Tony Johnson

Baseball is 90 per cent mental. The other half is physical.

Yogi Berra

And Damon Hill is coming into the pit lane, yes, it's Damon Hill coming into the Williams pit, and Damon Hill in the pit, no, it's Michael Schumacher.

Murray Walker

I would not say that David Ginola is the best winger in the Premier Division but there is none better.

Ron Atkinson

The three saddest words in the English language: Partick Thistle, nil.

Billy Connolly

Sport

In women's tennis, the Williamses hate the Hingises, the
Hingeses hate the Williamses, Davenport hates Mauresmo
and everybody hates Kournikova.

Simon Barnes

The entire secret of my success is not to play snooker with a
lefthanded Welsh miner.

Ted Ray

I spent all day yesterday wading through streams and
dropping hooks into deep water. That's the last time I'm
going to waste playing golf.

Tommy Cooper

I think I fail a bit less than everyone else.

Jack Nicklaus

You've got to time your babies for the off-season and get
married in the off-season. Baseball always comes first.

Liz Mitchell

In the Bowling alley of Tomorrow, there will even be
machines that wear rental shoes and throw the ball for you.
Your sole function will be to drink beer.

Dave Barry

We've signed five foreigners over the summer but I'll be on
hand to learn them a bit of English.

Denis Wise

Theatre and Criticism

I have knocked everything in this play except the chorus
girls' knees, and there God anticipated me.

Percy Hammond

If laughter is contagious, my son has found the cure.

Les Dawson's mother

You wouldn't get away with that if my script writer was
here.

Bob Hope

I saw the play under adverse conditions – the curtain was up.

Robert Benchley

If there are any of you at the back who do not hear me, there
is no use raising your hands because I am also near-sighted.

W.H. Auden

Chevy Chase couldn't ad-lib a fart after a baked bean dinner.

Johnny Carson

A first night audience consists of the unburied dead.

Orson Bean

Critics are like eunuchs in a harem; they know exactly how
it should be done – they see it being done every night, but
they can't do it themselves.

Brendan Behan

Waiting For Godot is a play in which nothing happens, twice.

Vivian Mercier

The impact of the play was like the banging together of two
damp dish-cloths.

Brendan Behan

Two things in the play should have been cut. The second act and that youngster's throat.

Noel Coward

My agent gets ten per cent of everything I get, except the blinding headaches.

Fred Allen

The play was a great success, but the audience was a disaster.

Oscar Wilde

No one can have a higher opinion of him than I have – and I think he is a dirty little beast.

W.S. Gilbert

There is absolutely nothing wrong with Oscar Levant that a miracle cannot fix.

Alexander Woollcott

The central problem in *Hamlet* is whether the critics are mad or only pretending to be mad.

Oscar Wilde

He played the King as if he was afraid that at any moment someone would play the ace.

Eugene Field

Robert Mitchum does not so much act as point his suit at people.

Russell Davies

Go on writing plays my boy. One of these days a London producer will go into his office and say to his secretary, 'Is there a play from Shaw this morning?' and when she says 'No,' he will say, 'Well, then we'll have to start on the rubbish.' And that's your chance my boy.

George Bernard Shaw

The Roly-Poly dancers on my show were built in the days when meat was cheap.

Les Dawson

One hypothesis claims that there are only seven jokes – in which case Hale and Pace have not yet heard six of them.

Victor Lewis-Smith

Men go to the theatre to forget; women, to remember.

George Nathan

I observe just one old showbusiness tradition – never fart in a dressing-room without windows.

Norman Caley

The theatre was so empty night after night, monks started using it as a short cut to vespers.

Les Dawson

Bernard Manning is a generous man – he'd give you the tent off his back.

Jimmy Tarbuck

Nuns sing in cloisters. Miss Andrews (who plays Maria) sings in her bedroom. Christopher Plummer sings in self-defense.

Philip Oakes

The play *Halfway to Hell* grossly underestimates the distance.

Brooks Atkinson

A hand-picked cast will bring my childhood to life. They will tastefully re-enact my wedding night and Norm's first urological accident.

Edna Everage

I've never much enjoyed going to plays. The unreality of painted people standing on a platform saying things they've said to each other for months is more than I can overlook.

John Updike

The first qualification for a dramatic critic is the capacity to sleep while sitting bolt upright.

William Archer

A pizza with breasts, Weisz walked through the part as if she had cotton wool in her ears and had refused to read the rest of the script on the grounds that she wanted to keep lunch down.

A.A. Gill

The first time I saw The Goons, it suddenly struck me that comedy needn't be funny.

Alexei Sayle

Dean Martin's acting is so poor that even his impersonation of a drunk is unconvincing.

Harry Medved

The only time my friends laughed at me was when I told them I was going to become a comedian.

Robin Greenspan

For a man linked with satire, Peter Cook was without malice to anyone, although he did admit to pursuing an irrational vendetta against the late great Gracie Fields.

Richard Ingrams

There was a vaudeville actor who died and left an estate of eight hundred hotel and Pullman towels.

W. C. Fields

Ballet means paying a lot of money just to see buggers jump.

Nigel Bruce

My performance in *Hamlet* was not as bad as the critics claimed. I neither waved to my friends in the audience nor walked through the scenery.

Kenneth Tynan

Demi Moore's breasts hang around *Striptease* like a couple of silicon albatrosses.

Mark Steyn

Acting is merely the expression of a neurotic impulse. It's a bum's life. The principal benefit acting has afforded me is the money to pay for my psychoanalysis.

Marlon Brando

I was planning to go into architecture, but when I arrived at college registration, architecture was filled up. Acting was right next to it, so I signed up for acting instead.

Tom Selleck

Lillian Gish may be a charming person, but she is not
Ophelia. She comes on stage as if she had been sent out for
to sew rings on the new curtains.

Mrs. Patrick Campbell

Jamie Lee Curtis has trouble learning her lines because
English is not her first language. She doesn't, unfortunately,
have a first language.

John Cleese

Those big empty houses do not scare me: I was in vaudeville.

Bob Hope

Never forget what I am going to tell you: actors are crap.

John Ford

An actor who drinks is in a bad way; but the actor who eats
is lost.

George Bernard Shaw

Godspell is back in London. For those who missed it the first
time, this is a golden opportunity to miss it again.

Michael Billington

I'm glad you liked my portrayal of Catherine the Great. I
like her too. She ruled over thirty million people and had
three thousand lovers. I do the best I can in two hours.

Mae West

Sean Connery has such a deep love of Scotland that he refuses to use anything other than a Scottish accent no matter what the role he is taking.

Graham Norton

Borstal Boy is a show that will run on and on like a gurrier's nosebleed.

Hugh Leonard

Dying is easy. Comedy is hard.

Edmund Gwenn

When I get hold of Bette Davis, I will tear every hair out of her moustache.

Tallulah Bankhead

I was on tour with a review that played the Palace at Westcliff-on-Sea in Essex; the review in the local paper was headlined, "Another nail in the Palace coffin".

Roy Hudd

Roman Polanski is the five-foot Pole you wouldn't want to touch anyone with.

Kenneth Tynan

The promoters of the new technology say that this marks the first time that an entertainer who is no longer living has headlined a concert. Oh really? Have they never seen the Royal Variety Performance?

Richard Morrison

To say that Michael Winner is his own worst enemy is to provoke a ragged chorus from odd corners of the film industry of "Not while I'm alive."

Barry Norman

God was very good to the world when He took Miriam Hopkins from us.

Bette Davis

The word agent is the most disgusting word in the English language.

Peggy Ramsay

Rod Hull is a man who spends his evenings with his arm up a tatty old bird.

Paul Merton

The most famous building in the heart of Dublin is the architecturally undistinguished Abbey Theatre, once the city morgue and now entirely restored to its original purpose.

Frank O'Connor

Once seen, Walter Matthau's antique-mapped face is never forgotten: a bloodhound with a head cold, a man who is simultaneously biting on a bad lobster and caught by the neck in lift doors, a mad scientist's amalgam of Wallace Beer and Yogi Bear.

Alan Brien

Last year I was voted the best ventriloquist in Britain – by the British Lipreaders' Association.

David Dixon

You have to admire Madonna. She hides her lack of talent so well.

Manolo Blahnik

When I saw Dylan Thomas's *Under Milk Wood* on television, I thought that the best thing in the programme was the 20-minute breakdown.

George Murray

Your play is delightful, and there's nothing that can't be fixed.

Gertrude Lawrence

I saw 'Midsummer Night's Dream', which I had never seen before nor shall ever see again, for it is the most insipid, ridiculous play ever I saw in my life.

Samuel Pepys

I'm very proud of you. You managed to play the first act of *Blithe Spirit* tonight with all the Chinese flair and light–hearted brilliance of Lady Macbeth.

Noël Coward

George Bernard Shaw was the first man to have cut a swathe through the theatre and left it strewn with virgins.

Frank Harris

As a comedian I've got a lot of laughs – but mostly in bed.

Steve Martin

You can't accept one individual's criticism, particularly if the critic is female: when they get their period it's difficult for them to function as normal human beings.

Jerry Lewis

I'm not the first straight dancer or the last.

Mikhail Baryshnikov

Some directors couldn't direct lemmings off a cliff.

Doug Brod

I've seen better plots than *Break a Leg* in a cemetery.

Steward Klein

Thank you very much ladies and gentlemen. You've been 50 per cent.

Max Wall

Sarah Bernhardt had a clause in her contract forbidding animal acts to play with her, but she permitted W.C. Fields.

Mae West

June Whitfield has supported more actors than the Department of Health and Social Security.

Barry Took

Miscellaneous

Miscellaneous

The realisation that one is to be hanged in the morning concentrates the mind wonderfully.

Samuel Johnson

There is only one way to find out if a man is honest – ask him. If he says 'yes' he's not honest.

Groucho Marx

Never kick a fresh turd on a hot day.

Harry S. Truman

The kilt is an unrivalled garment for fornication and diarrhoea.

John Masters

A filing cabinet is a place where you can lose things systematically.

T.H. Thompson

The snowdrop is more powerful than the Panzer.

Beverley Nichols

Princess Anne is such an active lass. So outdoorsy. She loves nature in spite of what nature did to her.

Bette Midler

It is always the best policy to tell the truth, unless of course you happen to be an exceptionally good liar.

Jerome K. Jerome

The reports of my death have been greatly exaggerated.

Mark Twain

One morning I shot an elephant in my pyjamas. How he got in my pyjamas I'll never know.

Groucho Marx

Miscellaneous

I know the answer! The answer lies within the heart of mankind! The answer is twelve? I must be in the wrong book.

Charles Schultz

Summer has set in with its usual severity.

S. T. Coleridge

See the happy moron, he doesn't give a damn. I wish I were a moron: my God, perhaps I am.

R. Fairchild

Rumpers was a little man. He made no secret of his height.

Alan Bennett

Just how big a coward am I? Well I was on the Olympic team.

Bob Hope

I have too much respect for the truth to drag it out on every trifling occasion.

Mark Twain

Always look out for number one and be careful not to step in number two.

Rodney Dangerfield

Too intense contemplation of his own genius had begun to undermine his health.

Max Beerbohm

I used to sell furniture for a living. The trouble was, it was my own.

Les Dawson

I'm not afraid of heights but I'm afraid of widths.

Steven Wright

Miscellaneous

There is nothing safer than flying – it's crashing that is dangerous.

Theo Cowan

One, two, three
Buckle my shoe.

Robert Benchley

A pedestrian is anyone who is knocked down by a motor car.

J.B. Morton

I never forget a face, but in your case I'm willing to make an exception.

Groucho Marx

One should try everything once, except incest and folk-dancing.

Arnold Bax

The trouble with this country is that there are too many people going about saying 'The trouble with this country is ...'

Sinclair Lewis

If dirt was trumps, what a hand you would hold!

Charles Lamb

I resigned from the army after two weeks service in the field, explaining I was 'incapacitated by fatigue' through persistent retreating.

Mark Twain

A committee is a cul-de-sac into which ideas are lured and then quietly strangled.

John A. Lincoln

Miscellaneous

On a Polar expedition begin with a clear idea which Pole
you are aiming at, and try to start facing the right way. Choose
your companions carefully – you may have to eat them.

W.C. Sellar

Go, and never darken my towels again.

Groucho Marx

The toilet paper was composed of quartered sheets of typing
paper, with holes in one corner. These were covered in messages, many of them marked 'Secret' and some of them
marked 'Top Secret'.

Peter Ustinov

The human race, to which so many of my readers belong …

G.K. Chesterton

The dog was licking its private parts with the gusto of an
alderman drinking soup.

Graham Greene

Such time as he can spare from the adornment of his person
he devotes to the neglect of his duties.

Samuel Johnson

Always remember the poor – it costs nothing.

Josh Billings

'I'm very brave generally,' he went on in a low voice: 'only
today I happen to have a headache.'

Lewis Carroll

No problem is insoluble, given a big enough plastic bag.

Tom Stoppard

Death is psychosomatic.

Charles Manson

Miscellaneous

I had a terrific idea this morning but I didn't like it.

Samuel Goldwyn

Self-decapitation is an extremely difficult, not to say dangerous thing to attempt.

W.S. Gilbert

I don't know what effect these men will have upon the enemy, but, by God, they terrify me.

Duke of Wellington

The most hazardous part of our expedition to Africa was crossing Piccadilly Circus.

Joseph Thomson

I admire Cecil Rhodes, I frankly confess it; and when the time comes I shall buy a piece of the rope for a keepsake.

Mark Twain

The biggest fool in the world hasn't been born yet.

Josh Billings

Guy Burgess had the look of an inquisitive rodent emerging into daylight from a drain.

Harold Nicolson

A large body of men have expressed their willingness to serve in the Army against Napoleon subject to the condition that they should not be sent overseas – except I presume in case of invasion.

William Pitt

What happens to the holes when the Swiss cheese is eaten?

Bertolt Brecht

The lion and the calf shall lie down together but the calf won't get much sleep.

Woody Allen

Another victory like that and we are done for.

Pyrrhus

I have bad reflexes. I was once run over by a car being pushed by two guys.

Woody Allen

I can believe anything as long as it is incredible.

Oscar Wilde

The man who would stoop so low as to write an anonymous letter, the least he might do is to sign his name to it.

Boyle Roach

A man cannot be in two places at the same time unless he is a bird.

Boyle Roach

'I will only shake my finger at him,' he said, and placed it on the trigger.

Stanislaw J. Lec

No man is an island but some of us are pretty long peninsulas.

Ashleigh Brilliant

Underground we have coal for 600 years. Above it we have Mr Shinwell. Reversal of these positions would solve our present troubles.

R.A. Whitsun

According to the Law of the West, a Colt 45 beats four aces.

Bill Jones

Thanks to the interstate highway system, it is now possible to travel across the country from coast to coast without seeing anything.

Charles Kuralt

Those who built fortifications, moats and defences around castles seem to have had a blind spot about every castle's really vulnerable point – the gift shop. All a determined enemy had to do was to overpower the two old ladies who work there and the whole castle was soon taken.

Bill Bailey

I would like to die from hypothermia brought about by the breeze from my slave girls' ostrich feather fans.

Daire O'Brien

Though extremely fat when he appears in public, in private life Mr Chesterton is in fact quite slim.

Stephen Leacock

Celebrities have an obligation to have a cause to live for – I chose gay rights. I joined it and worked for it and then I quit; why? Because that organisation is infiltrated with homosexuals.

Steve Martin

I don't understand the police – how can they expect me to show them my driving licence when they took it away last year?

Gracie Allen

Miscellaneous

The proper office of a friend is to side with you when you are in the wrong. Nearly anybody will side with you when you are in the right.

Mark Twain

In 1802 every hereditary monarch was insane.

Walter Bagehot

You can cover it up, but you can never quite forget it, as the woman said as she pulled the hat down over her son's third eye.

Heinrich Hoffmann

Two women shouting at each other across the street from their top windows can never agree, because they are arguing from different premises.

Sydney Smith

Work is the greatest thing in the world, so we should always save some of it for tomorrow.

Don Herold

If you don't miss a few planes every year you are spending too much time at airports.

Paul Martin

This agoraphobic skinhead said to me 'OK, in'.

Alexei Sayle

Miscellaneous

So many pedestrians, so little time.

Robin Williams

There is nothing in the world I wouldn't do for Bob Hope and there is nothing he wouldn't do for me. And that's the way we spend our lives, doing nothing for each other.

Bing Crosby

Tom Seaver asked me what time it was, I said 'You mean now?'

Yogi Berra

Mail your packages early so the post office can lose them in time for Christmas.

Johnny Carson

I'd cross an Alp to see a village idiot of quality.

Norman Douglas

Everything comes to him who waits, except a loaned book.

Kin Hubbard

A friend of mine, Joe Parts, joined the army. He was immediately promoted to corporal.

Andy Collins

No admittance. Not even to authorised personnel.

Douglas Adams

Rush hour is when the traffic is almost at a standstill.

J.B. Morton

I might give up my life for my friend, but he had better not ask me to do up a parcel.

Logan Smith

I make jail so unpleasant that they won't even think about doing something that could bring them back.

Joe Arpaio

If aliens land in Washington, and park illegally, we will definitely give them tickets.

Kenny Bryson

It is no coincidence that in no known language does the phrase "As pretty as an airport" appear.

Douglas Adams

Moses dragged us for forty years through the desert to bring us to the one place in the Middle East where there was no oil.

Golda Meir

Infamy, infamy, they've all go it in for me.

Kenneth Williams

Excess on occasion is exhilarating. It prevents moderation from acquiring the deadening effect of a habit.

Somerset Maugham

Miscellaneous

If there was a little room somewhere in the British Museum that contained only about twenty exhibits and good lighting, easy chairs, and a notice imploring you to smoke, I believe I should become a museum man.

J.B. Priestley

I checked into a hotel and they had towels from my house.

Mark Guido

Gunner Octavian Neat would suddenly appear naked in a barrack room and say, 'Does anybody know a good tailor?' or 'Gentlemen – I thinks there's a thief in the battery'.

Spike Milligan

Nature played a cruel trick on her by giving her a waxed moustache.

Alan Bennett

A lie is a very poor substitute for the truth, but the only one discovered to date.

Mark Twain

The only solution to the violence problem is to take all the violent people out and shoot them.

Emo Philips

You know it's not a good wax museum if there are wicks coming out of people's heads.

Rick Reynolds

I never put on a pair of shoes until I've worn them for a few months.

Samuel Goldwyn

People are more violently opposed to fur than leather because it's safer to harass rich women then motorcycle gangs.

Alexei Sayle

I'm not concerned with all hell breaking loose, but that a part of hell will break loose. That would be much harder to detect.

George Carlin

Why does the Air Force need expensive new bombers? Have the people we've been bombing over the years been complaining?

George Wallace

For a while I didn't have a car – I had a helicopter. I had no place to park it, so I just tied it to a lamp post and left it running.

Steven Wright

No matter where you go, there you are.

Bob Topping

Let's have some new cliches.

Samuel Goldwyn

Miscellaneous

The main quality for membership of Brook's Club Library Committee would appear to be illiteracy qualified by absenteeism.

Geoffrey Madan

Members of the public committing suicide from the 140–foot tower on my estate do so at their own risk.

Gerald Tyrwhitt-Wilson

Dancing with her was like moving a piano.

Ring Lardner

She was beheaded, chopped into pieces and placed in a trunk, but she was not interfered with.

Nick Reaney

The committee will be composed of open-minded people who agree with me.

Edward McKita

Have you ever noticed how anybody going slower than you is an idiot while anybody going faster than you is a maniac?

George Carlin

You know you've made the wrong decision when the notice advertising vacancies is screwed to the front gate of the hotel.

Pat Blackford

I refuse to travel on any airline where the pilots believe in reincarnation.

Spalding Gray

I had all the spots removed from my dice for luck, but I remember where they formerly were.

Damon Runyon

Some of my jokes would make rhubarb grow.

Roy Brown

I have a warm place for you Charles; not in my heart, in my fireplace.

W. C. Fields

The worst bit of gossip I ever heard about myself was that I was having a gay affair with Arthur Mullard.

Roy Hudd

At no time is freedom of speech more precious than when a man hits his thumb with a hammer.

Marshall Lumsden

He was madder than Mad Jack McMad, winner of last year's madman contest.

Rowan Atkinson

This car can turn on a sixpence: whatever that is.

Nubar Gulbenkian

Miscellaneous

Prussian Field Marshal Prince Gebhard Leberecht von Blucher, whose timely intervention sealed Wellington's triumph at Waterloo, was convinced that he was pregnant with an elephant, fathered on him by a French soldier.

Geoff Tibballs

The sign said, "This door is not to be used as an entrance or an exit."

Gerald Hazzard

Sleep is like death without the long-term commitment.

Lea Krinsky

I was hitchhiking the other day and a hearse stopped. I said "No thanks, I'm not going that far."

Steven Wright

I have seen better organised creatures than you running around farmyards with their heads cut off.

John Cleese

My wife came home and said she had some good news and some bad news about the car. I said, "What's the good news?" She said, "The airbag works."

Roy Brown

The early bird may get the worm, but the second mouse gets the cheese.

Steven Wright

Any walk through a park that runs between a double line of mangy trees by the ladies' toilet is invariably known as "Lovers' Lane".

F. Scott Fitzgerald

I landed at Orly airport and discovered my luggage wasn't on the same plane. My bags were finally traced to Israel where they were opened and all my trousers were altered.

Woody Allen

Public transport should be avoided with exactly the same zeal that one accords to the avoidance of Herpes II.

Fran Lebowitz

If the remarks with which I am credited and never made are really good, I acknowledge them. I generally work myself into the belief that I originally said them.

Noel Coward

In the city a funeral is just a traffic obstruction; in the country it is a form of entertainment.

George Ade

Experience teaches that it doesn't.

Norman McCaig

Miscellaneous

World War Two wasn't good for much except for destroying Hitler and furthering Vera Lynn's career.

Alexei Sayle

When you have got an elephant by the hind leg, and he is trying to run away, it is best to let him run.

Abraham Lincoln

Hate mail is the only kind of letter that never gets lost by the Post Office.

Philip Kerr

You don't need to use a sledgehammer to crack a walnut, but it's a lot of fun trying.

Graham Keith

I'm a hero with coward's legs.

Spike Milligan

Show me a man with both feet on the ground and I'll show you a man who cannot put his pants on.

Arthur Watson

When just about everything is coming your way, you're obviously in the wrong lane.

Michael Caine

Nostalgia ain't what it used to be.

Yogi Berra

My last comment on leaving the Titanic was, "I rang for ice, but this is ridiculous."

Madeline Astor

Whenever I think of the past, it brings back so many memories.

Steven Wright

Eleven men well armed will certainly subdue one single man in his shirt.

Jonathan Swift

As the horsepower in modern automobiles steadily rises, the congestion of traffic steadily lowers the possible speed of your car. This is known as Progress.

Sydney J. Harris

The future ain't what it used to be.

Yogi Berra

Cavalry should be used in modern warfare to add a little tone to what would otherwise be a vulgar brawl.

Richard Winward

I knew I was going to take the wrong train, so I left early.

Yogi Berra

The most stupid thing I ever did was to put a knife in the fork drawer.

Bob Mortimer

I am not superstitious but I would not sleep thirteen to a bed on a Friday night.

Chauncey Depew

My grandfather fought in the First World War. He was shot in the Dardanelles: very painful.

Frankie Howerd

An unbiased opinion is always absolutely valueless.

Oscar Wilde

What is yellow and lies at the bottom of the Atlantic Ocean? Sand!

Rick Mayall

I am not arguing with you: I am telling you.

James McNeill Whistler

I wear a zebra: that's twenty-six sizes larger than an A bra.

Jo Brand

We are not retreating, merely advancing in another direction.

Douglas Adams

Garden catalogues are as big liars as house agents.

Rumer Godden

"Fragile" is usually interpreted by postal workers as "please throw underarm".

Morey Amsterdam

It is truth you cannot contradict; you can without any difficulty contradict Socrates.

Plato

In Connecticut, a prisoner on death row has gone on hunger strike. Now there's a problem that pretty much takes care of itself.

Jay Leno

He who lives by the sword will eventually be wiped out by some bastard with a sawn-off shotgun.

Steady Eddy

Club 18-30 holidays: you know they're referring to I.Q. there, don't you?

Ben Elton

The other day I... No, that wasn't me.

Steven Wright

I am confused as a baby in a topless bar.

Betty Black

You can't learn too soon that the most useful thing about a principle is that it can always be sacrificed to expediency.

Somerset Maugham

A doorman is a genius who can open the door of your car with one hand, help you in with the other, and still have one left for the tip.

Dorothy Kilgallen

Cab drivers are living proof that practice does not make perfect.

Howard Ogden

The quietest place in the world is the complaint department at the parachute packing plant.

Jackie Martling

Airline hostesses show you how to use a seat belt in case you haven't been in a car since 1965.

Jerry Seinfeld

There is only one thing about which I am certain and that is that there is nothing about which one can be certain.

Somerset Maugham

Never approach a bull from the front, a horse from the rear or a fool from any direction.

Ken Alstad

I was reading in this book that the first tube station ever opened was Baker Street in 1863. What was the point of that? Where would you go?

Paul Merton

I went into the hardware store and bought some used paint. It was in the shape of a house.

Steven Wright

He called me a fatalist, but I'd never collected a postage stamp in my life.

Yogi Berra

The most difficult things for a man to do are to climb a wall leaning towards you, to kiss a girl leaning away from you, and to make an after-dinner speech.

Winston Churchill

I pray that there's intelligent life somewhere out there in space because there's bugger all down here on earth.

Eric Idle

All cats should be muzzled outside to stop the agonising torture of mice and small birds.

Viscount Monckton

The Devil himself has probably redesigned Hell in the light of information he has gained from observing airport layouts.

Anthony Price

My daughter was tragically abducted by wombats.

Edna Everage

A special evacuation medal should be presented to all survivors of the Crete campaign. It should be inscribed simply EX CRETA.

Evelyn Waugh

Queen Victoria is more of a man than I expected.

Henry James

How is it that the first piece of luggage on the airport carousel never belongs to anyone?

George Roberts

The first rule of comedy is not to perform in a town where they still point at aeroplanes.

Bobby Mills

On one occasion I drove a car into the wall of my house which failed to take evasive action.

John Mortimer

Soldiers who wish to be a hero
Are practically zero.
But those who wish to be civilians
Jesus they run into millions.

Norman Rosten

It is not a bomb; it is a device which is exploding.

Jacques Le Blanc

Miscellaneous

At Houdini's funeral I bet a hundred bucks that he wasn't in the coffin.

Charles Dillingham

Most of us know instinctively that the phrase 'trust me, light this fuse' is a recipe for disaster.

Wendy Northcutt

The most dangerous thing in a combat zone is an officer with a map.

Patrick Murray

Captain Hook died because he wiped with the wrong hand.

Tommy Sledge

He had a fine head of dandruff.

Spike Milligan

Wife unable to obtain bidet for shipment from Paris. Suggest handstand in shower.

Billy Wilder

Being a hero is one of the shortest-lived professions there is.

Will Rogers

If we lose this war, I'll start another in my wife's name.

Moshe Dayan

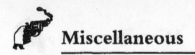

Courage is often lack of insight, whereas cowardice in many cases is based on good information.

Peter Ustinov

It is time for the human race to enter the solar system.

Dan Quayle

In response to a holiday query, I received the following reply: 'Standing among savage scenery, the hotel offers stupendous revelations. There is a French widow in every bedroom, affording delightful prospects.'

Gerard Hoffnung

Every night for the last eight years I've sat in my house staring at the rug trying to move it by telekinesis. It hasn't moved an inch. But the house is gone.

Steven Wright

It gets late early out here.

Yogi Berra

I have just read in your magazine that I am dead. Don't forget to delete me from your list of subscribers.

Rudyard Kipling

This guy came up to me in the street and said, 'Do you mind if I ask you a question?' I said to him 'Didn't give me much of a choice there buddy, did you?'

Steven Wright

I met Colonel House, the great little man who can be silent in several languages.

James Harbord

The results of psychology experiments apply only to the participants – first-year college psychology students.

Patrick Murray

I like to skydive horizontally.

Steven Wright

Mrs Santa Claus is very upset because her husband has a list of the names of all the really bad girls.

Robin Williams

If you tell a joke in the forest, but nobody laughs, was it a joke?

Steven Wright

It doesn't beggar well for the future.

Henry McLeish

Have you noticed that all hot-water bottles look like Henry the Eighth?

Max Beerbohm

If you can't imitate him, don't copy him.

Yogi Berra

It was a three-star hotel – I could see them through the roof.

Frankie Howard

I started using Grecian 2000 and now I look like a 2000-year-old Greek.

Roy Brown

Airplane travel is Nature's way of making you look like your passport photograph.

Al Gore

Whose cruel idea was it for the word 'lisp' to have an 's' in it?

Chris Maude

In the army I joined the Tank Corps because I preferred to go into battle sitting down.

Peter Ustinov

Put procrastination off until tomorrow.

Steven Wright

I picked up the phone and said, 'Is this the local swimming baths?' A voice said, 'That all depends where you're ringing from.'

Tommy Cooper

I always wear battledress. It is practical, simple, cheap and does not go out of fashion.

Fidel Castro

Miscellaneous

You can take a horse to water, but a pencil must be lead.

Stan Laurel

Wars teach us not to love our enemies but to hate our allies.

W. L. George

Don't use shampoo – use the real thing.

Rodney Dangerfield

His eminence was due to the flatness of the surrounding landscape.

John Stuart Mill

A tombstone is the only thing that can stand upright and lie on its face at the same time.

Mary Little

Ferdinand Foch is just a frantic pair of moustaches.

T. E. Lawrence

Never get yourself into a position where the only escape route is vertically upwards.

George Patton

Why do they lock gas station bathrooms? Are they afraid someone will clean them?

Jerry Seinfeld

Miscellaneous

No man is an island, but six men bound together make quite an effective raft.

Jo Brand

The models were so nervous backstage they were keeping their food down.

Jack Dee

You know something? Dogs go through life and they never have any money. Not a cent! And do you know why? No pockets.

Jerry Seinfeld

I don't dance, but I'd love to hold you while you do.

Leslie Phillips

The bowling ball is the natural enemy of the egg.

Michael Davis

According to most studies, people's number one fear is public speaking. Number two is death.

Jerry Seinfeld

Jeremy Clarkson claims to be able to tell the make of car he is driving while blindfolded.

A. A. Gill

Miscellaneous

Imagine if there were no hypothetical situations.

John Mendosa

I've often wondered, do kippers swim folded or flat?

Ken Dodd

Matt Busby was the eternal optimist. In 1968 he still hoped Glenn Miller was just missing.

Pat Crerand

A legend is a lie that has attained the dignity of age.

H. L. Mencken

I don't give a damn what colour you are so long as you get out there and kill those sonsofbitches in green suits.

George S. Patton

We who are about to die are going to take one hell of a lot of bastards with us.

Joel Rosenberg

Something tells me that they probably screwed up and named Murphy's Law after the wrong guy.

Doug Finney

Index

Index

Abbey, Edward 223
Abernathy, F.W. 147
Abernathy, Ralph 381
Ace, Jane 301
Achard, Marcel 218
Acheson, Dean 29
Adams, Douglas 64, 74, 387, 518, 519, 528, 539
Adams, Franklin P. 65, 150, 159, 385
Adams, Henry 400, 411
Adams, James T. 147
Adams, Joey 32, 157, 169
Adams, Scott 37, 159, 351, 390, 460
Adams, Tony 65
Addison, Joseph 146
Ade, George 68, 148, 251, 252, 314, 315, 462, 468, 525
Adler, Alfred 212
Adler, Richard 275
Aesop 389, 403
Aga Khan III 51
Agate, James 39, 204, 254, 289, 453
Agee, James 267, 289
Aitken, Jonathan 87
Alas, Leopoldo 74
Alexander, Hilary 15
Algren, Nelson 467
Ali, Mohammed 476, 477
Allen, Dave 407
Allen, Fred 49, 107, 109, 251, 257, 263, 297, 471, 499
Allen, George 469
Allen, Gracie 98, 129, 171, 223, 311, 516
Allen, Steve 276
Allen, Woody 17, 26, 27, 68, 70, 83, 109, 111, 148, 151, 176, 179, 198, 199, 201, 203, 204, 205, 206, 216, 272, 284, 294, 314, 340, 351, 357, 371, 410, 411, 413, 417, 444, 468, 475, 515, 525
Allen Smith, H. 54
Alsop, Joseph 402
Alstad, Ken 237, 305, 530
Altman, Steve 59
Altringham, Lord 414
Aman, Reinhold 360
Amis, Kingsley 49, 63, 188, 324, 351, 370, 410

Amory, Cleveland 24
Anderson, Pamela 273
Anderson, Sherwood 133
Annan, Lord 85
Arafat, Yasser 345, 384
Arbuthnot, John 381
Aristotle 415
Armey, Richard 343
Armor, Joyce 179
Armour, Richard 93, 190
Armstrong, Louis 427
Armstrong, Robert 404
Arnold, Tom 82, 130, 211
Arthur, Jean 276
Ash, Russell 129
Ashcroft, Linda 17
Asimov, Isaac 79, 124
Asquith, Cyril 19
Asquith, Margot 448, 454
Astor, Madeline 527
Astor, Mary 283
Astor, Nancy 207
Atell, Dave 161
Athenaeus 52
Atkinson, Ron 493, 494
Atkinson, Rowan 54, 134, 164, 346, 437, 523
Attenborough, Richard 404
Aubrey, John 310
Auden, W.H. 94, 130, 498
Augustine, St 200, 245
Austin, Alfred 230

Bagehot, Walter 517
Bagley, Desmond 69
Bailey, Bill 516
Bailey, Sydney B. 392
Bainbridge, Beryl 126
Baker, Danny 270
Baker, James 407
Baker, Russell 178, 362, 390
Baldwin, Stanley 78
Ball, Lucille 90, 159
Ball, Zoe 220
Ballesteros, Seve 84
Balzac, Honoré de 198, 201, 344, 452
Bankhead, Tallulah 85, 157, 258, 289, 445, 451, 504

Index

Banks-Smith, Nancy 77, 444
Barbi, Shane 282
Bareham, Lindsey 96
Barfield, Mike 97, 175, 267
Barr, Roseanne 172, 177, 199, 225, 228, 233, 234, 241, 243, 304, 428
Barrie, J.M. 146, 486, 487
Barry, Dave 14, 21, 38, 60, 61, 73, 93, 105, 111, 163, 173, 175, 179, 182, 189, 192, 193, 222, 235, 239, 262, 277, 278, 300, 306, 349, 350, 354, 388, 389, 415, 436, 439, 470, 478, 483, 495
Barrymore, John 218
Bartholomew, Cecilia 122
Baruch, Bernard 185
Barzan, Gerald 37
Bassett, Dave 475
Bateman, Michael 338
Bateson, Dingwall 110
Battie, William 444
Baudelaire, Charles 117, 366
Baughman, Dale 193
Baxter, Alida 206
Baxter, Beverley 255
Bean, Sean 482
Beardsley, Peter 477
Beckett, Samuel 70, 132, 174
Beckham, David 426
Beckham, Victoria 491
Beecham, Thomas 13, 51, 314, 315, 316, 317, 321, 323, 325, 327, 330, 370
Beerbohm, Max 13, 83, 94, 116, 128, 139, 147, 209, 251, 511, 535
Beerbohm Tree, Herbert 252, 294, 422
Beethoven, Ludwig van 316
Behan, Brendan 46, 102, 118, 135, 182, 210, 251, 267, 292, 329, 336, 337, 339, 340, 353, 412, 419, 422, 423, 454, 462, 498
Behan, Brian 54
Behan, Dominic 428
Behan, Stephan 169
Bell, Ian 58
Belloc, Hilaire 132
Benaud, Richie 484
Benchley, Robert 64, 83, 109, 115, 177, 354, 446, 467, 498, 512

Bennett, Alan 72, 114, 125, 147, 307, 459, 511, 520
Bennett, Arnold 161
Bennett, Billy 232
Bennett, James 289
Benny, Jack 206
Benson, A.C. 418
Bentley, Dick 192
Bergman, George 449
Bergman, Ross 307, 329
Bergman, Stefan 68
Berk, Ronald 141
Berkman, Marcus 133
Berle, Milton 38, 55, 133, 174, 191, 233, 285, 304, 363, 423
Berlin, Irving 328
Bernal, John 417
Bernard, Jeffrey 51, 53, 56, 277, 292, 358, 419
Bernard, Peter 275
Berne, Eric 309
Bernstein, Sheryl 37
Bernthsen, Pierre 105
Berra, Yogi 32, 91, 211, 260, 320, 450, 466, 469, 470, 472, 474, 479, 483, 494, 518, 526, 527, 531, 534, 538
Best, George 51, 58, 273, 485, 492
Beswick, Richard 130
Betts, Hannah 195
Bevin, Ernest 187, 404
Bhoy, Danny 59, 369
Bierce, Ambrose 32, 48, 62, 71, 85, 140, 175, 180, 194, 204, 205, 207, 314, 341, 400, 444
Billings, Josh 27, 65, 194, 210, 414, 514
Billington, Michael 503
Binder, Mike 239
Bing, Rudolf 330
Binstead, Arthur 175
Bishop, Jim 147
Bissonette, David 229
Björk 480
Blackford, Pat 522
Blair, Tony 391
Blezard, William 316
Blom, Eric 317
Blount, Roy 21

Index

Blundell, William 130
Blunt, Wilfred 13
Boardwell, Geoff 321
Body, Sidney 307
Bogart, Humphrey 287
Bohr, Niels 432
Bolitho, William 370
Bombeck, Erma 150, 156, 159, 165, 172, 189, 192, 195, 243, 302
Boone, Pat 218
Boorstin, Daniel J. 255
Boothroyd, Basil 170, 184
Boren, Jim 308
Borenstein, David 304
Borge, Victor 153, 319
Borges, Jorge Luis 125
Boswell, James 141
Boucicault, Dion 201
Boulez, Pierre 319
Boulton, Adam 460
Bowie, David 326
Bowler, Sheila 266
Bowles, Colin 292
Bowra, Maurice 203, 242, 459
Boxer, Barbara 366
Boyd, Tommy 329
Boyle, Hal 216
Bradbury, Grace 232
Bradbury, Malcolm 163, 382
Braddon, Russell 121
Brand, Jo 55, 94, 131, 135, 185, 189, 193, 211, 226, 229, 231, 242, 247, 310, 403, 423, 528, 538
Brando, Marlon 428, 502
Branson, Richard 35, 38
Brayfield, Celia 136
Brecht, Bertolt 514
Breden, Bernard 120
Brenan, Gerald 139
Brenner, David 96
Bresson, Robert 318
Brien, Alan 70, 505
Brilliant, Ashleigh 515
Britton, Noel 92
Brodie, John 41
Brogan, Denis 171, 396
Brooks, Mel 97, 143, 168, 281, 427

Brooks, Tony 399
Brougham, Henry 103
Broughton, James 208
Broughton, Rhoda 218, 456
Broughton, Robert 129
Brown, Arnold 246
Brown, Craig 137
Brown, George 413
Brown, Joe E. 228
Brown, Larry 216
Brown, Rita Mae 20, 433
Brown, Roy 'Chubby' 57, 94, 188, 202, 219, 247, 467, 523, 524, 536
Brown, Tom 52
Bruce, Nigel 502
Bruce, Peter 326
Bruno, Frank 479
Bryne, Jason 309
Bryson, Bill 143, 357, 365, 373
Buchan, John 356
Buchwald, Art 393
Buckley, William F. 30, 34
Bukowski, Charles 270
Buñuel, Luis 412
Burchill, Julie 14, 210, 235, 282
Burden, Martin 48
Buren, Abigail Van 214
Burford, Anne 364
Burgen, Stephen 60
Burgess, Anthony 136, 198
Burgess, Tony 99
Burns, George 43, 52, 91, 152, 153, 154, 172, 175, 177, 185, 186, 214, 215, 229, 297, 456, 461
Burns, Robert 130
Bus, Ralph 146
Bush, George W. 36, 187, 406
Butler, Samuel 54, 150, 240, 363, 410
Butler, Tony 48, 341
Buttons, Red 186
Bygraves, Max 349
Byrne, Robert 162, 199

Caen, Herb 99, 417
Caine, Michael 526
Callow, Simon 284
Calsher, Hortense 226

Cameron, James 286
Cameron, Simon 379
Campbell, Mrs Patrick 204
Campbell, Roy 139
Campbell, Thomas 135
Camus, Albert 157
Cannon, Dyan 254
Cape, Jonathan 133
Caplan, Mortimer 31
Capone, Al 338
Capote, Truman 116, 123, 366
Capp, Al 12
Caracciolo, Francesco 336
Carey, Mariah 365, 366
Carlin, George 64, 180, 274, 344, 521, 522
Carlin, Kim 134
Carlyle, Thomas 79, 355
Carpenter, Humphrey 143
Carr, Barbara 402
Carritt, David 16
Carrott, Jasper 277
Carson, Ciarán 349
Carson, Frank 240, 353, 367
Carson, Johnny 184, 221, 360, 372, 498, 518
Carter, Billy 62, 195
Carter, Judith 216
Carter, Lillian 192, 382
Caruso, Dorothy 327
Cary, Joyce 198
Cassel, Paul 281
Cecil, Mary 220
Cerf, Bennett 70
Chamfort, Sébastien Roch Nicolas 127
Chan, Charlie 92, 434
Chandler, Raymond 278, 347, 457
Chanel, Coco 223
Chandler, Raymond 199
Chaplin, Charlie 427
Chappell, Ian 18
Charlton, Jack 347
Cheever, John 304
Chekhov, Anton 13, 19, 103
Cher 166
Cherry, Don 469
Chesterfield, Lord 171, 202
Chesterton, G.K. 18, 410, 411, 412, 419, 424, 445, 513

Chiene, John 292
Christenson, Gary 243
Christie, Linford 480
Churchill, Randolph 397
Churchill, Winston 16, 57, 76, 84, 178, 345, 356, 380, 383, 384, 385, 388, 402, 406, 418, 446, 531
Ciampi, Carlo 395
Ciardi, John 49
Cicero 142
Clancy, Tom 140, 284, 388
Clark, Alan 54, 82, 167, 181
Clark, Jane 236, 454
Clark, Steven 73
Clarke, John 76
Clarkson, Jeremy 58, 107, 168, 240, 311, 364, 368
Cleary, Dominic 367, 384
Cleese, John 269, 503, 524
Clemenceau, Georges 337
Cleveland, John 359
Clough, Brian 364, 481
Cobb, Irvin 295
Cockburn, Claud 257
Coe, Sebastian 473
Coffin, Harold 73, 76
Cohen, George M. 275
Cohen, Marvin 469
Coke, Desmond 485
Coleman, David 259, 474
Coleridge, S.T. 314, 511
Coles, Joanna 110
Collins, J.C. 69
Collins, Phil 240
Collins, Wilkie 215
Collinson, Stuart 361
Colombo, John Robert 336
Colton, Charles 418
Colum, Padraig 207
Congreve, William 241, 422
Conley, Brian 237, 367
Connelly, Mary 330
Connery, Sean 265
Connolly, Billy 36, 60, 363, 494
Connolly, Cyril 123, 345, 444
Conway, Tim 216
Coogan, Steve 352

Index

Cook, Sherwin 387
Cooke, Alistair 241
Coolidge, Calvin 380
Cooper, Diana 298
Cooper, Gary 274
Cooper, Jilly 131, 154
Cooper, Tommy 12, 231, 310, 491, 492, 495, 536
Cope, Wendy 228, 241
Copland, Aaron 320, 339
Coren, Alan 28, 35, 349
Cornford, Francis 85
Cosby, Bill 39, 86, 190
Costello, Lou 241
Coward, Noel 19, 46, 127, 128, 148, 223, 227, 252, 253, 270, 271, 294, 324, 325, 331, 343, 447, 455, 457, 499, 506, 525
Cox, Chris 321
Craddock, Johnny 97
Crawford, Joan 258, 269
Crerand, Pat 539
Crisp, Quentin 19, 26, 103, 124, 146, 157, 180, 181, 212, 225, 338, 339, 360, 424, 449, 473
Critchley, Julian 119
Crompton, Colin 105
Crooks, Garth 482
Crosby, Bing 518
Crosland, T.W. 340
Crow, Frank 295
cummings, e.e. 117
Cummins, Danny 333
Cuppy, Will 198, 200, 303
Curran, John F. 104
Curry, Tim 434
Curtis, Jamie Lee 85
Curtis, Tony 230, 272, 478
Cytron, Sara 110

Dahlberg, Edward 181
Dale, Iain 349, 385
Dali, Salvador 12, 16, 21
Daly, Mary 232
Dane, Frank 134, 384
Dangerfield, Rodney 31, 91, 149, 192, 199, 221, 226, 238, 242, 244, 268, 296, 308, 469, 511, 537

Davenport, Lizzi 321
Davidson, Brenda 80, 82, 178, 233
Davies, Alan 77, 96, 108
Davis, Angela 405
Davis, Bette 229, 250, 505
Davies, Bob 63
Davies, Edward 108
Davies, Hunter 176
Davies, Robertson 78, 142
Davies, Russell 499
Davies, Stan Gebler 355
Davis, Bette 200, 269
Davis, Bob 134
Davis, Sammy Jr 326
Davis, Steve 476
Dawson, Les 156, 176, 205, 207, 208, 214, 224, 308, 463, 500, 511
Day, Clarence 354
Day, Lillian 199, 365
De Gaulle, Charles 179, 345, 356, 362
de Havilland, Olivia 226
de Manio, Jack 253
De Mille, Cecil B. 140
de Witt, George 117
Deayton, Angus 278, 493
DeBarri, Girald 371
Debussy, Claude 331
Dedopulos, Tim 108, 219
Dee, Jack 32, 538
Deering, Jo-Ann 106
Deford, Frank 257
Degas, Hilaire 18
DeGeneres, Ellen 184
DeLillo, Don 228
Denham, John 137
Denning, Lord 107
Dent, Alan 316
Depardieu, Gerard 240
Desmond, Barry 403
Deukmejian, George 401
Deutsch, André 35
Dewar, Isla 184
Dewar, Lord 107
Diabolus, Dick 314
Dickens, Charles 27, 110, 161, 238, 355
Dickey, James 140
Dicks, Terence 350

Index

Dickson, Paul 84
Dickson, Rhonda 245
Dietrich, Marlene 263
Dietz, Howard 323
Diller, Phyllis 41, 71, 146, 147, 154, 156, 157, 183, 195, 206, 208, 229, 236, 238, 245, 277, 308, 428
Dillon, James 379
Dimmet, Ernest 20
Dior, Christian 235
Disraeli, Benjamin 116, 118, 381, 457
Dix, Dorothy 202
Dixon, John 39
Dobie, J.F. 69
Docherty, Tommy 165, 218, 471, 472
Dodd, Ken 43, 68, 171, 234, 296, 539
Dodds, Bill 111
Dole, Bob 351
Douglas, Kirk 259
Douglas, Michael 289
Drake, Francis 470
Driscoll, Margarette 395
Driver, Christopher 90
Dumas, Alexandre 207, 214, 448
Dunne, Finley Peter 27, 35, 187, 301, 419, 468
Dunne, Philip 276
Dunstan, Keith 351
Durant, Will 394
Durante, Jimmy 106, 130, 151, 325
Durrell, Gerald 128
Durrell, Lawrence 71
Durst, Will 203
Dutton, Dave 49

Eagleton, Terry 326, 363, 366
East, Ray 398
Eastwood, Clint 280
Eaton, Hal 257
Ebersole, Lucinda 425
Eclair, Jenny 187, 309
Eco, Umberto 441
Edgeworth, Maria 357
Edwards, Bob 380
Edwards, David 422
Edwards, Jimmy 358
Edwards, Oliver 412
Ehrenreich, Barbara 82, 175, 327, 396

Eisenhower, Dwight D. 412
Eliot, Charles W. 71
Eliot, T.S. 115, 135, 137, 166, 326
Ellis, H.F. 432
Elton, Ben 529
Emerson, Ralph Waldo 72, 79, 385, 449
Enderbery, Keppel 347
English, Alan 122
Enright, D.J. 123
Erasmus, Desiderius 428
Erskine, Lord 32
Ertz, Susan 411
Esar, Evan 160
Espy, Willard 304
Estrada, Joseph 221
Ettinger, Bob 243
Euripides 446
Evans, Edith 205
Evarts, William 59
Everage, Edna 128, 162, 297, 306, 501, 531
Ewing, Sam 166
Ewing, Winnie 405

Fadiman, Clifton 138
Falwell, Jerry 253
Farmer, Tom 174
Faulkner, William 60
Fawlty, Basil 480
Fay, Liam 276
Fechtner, Leopold 191
Fegg, Eugene 165
Feldman, Marty 453
Felton, Bruce 50
Fiebig, Jim 319
Fielding, Fenella 217
Fielding, Henry 199, 213
Fields, D. 253
Fields, Totie 95, 96
Fields, W.C. 26, 33, 34, 46, 47, 48, 50, 54, 55, 56, 57, 58, 59, 60, 61, 63, 64, 90, 148, 149, 151, 164, 166, 167, 169, 182, 200, 209, 219, 220, 223, 240, 270, 300, 301, 322, 352, 353, 370, 379, 411, 436, 446, 455, 463, 502, 523
Finney, Doug 539
Fischer, Martin 302, 311
Fisher, Geoffrey 108

Index

Fiterman, Linda 245
Fitzgerald, F. Scott 48, 420, 525
Flaherty, Joe 57
Flanner, Janet 460
Flaubert, Gustave 319
Fleming, Alexander 438
Fleming, Peter 19
Flintstone, Fred 487
Flowers, Gennifer 282
Floyd, Keith 62
Follian, John 302
Fonda, Henry 286
Foote, Samuel 47
Forbes, Malcolm S. 450
Ford, Gerald 483
Ford, Harrison 273, 371
Ford, Henry 433
Ford, John M. 162, 5-3
Foreman, George 476
Forsyth, Bruce 323
Fountain, John 341
Fowler, Gene 115
Fowler, Mark 344
Fox, Henry 38
Fox, Michael J. 306, 418
Foxworthy, Jeff 73
Foy, Christopher 97
Francis, Gerry 268
Francis, Neil 478
Francis, Stu 55, 324
Frankau, Pamela 342
Franklin, Benjamin 24, 156
Fraser, Kenneth 343
Freed, Arthur 370
Freud, Clement 458
Freud, Sigmund 178, 234, 440
Friedman, Kinky 57
Frost, David 168
Frost, Robert 28, 116
Frye, David 382
Fuentes, Carlos 342
Fuglie, Lisa 319
Fuller, Thomas 83
Furgol, Ed 25

Gabor, Zsa Zsa 170, 204, 211, 216, 224, 227
Galbraith, J.K. 32, 395

Gallagher, Tom 264
Galsworthy, John 246
Gandhi, Mahatma 341
Gardner, Hy 173
Garland, Judy 257
Garner, J.N. 383, 407
Gasset, Jose Ortega y 358
Gathorne-Hardy, Jonathan 359
Gauguin, Paul 13
Geiss, Ralph 125
Geneen, Harold 39
Generis, Ellen de 155
George I, King 21
George V, King 199
George, Charlie 226
George, Raymond 50, 56
Gerard, Jasper 324
Getty, Estelle 212
Getty, J. Paul 39, 40
Giachini, Walt 295
Gibbon, Edward 407
Gibson, Mel 282
Gide, André 343
Gilbert, W.S. 304, 333, 386, 499, 514
Gill, A.A. 16, 81, 93, 209, 258, 261, 262, 263, 265, 268, 269, 280, 281, 353, 365, 440, 488, 501, 538
Gillespie, Dizzy 331
Gingold, Hermione 228, 231
Ginsberg, Allen 360
Glass, Senator 406
Gleason, Jackie 301
Glyn, Elinor 348
Gobel, George 57
Godard, Jean-Luc 17, 253
Goddard, Bob 237
Gogarty, Oliver St. John 361, 373
Goldman, William 33
Goldsmith, James 201
Goldwyn, Samuel 19, 25, 31, 125, 251, 252, 254, 255, 259, 261, 263, 264, 265, 271, 276, 286, 294, 299, 332, 333, 470, 514, 521
Goncourt, Edmond de 90
Gooch, Graham 489
Gordon, George 340
Gordon, Richard 236, 294, 303, 305

Gore, Arthur 102
Gorman, Teresa 391
Gow, Ian 165
Grade, Lew 288
Graffoe, Boothby 361
Graham, Billy 102
Graham, Harry 148
Grant, C.K. 27
Grant, Cary 37, 294
Grant, Lee 387
Grant, Ulysses S. 323
Graves, Robert 140
Green, Benny 467
Green, John 401
Greene, Graham 288, 456, 513
Greener, Bill 253
Greenspan, Robin 501
Greer, Germaine 103, 227, 230, 365
Gregory, Dick 49, 374
Grizzard, Lewis 95, 96, 172, 185, 193, 235
Groening, Matt 386
Guardia, Fiorello la 396
Guftason, John 402
Guichard, Jean 200
Guinness, Alec 117
Guitry, Sacha 203
Gulbenkian, Nubar 523
Gunther, John 177, 362

Hackett, Buddy 97
Hagen, Walter 34
Hagman, Larry 378
Haig, Douglas 371
Hailey, Arthur 40
Hall, Albert 216
Halsey, Margaret 342
Hamilton, Alex 14, 15
Hancock, Tony 143, 303
Hand, Eoin 479
Handelsman, David 75
Handey, Jack 60, 77, 105, 158, 244, 298, 321, 456
Hanley, Clifford 417
Hardiman, Larry 389
Harding, Mike 47, 95, 332, 478
Hardy, Thomas 396
Harney, Bill 98

Harris, Frank 506
Harris, George 78, 85
Harris, Joel C. 183
Harris, Phil 49
Harris, Nikki 18
Harris, Sydney 435, 527
Harrison, George 323
Hart, Gary 398
Hartford, Robert 320
Haskins, Ernest 42
Hassett, Neil 275
Hastings, Max 252
Hastings, Selina 98
Hatherill, G.H. 205
Hawkes, Nigel 435
Hawkins, Anthony 421
Hawkins, Paul 56, 64
Healey, Denis 380, 400, 406
Healy, Maurice 106
Healy-Rae, Jackie 357
Hecht, Ben 250
Heffer, Eric 379
Hegel, G.W. 413
Heifetz, Jascha 321
Heine, Heinrich 12, 293, 447
Heller, Joseph 310
Helms, Jesse 51
Helpman, Robert 369
Hemingway, Ernest 131, 257
Henderson, Leon 26
Henry, Lenny 358
Henry, O. 447
Henry, Simon 368
Hepburn, Katharine 227
Herbert, A.P. 20, 109, 250, 252, 400
Herbert, James 395
Herford, Oliver 52, 114, 156, 201, 336
Herold, Don 293
Heston, Charlton 286
Heyhoe-Flint, Rachel 486
Hicks, Seymour 26
Hill, Benny 250, 281
Hill, Harry 186, 440
Hills, Dick 241
Hills, Reginald 128
Hilton, Nicky 207
Hirohito, Emperor 338

 **Index**

Hirschfeld, Al 21
Hirst, Damien 17, 21
Hislop, Ian 480
Hitchcock, Alfred 285
Hitler, Adolf 12, 382
Hoban, Russell 329
Hobbes, Halliwell 77
Hobsbawm, Eric 346
Hoffnung, Gerard 367, 534
Hoggart, Paul 217, 325
Hoggart, Simon 152
Holden, William 142
Hollander, John 90
Hood, Thomas 99, 348
Hoover, Herbert 27
Hope, Bob 42, 153, 158, 165, 172, 183, 200,
    220, 276, 281, 284, 287, 328, 341, 411,
    484, 498, 503, 511
Hoppe, Art 415
Hornby, Nick 488
Horne, Harriet van 273
Housman, A.E. 434
Houston, Sam 382
Howard, Frankie 528, 536
Howard, Jane 152
Howard, Michael 461
Howard, Philip 375
Howe, Edgar 84, 160, 161, 162
Howlett, Steven 53
Howse, Christopher 59
Hubbard, Elbert 87, 159
Hubbard, Kin 29, 105, 155, 161, 162, 184,
    215, 315, 323, 405, 467, 474, 518, 535
Hudd, Roy 523
Huffman, Sheila 272
Hughes, Edward 342
Hughes, Howard 265
Hughes, John 474
Hughes, Rupert 203
Hugo, Victor 74
Hume, Paul 322
Humphries, Barry 78
Hussein, Saddam 384, 391
Huston, John 181
Hutcheon, David 324
Huxley, Aldous 295
Hynes, Michael 254

Ifans, Rhys 367
Imhoff, John 27
Ince, W.R. 116
Ingersoll, Robert G. 149, 416
Ingrams, Richard 445, 502
Irons, Jeremy 288
Ivins, Molly 260

Jackson, Steve 400
Jackson, Walthall 14
James I, King 116
James, Alan 329
James, Brian 143
James, Clive 253, 265, 272, 381, 475
James, Henry 133, 532
James, Martin 268
James, P.D. 344
Jameson, Rex 50
Jarvis, Charles 98, 308
Jeavons, Clyde 286
Jeffay, Bob 28
Jefferson, Thomas 262
Jellinek, Roger 382
Jerome, Jerome K. 28, 457, 510
Jerrold, Douglas 105
John, Elton 201
Johnson, Alva 266
Johnson, Lyndon 232, 264, 378, 382, 384,
    400
Johnson, Ron 328
Johnson, Samuel 52, 61, 90, 114, 115, 118,
    148, 336, 338, 339, 340, 351, 375, 412,
    469, 510, 513
Johnson, Sterling 359
Johnston, Paul 288
Jones, C.T. 24
Jones, Franklin P. 415
Jones, Jack 403
Jong, Erica 203, 425
Joplin, Janis 322
Joseph, Joe 272, 393
Joyce, James 115, 127, 176, 361, 413
Joyce, Nora 133

Kael, Pauline 274, 277
Kahn, Alice 111, 244
Kane, Robert 363

Index

Kant, Immanuel 82
Kashfi, Anna 279
Kauffman, Max 171, 229
Kaufman, George S. 26, 129
Kaufman, Gerald 327, 397
Kaufman, Jean-Claude 239
Kavanagh, Patrick 129, 202, 339
Keating, Kenneth 399
Keating, Paul 394
Keats, John 139
Keegan, Kevin 309
Keillor, Garrison 63, 155
Kelly, Gerard 264
Kelly, Jack 469
Kelly, James 223
Kelly, Terri 233
Kennedy, Charles 407
Kennedy, Sarah 220
Kennedy, Teddy 391
Kenny, Jon 331
Kent, Edward 29
Kerr, Deborah 217
Kerr, Jean 154, 177, 293
Kerr, M.E. 109
Ketcham, Hank 92
Keyes, Marian 302
Keynes, John Maynard 394
Khrushchev, Nikita 378
Kieslowski, Krzystof 273
Kifner, John 393
Kiley, Brian 87, 187, 240
Kilvert, Francis 359
Kingsley, Ben 254
Kington, Miles 25
Kinison, Sam 228
Kirchner, Paul 259
Kirwan, Jack 131
Kiser, Joan 182
Kissinger, Henry 343
Kitman, Marvin 276
Klein, Allen 190
Klimek, Lester 195
Knight, Wayne 75
Knoll, Erwin 250
Knott, Blanche 91
Knott, Helen 220
Knox, Ronald 410

Kolinsky, Sue 159, 353
Kornheiser, Tony 180
Kovacs, Ernie 250
Kraus, Karl 123, 288
Krauthammer, Charles 299
Kruger, E.K. 317
Kurnitz, Harry 288
Kyne, Thomas 449

La Bruyère 156
Lake, Anthony 75
Lake, Brian 135
Lamarr, Hedy 368
Lamb, Charles 25, 339, 424, 512
Lamott, Anne 178
Lancaster, Burt 260, 273
Lancaster, Osbert 459
Landers, Ann 150, 173, 230
Landesman, Cosmo 138
Landor, Walter Savage 136
Lang, Andrew 433
Langer, Agnes 244
Lansky, Bruce 86, 189, 190, 191
Lardner, Ring 52, 71, 117, 447, 468, 468,
    473, 489, 522
Larson, Doug 251
Larkin, Philip 143, 172, 375
Larsen, Garry 255
Laughton, Charles 256
Laurel, Stan 390, 537
Laurie, Hugh 436
Lawrence, T.E. 537
Lawrenson, Helen 398
Lawson, Nigella 84
Layton, Irving 337
Le Gallienne, Richard 142
le Pen, Jean-Marie 397
Leacock, Stephen 18, 70, 268, 299, 372,
    412, 432, 477, 516
Lear, Amanda 453
Lear, Edward 151
Leary, Denis 63, 99, 111, 244, 330, 361
Leavis, F.R. 142
Leblanc, Felix 305
Lebowitz, Fran 68, 92, 97, 127, 163, 174,
    181, 188, 189, 192, 247, 262, 304, 338,
    429

 **Index**

Lebrecht, Norman 324
Lee, Larry 212
Lees-Milne, James 426
Lehrer, Tom 42, 68, 74, 317
Leifer, Carol 229
Leigh, Ray 153
Lemmon, David 470
Lenclos, Ninon de 177
Lenin, V.I. 378
Leno, Jay 94, 269, 399, 529
Leonard, Hugh 40, 62, 231, 283, 311, 344,
    444, 453, 461, 483, 504
Leonardo da Vinci 202
Lerner, Alan Jay 371
Lerner, Max 183
Leslie, Shane 56, 65
Lette, Kathy 242, 309
Letterman, David 30, 39, 79, 261, 263, 301,
    346, 348, 372, 479
Levant, Oscar 231, 316, 318, 320, 331, 333
Levenson, Sam 146
Levi, Dino 150
Levin, Alex 350
Levin, Bernard 458
Levine, Joseph E. 255
Levison, Leonard 195
Lewin, David 425
Lewis, Arthur J. 48
Lewis, C.S. 156
Lewis, Jerry 507
Lewis, Joe E. 33, 34, 60, 296
Lewis, Sinclair 143
Lewis-Smith, Victor 104, 158, 258, 260,
    261, 262, 296, 318, 347, 384, 475, 476,
    500
Libermann, Max 16
Lieberman, Gerald F. 182
Liebling, A.J. 266
Lilley, Peter 407
Lincoln, Abraham 385, 526
Lincoln, John A. 512
Lineker, Gary 485
Linklater, Eric 206
Lipman, Maureen 276, 369
Lloyd-George, David 33, 393
Lockhart, John 129
Lodge, David 360

Loewe, Frederick 328
Logue, Christopher 384
Lollobrigida, Gina 225
Lombard, Carole 232
Long, Huey 397
Long, J.L. 43
Looby, Dan 185
Loos, Anita 205
Lord, Francis 208
Lorenz, Konrad 435
Lowell, Robert 25
Lucan, Arthur 187
Lucas, E.V. 425
Luckman, Charles 356
Luna, Francisco 106
Lundquist, James 142
Luttrel, Henry 160
Lynch, Mary 231
Lynd, Robert 422
Lyon, Ben 42
Lyttelton, George 420

Mabley, Moms 244
Macaulay, Thomas B. 123, 137
MacCampbell, Donald 141
MacCarthy, J.J. 472
MacColl, D.S. 76
Macdiarmuid, Hugh 81
MacDonald, Dwight 286
MacDonald, John D. 40
MacDougall, Donald 372
MacHale, Des 135
Machiavelli, Niccolo 413
Mackenzie, Compton 233
MacKenzie, Kelvin 271
MacLaine, Shirley 271, 278, 387
MacLiammoir, Michael 238
MacManus, Seumas 202, 204
Madan, Geoffrey 62, 107, 418, 459, 522
Madariaga, Salvador de 413
Maguire, William 209
Mahaffy, John P. 298
Mailer, Norman 127
Mair, Eddie 275
Maloney, Doris 333
Maloney, John 300
Mandel, Howie 270

Manes, Stephen 263
Manning, Bernard 345, 482
Manson, Charles 513
Marceau, Sophie 369
Marcos, Imelda 160
Margolyes, Miriam 414
Marquis, Don 114, 252
Marsano, William 75
Marsh, Ngaio 185
Marshall, Arthur 71, 356
Marter, Barry 99
Martin, Dean 46, 49
Martin, Judith 450
Martin, Paul 517
Martin, Steve 388, 507, 516
Martin, Thomas L. 49
Martling, Jackie 236, 305
Marvin, Lee 254
Marx, Groucho 37, 38, 54, 57, 76, 99, 122,
    153, 163, 166, 192, 207, 211, 213, 218,
    223, 224, 229, 230, 242, 245, 250, 265,
    268, 287, 292, 296, 435, 455, 462, 463,
    510, 512, 513
Marx, Harpo 323
Marx, Jenny 27
Mason, Andrew 451
Mason, Jackie 36, 43, 222, 357
Mason, Roy 369
Masson, Tom 194
Masters, George 280
Matisse, Henri 18
Matthau, Walter 238, 239, 285, 293
Maugham, Somerset 119, 130, 138, 148,
    206, 318, 519, 529, 530
Maxwell, Robert 251
Maynard, John 110
McAdoo, William 381
McAleese, Mary 386
McCarthy, Charlie 164
McCarthy, Desmond 390
McCarthy, Edward 390
McCord, David 107
McCormack, Mark 87
McDonald, Dwight 353
McEvoy, Andrew 16
McFarland, Thomas 87
McGavran, James 217

McGill, Donald 368
McGonagall, W.M. 134
McGoorty, Danny 448
McGowan, Alastair 330
McGrath, John 29, 175
McGuane, Tom 208
McKenzie, E.C. 177, 179, 233, 237
McKeown, Jimeoin 368
McKeon, James 194
McLaren, Bill 472
McLaughlin, Mignon 207
McLeish, Henry 403
McLeod, Virginia 198
McLuhan, Marshall 24, 85, 136, 315
McMurty, Larry 178
McNally, Frank 43, 401
McPherson, Ian 354
McQueen, Mike 141, 189, 243
Mead, Margaret 182
Meade, Taylor 25
Meades, Jonathan 92
Meaney, Kevin 53
Meany, George 110
Mein, Tommy 306
Meir, Golda 519
Melba, Nellie 271
Mellor, David 110
Melly, George 332
Melnyk, Ralph 70
Mencken, H.L. 111, 150, 165, 173, 204,
    209, 236, 257, 280, 299, 306, 378, 383,
    386, 396, 399, 416, 419, 446, 539
Mendosa, John 539
Menino, Thomas 373
Mercer, Johnny 314
Merton, Mrs 35, 300, 400
Merton, Paul 181, 404, 420, 505, 530
Metalous, Grace 139
Metz, Milton 42
Meur, Tony de 201
Michaels, Andrea 309
Midler, Bette 245, 364, 510
Mikes, George 303, 337, 348, 369
Milius, John 279
Mill, John Stuart 537
Miller, Arthur 29
Miller, Dennis 222, 243, 322

Index

Miller, Henry 91, 126
Miller, Johnny 466
Miller, Jonathan 256
Miller, Mike 301
Miller, Olin 219, 421
Milligan, Spike 25, 68, 80, 104, 155, 157, 174, 215, 259, 292, 293, 295, 299, 300, 301, 328, 338, 361, 418, 436, 520, 526, 533
Mills, Bobby 532
Milne, A.A. 460
Mindess, Harvey 127
Mintzberg, Henry 41
Mitchell, Julian 190
Mitchum, Robert 237, 257, 279, 281, 285, 286, 287
Mitford, Jessica 102
Mitford, Nancy 116, 146, 343, 354, 383
Mizner, Wilson 65, 118, 151, 254
Molnar, Ferenc 141
Monkhouse, Bob 236
Montagu, Elizabeth 232
Montagu, F.A. 433
Montand, Yves 212, 247
Montgomery, Robert 283
Mooney, Sheila 139
Moor, George 419, 452
Moore, Brian 471
Moore, Eric 162
Moore, George 118, 126, 139, 340, 445
Moore, Julia A. 121
Moore, Patrick 435
Moore, Roger 186, 288
Moore, Thomas 121
Moran, Dylan 17, 440
Morley, Lord 137
Morley, Robert 25
Morley, Sheridan 139, 318
Morris, William 343
Morrissey, Eamon 52
Mortimer, Bob 527
Mortimer, John 86, 91, 102, 132, 308, 403, 532
Morton, J.B. 69, 102, 316, 341, 414, 512, 519
Mosley, Diana 405
Moss, Norman 266
Moulton, David 56

Mountbatten, Louis 382
Moynihan, Daniel P. 393
Mozart, W.A. 316
Muggeridge, Malcolm 117, 142, 338, 421, 427
Muir, Edwin 359
Muir, Frank 98, 309
Mull, Martin 65, 151
Mumford, Ethel 462
Munro, H.H. 53, 90, 208, 214, 347, 423, 454, 456
Murdoch, Rupert 285
Murphy, John A. 359
Murphy, Robert 437
Murray, Jim 471
Murray, Patrick 13, 72, 132, 140, 153, 202, 204, 217, 245, 252, 292, 318, 390, 394, 417, 492, 533, 535

Naiman, Arthur 30
Nairn, J. 82
Nash, Ogden 168, 193, 310
Nastase, Ilie 26
Nathan, George J. 55, 119, 156, 283, 500
Neal, Phil 476
Needham, Richard 29, 31
Nelms, Cynthia 225
Nesbitt, Rab C. 62, 298
Nesen, Ron 388
Neumann, Alfred E. 386
Newton, Isaac 432
Nichols, Beverley 315
Nicklaus, Jack 495
Nicolson, Harold 514
Nietzsche, Friedrich 411
Niven, David 59
Nixon, Richard 381, 382, 389
Noakes, Jeremy 436
Norman, Barry 505
Norris, David 269
Northcutt, Wendy 441
Norton, Graham 355, 504
Nown, Graham 452
Nyulund, Rose 95

O'Brien, Conan 282
O'Brien, Daire 208, 516

O'Brien, Flann 28, 127, 305, 374, 448
O'Carroll, Brendan 182
O'Connor, Sandra 107
O'Connor, Sinead 426
O'Donnell, Michael 307, 362
Ogilvie, Heneage 432
O'Hanlon, Ardal 98, 186, 188
O'Hara, Joan 281
O'Keeffe, Georgia 18
O'Keeffe, John 322
Onassis, Aristotle 41
O'Neill, Eugene 339
Orben, Robert 30, 167
O'Reilly, Bill 487
Ormathwaite, Lord 154
O'Rourke, Brian 61
O'Rourke, P.J. 96, 137, 149, 164, 170, 171, 172, 174, 188, 194, 210, 227, 246, 337, 348, 350, 356, 364, 370, 375, 406, 416, 449, 458, 483
Orton, Joe 151, 247
Orwell, George 125, 141, 416, 429
Osborne, John 115, 283
Osgood, Peter 481
Osler, William 294, 298
O'Toole, Peter 280
Otter, Frank 149
Owen, Antonia 167
Ozark, Danny 391

Paget, Clarence 278
Paget, reginald 401
Paglia, Camille 210
Palmer, Arnold 466
Palmer-Tomkinson, Tara 34, 83
Parker, Dorothy 77, 115, 125, 129, 142, 217, 238
Parker, Robert 78
Parkinson, C.N. 378
Parkinson, Michael 351, 467
Parr, Jack 282
Parton, Dolly 240
Parton, James 354
Patrick, G. 152
Patten, Chris 392
Patterson, Jennifer 81
Patton, George 369, 414, 537, 539

Paulsen, Pat 387
Pavarotti, Luciano 322
Pearce, Stuart 473
Peers, Joe 41
Penn, William 420
Pepys, Samuel 103, 506
Percival, Nick 434
Perelman, S.J. 33, 37, 213, 280, 282, 284, 306
Perlis, Jack 316
Perrett, Gene 104, 173
Persaud, Raj 176
Peter, Laurence J. 157, 367
Petroviv, Stephan 365
Philips, Emo 39, 43, 93, 147, 148, 154, 155, 170, 203, 211, 218, 225, 471, 520
Phillips, Bob 90, 148, 410
Phillips, Guy 455
Picasso, Pablo 20, 40
Pickering, Ron 273
Pickford, Mary 165
Pierce, Andrew 80
Pierce, Charles 146
Pierrepoint, Albert 368
Piggot, Lester 484
Piggy, Miss 239, 455
Pilling, Michael J. 266
Pindar, Peter 132
Pinker, Steven 332
Pitt, William 514
Plasset, Norton 104
Plato 402, 529
Player, Gary 194
Plomer, William 21
Plomp, John 191
Plunkett, James 429
Podhoretz, John 138
Pompadour, Madame de 340
Pope, Alexander 105
Porson, Richard 115, 120
Portago, Barbara De 302
Porter, Edward 275
Potter, Mick 107
Potter, Stephen 53, 118, 336, 455, 461
Potts, Paul 125
Poundstone, Paula 296
Pratt, Denis 446

Press, Bill 386
Prichard, Michael 162
Priestley, J.B. 339, 417, 520
Prinze, Freddie 149
Pritchett, Oliver 306
Prochnow, Herbert 109, 177
Puckett, U.J. 104
Putin, Vladimir 403
Puxley, Alan 55
Puzo, Mario 106

Quarles, Francis 311
Quayle, Dan 379, 383, 389, 395, 404, 534
Quindlen, Anna 191
Quinton, John 392

Rabelais, François 24, 47
Rado, James 379
Raphael, Frederic 21, 79, 206
Rathbun, R.K. 69
Rattigan, Terence 238
Rattle, Simpon 330
Rautianien, Pasi 65
Reagan, Ronald 386, 395
Rector, Charles 92
Redmond, Michael 34, 294, 420
Reed, Henry 136
Reed, Rex 256
Reels, Larry 439
Rees-Mogg, Jacob 396
Reger, Max 115
Regnier, Henri de 198
Reich, Wilhelm 123
Reinhart, Ed 15
Renan, Joseph Ernest 341
Renard, Jules 143, 163
Reston, James 274, 387
Reynolds, Burt 257
Reynolds, Richard 520
Rhodes, Cecil 336, 367
Richards, Gordon 472
Richards, Keith 321
Richards, Lord 401
Rickles, Don 53
Ridge, William 462
Rifkind, Malcolm 407

Rivers, Joan 34, 36, 150, 161, 166, 169, 173, 179, 188, 193, 198, 199, 200, 211, 221, 242, 244, 271, 283, 285, 295, 305, 311, 439
Roach, Boyle 515
Robbins, Miriam 183
Robbins, Tom 30
Roberts, Paddy 326
Robinson, Hercules 402
Robinson, Tom 469
Robson, Bobby 331
Roche, Arthur 161
Rodin, Auguste 16
Rodriguez, Chi Chi 91
Rogers, Will 28, 54, 80, 109, 176, 179, 200, 267, 325, 358, 378, 379, 383, 385, 387, 390, 406, 533
Romains, Jules 305
Ronay, Egon 95
Rooney, Andy 92
Rooney, John 81
Rooney, Mickey 35, 171, 203, 265
Roope, George 489
Roosevelt, Alice 446
Roosevelt, Franklin D. 72
Roosevelt, Theodore 69, 399, 461
Roque, Jacqueline 15
Rose, Don 215
Rose, Simon 132, 266, 277, 279
Rosenberg, Howard 326
Rosenberg, Joel 160, 451, 539
Ross, Jonathan 99
Rossini, Gioacchino 315, 320
Rosten, Leo 31, 94, 261, 319, 347, 415
Rosten, Norman 532
Roth, David 332
Rowland, Helen 152, 155, 237, 246
Royko, Mike 386
Rubin, Bob 294
Rubin, Jerry 429
Rudner, Rita 26, 147, 166, 169, 175, 180, 183, 205, 212, 217, 219, 221, 222, 239, 241, 242, 267, 278, 325, 422
Runyon, Damon 211, 466, 469, 523
Rushton, William 252, 346, 362
Ruskin, John 328
Russell, Bertrand 64, 427
Russell, George 152

Index

Sackville-West, Vita 154
Saefer, Morley 159
Safian, Louis A. 152
Safire, William 75
St. Johns, Adela Rogers 202
Saki 247, 426
Salisbury, Lord 275, 400
Samuel, Herbert 389
Samuels, Jim 213, 256, 350
Sanders, George 352, 404
Sandburg, Carl 289
Sansom, Ruth 194
Sargent, Claire 392
Sartre, Jean-Paul 128
Saunders, Ernest 33
Sayle, Alexei 93, 160, 350, 393, 501, 517, 521, 526
Schaffer, Bob 42
Schoenstein, Ralph 183
Schopenhauer, Arthur 201, 219
Schreiner, Lee 297
Schultz, Charles 152, 346, 511
Scott, C.P. 256
Scott, Liz 50
Secombe, Harry 355
Seinfeld, Jerry 43, 58, 94, 106, 108, 167, 246, 287, 537, 538
Selleck, Tom 502
Selsdon, Esther 307
Sewell, Brian 18
Shakespeare, William 307, 317
Shwarzenegger, Arnold 41
Shakes, Ronnie 162
Shandling, Gary 203, 210, 214, 223
Shankly, Bill 466, 467, 490
Shanley, Vin 72
Shapiro, Karl 134, 299
Sharp, Dolph 42
Shaw, George Bernard 12, 36, 81, 87, 102, 114, 122, 169, 319, 325, 330, 361, 374, 385, 397, 429, 448, 456, 499, 5-3
Shaw, Karl 262, 297, 346, 352
Shaw, Peter 210
Sheed, Wilfrid 262, 352, 360, 364
Sheen, Fulton J. 168, 412, 419
Sheridan, John D. 169
Sheridan, Richard Brinsley 38, 452

Shilton, Peter 470
Shoenberg, Fred 167
Shore, Dinah 331
Shorten, Caroline 404
Shy, Timothy 71
Sickert, Walter 463
Signoret, Simone 283
Silver, Joel 254
Simmons, John 351
Simon, John 287
Simon, Neil 266
Simpson, Homer 158, 461
Simpson, John 221
Simpson, N.F. 46
Simpson, Wallis 40
Singer, Steven Max 213
Siskel, Gene 278
Sitwell, Edith 124, 253, 451
Skelton, Red 221
Skinner, Cornelia Otis 310
Skinner, Dennis 406
Skinner, Frank 481
Slick, Alec 30
Sloan, John 420
Slovotsky, Walter 164
Smart, Christopher 119
Smirnoff, Yakov 64, 180, 265
Smith, Arthur 307
Smith, Elinor 170
Smith, Godfrey 76, 106, 157
Smith, Ian 398
Smith, Mel 424
Smith, Patti 428
Smith, Sydney 87, 114, 121, 207, 222, 308, 358, 373, 517
Smith, Wes 433
Smullyan, Raymond 410
Snow, Peter 346
Socrates 150
Sokolov, Raymond 375
Somervell, David 345
Somoza, Anastasio 394
Soper, Lord 421
South, Jack 224
Spaeth, Duncan 341
Spark, Muriel 426
Spellman, Francis 150

Index

Spencer, Herbert 425
Spencer, Raine 304
Spendlove, Scott 189
Spock, Benjamin 151
Stack, Peter 259
Stallings, Laurence 251
Stallone, Sylvester 274, 277
Stanshall, Vivian 61
Starr, Freddie 96
Stead, Christina 193
Steel, F.A. 364
Steele, Richard 422
Steffens, Lincoln 289
Steinbeck, George 124
Steinem, Gloria 237
Stephanopolous, George 391
Stephens, James 317
Stevens, Thaddeus 103
Stevenson, Adlai 164, 250, 251, 383, 391, 401
Stevenson, Robert Louis 296
Steyn, Mark 502
Stillwell, Michael 437
Stoppard, Tom 16, 513
Strachey, Carrington 217
Strachey, John 429
Strachey, Lytton 70, 124, 138
Street, C. 317
Streifer, Philip 80
Strong, Roy 19
Sturge Moore, T. 119
Sullivan, Arthur 327
Sullivan, Frank 155
Summers, Lawrence 349
Sutch, Lord 397, 401
Sutton, Willie 26, 31
Swanson, Gloria 133
Swanton, H.N. 131
Swift, Jonathan 47, 90, 220, 340, 349, 453, 459, 527
Sylvester, Robert 119

Talleyrand, Charles de 212
Tammeus, Bill 30
Tanner, Jack 362
Tarbuck, Jimmy 500
Tarrant, Chris 264

Taussik, Tom 337
Taylor, A.J.P. 73, 284
Taylor, Deems 327
Taylor, Denis 358
Taylor, Elizabeth 287, 423
Taylor, H.S. 414
Taylor, Lawrence 301
Templeton, Brad 323
Terry, Ellen 224
Thackeray, William M. 134, 170
Thatcher, Carol 138
Thatcher, Denis 56
Thatcher, Margaret 365, 380, 392, 394, 405, 411
Theroux, Paul 405
Thomas, Allen D. 49
Thomas, Dylan 20, 46, 359, 449
Thomas, George 296, 298, 299
Thomas, Glan 102
Thomas, Gwyn 337
Thomas, Lowell 261
Thompson, Bobby 176
Thompson, Daley 489
Thompson, Damien 417
Thompson, Hunter S. 47
Thompson, Ken 178
Thompson, Nix 279
Thomson, David 285
Thomson, Roy 258
Thoreau, Henry D. 126, 421
Thurber, James 46, 136, 153, 170, 186, 207, 227, 256, 258
Tibballs, Geoff 20, 309, 462, 524
Tillman, Henry J. 161
Timberlake, Lewis 29
Titian 20
Toibin, Niall 57, 181, 355
Toksvig, Sandy 50
Tonto 253
Took, Barry 507
Tookey, Christopher 259, 261, 267
Toscanini, Arturo 203, 333
Townsend, Robert 36
Tracy, Spencer 273
Tremayne, Sydney 295
Trevino, Lee 466, 467, 468, 471, 473, 477, 490

Trillin, Calvin 91
Trinder, Tommy 373
Trollope, Anthony 74
Trueman, Fred 488
Truman, Harry S. 383, 399
Trump, Ivana 36
Tucholsky, Kurt 375
Tucker, Sophie 486
Tucker, Sophie 24
Turnbull, Heather 370
Turner, Lana 205
Turner, Stuart 185
Tutu, Desmond 342
Twain, Mark 24, 27, 86, 104, 109, 117, 120, 125, 141, 149, 157, 167, 184, 194, 200, 201, 225, 239, 293, 311, 315, 318, 320, 336, 338, 342, 344, 345, 370, 371, 380, 415, 427, 428, 433, 446, 450, 451, 454, 455, 459, 460, 510, 511, 512, 514, 517, 520
Tynan, Kenneth 252, 272, 380, 502, 504
Tyron, Edward 437
Tyson, Mike 486, 490

Ueland, Brenda 235
Underhill, Frank 402
Unwin, Stanley 39
Updike, John 41, 83, 287, 501
Updike, Simon 17
Ustinov, Peter 274, 341, 362, 398, 513, 534, 536

Vale, Jerry 48
Valéry, Paul 392, 410
Van Dyke, Henry 314
Vanbrugh, John 421
Vance, Patricia 389
Varano, Frank 64
Vaughan, Bill 388
Verdi, Giuseppe 333
Vertosick, Frank 303, 306
Victoria, Queen 405
Vidal, Gore 72, 79, 117, 375, 462
Vidor, King 285
Voltaire 108, 292, 378, 445
Vonnegut, Kurt 350
Vries, Peter de 147, 227, 441

Wade, Harry 264
Wagner, Jane 163, 302
Wagner, Richard 333
Walden, George 61
Waldegrave, William 434
Walker, Murray 481, 492, 493, 494
Walker, Stanley 119
Wall, Max 507
Wallace, Edgar 69
Wallace, George 521
Wallach, Eli 255
Wallach, Ira 26
Wallance, Judge Gregory 103
Wallis, Richard 374
Walpole, Horace 215
Walters, Julie 32
Walton, Sam 41
Warner, Charles D. 432
Warner, Jack 366
Waterhouse, Keith 204, 372
Watson, M.F. 366
Watson, Peter 209
Watson, Roland 393
Watterson, Bill 437
Waugh, Auberon 246, 374, 397
Waugh, Evelyn 15, 50, 51, 58, 59, 68, 69, 70, 72, 74, 75, 84, 87, 111, 120, 122, 126, 136, 138, 140, 167, 174, 187, 193, 198, 214, 258, 344, 348, 363, 368, 416, 426, 448, 451, 532
Wax, Ruby 42, 104
Wayne, John 62, 270, 284
Webster, Noah 253
Weidman, John 226
Welby, Thomas E. 97
Weldon, Fay 171
Welles, Orson 163
Wellesley, Arthur 360, 393
Wells, H.G. 223, 254, 487
Welsh, Joan 71
Werb, Mike 242
West, Mae 40, 205, 208, 230, 236, 238, 241, 272, 503, 507
West, Rebecca 206, 225
Westcott, Edward 452
Weston, Harry 439
Wharton, Edith 12

Index

Whistler, James McNeill 13, 149
White, E.B. 132, 303, 399
Whitehorn, Katherine 35, 151, 228, 342, 413, 438, 448, 455
Whitton, Charlotte 149
Wilde, Larry 80
Wilde, Oscar 12, 14, 15, 17, 24, 25, 33, 47, 55, 71, 77, 78, 81, 84, 86, 91, 95, 114, 116, 118, 120, 121, 122, 123, 124, 131, 146, 152, 168, 182, 200, 201, 216, 231, 316, 324, 337, 342, 357, 414, 418, 421, 424, 444, 445, 447, 449, 450, 451, 454, 457, 463, 466, 467, 499, 515, 528
Wilder, Billy 256, 264, 266, 533
Will, George 398
Williams, J.P.R. 468
Williams, Jimmy 239
Williams, Kenneth 519
Williams, Robin 37, 48, 215, 222, 246, 382, 518, 535
Williamson, Malcolm 322
Willocks, David 328
Wilson, Bryan 86
Wilson, Charles 343
Wilson, Earl 279
Wilson, Henry 392
Wilson, Woodrow 84
Winchell, Walter 251, 263
Winner, Michael 98, 99
Winokur, Jon 119
Winstead, Liz 243
Winston, Liz 342
Winters, Shelley 224
Wodehouse, P.G. 137, 213, 340
Wogan, Terry 284
Wolfe, Gene 81
Wolstenholme, Suzanne 234
Womersley, David 86
Wood, Mary Augusta 414

Wood, Natalie 209
Wood, Victoria 97, 234
Woods, Tiger 490
Woolcott, Alexander 253, 259, 426
Woolf, Virginia 126, 339
Woollcott, Alexander 116
Woosnam, Phil 468
Wordsworth, Christopher 282
Wordsworth, William 120
Wright, Charlotte 95
Wright, Frank Lloyd 13, 17, 348
Wright, Ian 63
Wright, Steven 14, 38, 53, 73, 76, 83, 103, 108, 110, 134, 158, 160, 190, 191, 219, 280, 295, 303, 310, 329, 332, 422, 425, 433, 435, 438, 511, 524, 525, 527, 529, 531, 534, 535, 536
Wuhl, Robert 332
Wulston, David 353
Wyatt, Woodrow 398

Yankovic, Al 300
Yeats, W.B. 48, 126, 411
Yelton, Jack 31
Yeltsin, Boris 371
Young, Brigham 413
Young, G.M. 256, 356, 394, 420
Youngman, Henny 24, 47, 65, 79, 168, 308, 355, 466

Zanuck, Darryl F. 19
Zappa, Frank 15, 56, 314
Zellerbach, Merla 98
Zera, Richard S. 152
Zhou Enlai 83
Ziegler, Larry 186
Zigman, Laura 230
Zito, Nick 490
Zola, Emile 49